EVERYONE IS TALKING ABOUT "THE NEW COMICS"!

"Remember the comic books of your youth? They've grown up . . . And that's not all. The comics are also winning new respect: Literary honors, respectful reviews, museum exhibits—and even academic attention."
—*U.S. News & World Report*

"Comic books are flourishing . . . It has been awhile since comics were strictly for kids, and these days the racks are full of books that warrant adult perusal."
—New York *Daily News*

"Grown-ups flock to comics . . . Everyone in the industry— from publishers to distributors to retailers—agrees that the future of comic books lies in the adult market."
—*New York Times*

"At their best, grown-up comics such as 'Dark Knight' are almost cinematic in their artistic scope, blending full-page illustration with smaller frames of rapid-fire action."
—*Newsweek*

"American comic books are finally growing up, and the new generation of comic creators is rocking out, going gonzo and getting hip!"
—*Infashion* magazine

THE NEW COMICS

Edited by Gary Groth and Robert Fiore

Interviews from the pages of
THE COMICS JOURNAL

Notes and Bibliography by Robert Fiore

BERKLEY BOOKS, NEW YORK

THE NEW COMICS

A Berkley Book/published by arrangement with
Fantagraphics Books

PRINTING HISTORY
Berkley trade paperback edition / November 1988

CONTENTS

PART IV: THE NEW COMICS 181

THE NEW COMICS

THE COMICS JOURNAL AND THE NEW COMICS

BY GARY GROTH

DWIGHT MACDONALD, THE RENOWNED POLITICAL AND CULTURAL ESSAYIST, published a journal called *Politics* in the 1940s; referring to it, he once wrote: "We need specialists in abuse, technicians in villification, expert mudslingers." To MacDonald, villification was an essential weapon with which to assault a mendacious and increasingly impotent political establishment, mudslinging a way of getting at the truth; criticism was, for him, an attempt to define and articulate values.

The Comics Journal began publishing in July 1976; prior to this time, magazines about comics were amateur undertakings called fanzines (a term conflating *fan* and *magazine*), little more than puff sheets reflecting the uncritical enthusiasm of their young, impassioned publishers. The *Journal*, circumscribed by its subject matter and more modest in its intellectual achievement, nonetheless was to comics what *Politics* was to politics. The *Journal* was the first magazine to assert the need for critical standards in a profession and an artform until then unfamiliar with (and, as it turned out, downright hostile to) such standards. The *Journal*'s two consistent editorial imperatives were, first, to discuss (and debate) the merits of particular comics artists as well as the artistic capacities of the medium itself, and second, to illuminate (and usually to oppose) the various social and business instrumentalities that made comics the medium it was—and prevented comics from becoming the medium it was not.

The comics profession, represented at the time predominantly by Marvel and DC Comics, and therefore composed overwhelmingly of hacks, was outraged and appalled by the *Journal*'s nervy challenge to the artistic and ethical status quo of an industry with which they had grown comfortable.

Complaints, denunciation, and lawsuits became commonplace as the *Journal* continued to examine serious issues, challenge preconceptions upon which the industry was founded over fifty years ago, expose examples of plagiarism, conduct adversarial interviews, and generally become an irritant in a profession not known for its artistic standards or moral spine.

The *Journal*'s editorial point of view was unified by its singular commitment to raise the artistic level of the medium; but because the *Journal* was by no means simplistic or orthodox in its approach, because we allowed a wide disparity of opinions to be aired in our pages, because there were no party lines or marching orders, professionals and fans were often puzzled. We weren't always procreator and antimanagement. Broadly speaking, we advocated the essential dignity and rights of the creative individual while insisting that the creator place his talent in the service of a cultivated conscience instead of at the behest of the infantile and formulaic stick-in-trade of the comics industry. An unpopular position insofar as most comics artists and writers made their living by recycling clichés memorized in their childhood. But, we insisted upon imposing a cultural and artistic responsibility on both the creators and the companies that neither party had ever been asked to assume, indeed, had never even considered.

By the early '80s, the *Journal* had defined its journalistic and critical perspective; at about the same time, perhaps not so coincidentally, artists had begun to emerge (or flourish) who appreciated the values espoused by the magazine. art spiegelman, Will Eisner, Robert Crumb, Harvey Pekar, Gilbert and Jaime Hernandez, and other cartoonists found the demanding nature of the *Journal* to be compatible with and sympathetic to their own more serious-minded view of the potential of the comics form. Underground cartoonists, relegated to obscurity from the mid '70s to the early '80s, began appearing in magazines such as art spiegelman and Françoise Mouly's *RAW* and Robert Crumb's *Weirdo*; cartoonists such as the Hernandez Brothers, Peter Bagge, Drew Friedman, Rick Geary, and Dave Sim began publishing; Kitchen Sink Press began publishing new work by Will Eisner. Alternative cartoonists had found alternative publishers whose artistic principles mirrored their own. Marvel's and DC's strategy to tap into this trend was to revamp their super-hero lines; and as the two major companies became less relevant, the *Journal* became more vigorous in its efforts to call attention to creators who were broadening the horizons of the medium.

The interviews reprinted here represent the *Journal*'s more "constructive" attempt to inform the reading public (and rehabilitate the public's perception) as to the legitimacy of the comics form as a bona fide art. The selection of artists and writers in this book is the editors' attempt at objectively identifying those creators who a curious member of the reading public would find most worthy of their attention. A few words offering an historical context are in order.

If we define a hack by his willingness to subordinate his talent to purely commercial dictates, we find that the comics industry has been dominated by hacks since its inception. Although there was the occasional brilliant artist, such as Harvey Kurtzman or Carl Barks, and many remarkable craftsmen, the great bulk of comic books was puerile junk, shoddily produced, and marketed to children. The traditional artistic context of the comic book industry was shattered by the underground comics movement in the late '60s, represented in this volume by such pioneering cartoonists as Gilbert Shelton, Robert Crumb, Kim Deitch, and Bill Griffith. This was the only time in the history of the comic book when meaningful change was not the result of predominantly economic motives; the underground cartoonists worked out of an inner need, from the social and cultural matrix, not from the economic one.

Prior to the underground comics movement, cartoonists were routinely exploited in the comics industry. Comic book companies refused to allow cartoonists to retain ownership of their own work; in order to work within the comics business, cartoonists had to relinquish all rights to their work. This sleazy tradition was also shattered in the '60s; underground cartoonists retained ownership of their work, and underground comics publishers paid the cartoonists a royalty for every copy of a comic sold.

Underground comics publishing waned in the mid '70s; at the same time, paradoxically, comic book specialty stores sprang up all over the country, slowly at first, but growing to a sizable number by the early '80s. These stores catered primarily to comic book collectors and hard-core fans of super-heroes, which was the predominant genre at the time (as it is now). In short order, comic book specialty distributors followed naturally, catering to the specific needs of the comic book specialty stores. This opened a new market, as the economists would say, and by the early '80s independent (or alternative) publishers began publishing comic books distributed exclusively to this network of comic book stores. In order to compete with Marvel and DC, companies such as Pacific Comics lured artists away from the established companies by offering ownership rights and royalties—the same rights underground cartoonists enjoyed a dozen years ago, but which were still unavailable from Marvel and DC.

This altered the landscape of publishing activity in the comics profession; comic book specialty stores and independent publishers, catering to a more fanatical and obsessive readership, eventually bestowed celebrity status upon mainstream comics creators and created a star system of sorts. For the first time in the history of the mass-market comic book, mainstream artists and writers were in a better position to bargain for higher rates and more rights.

This new and burgeoning market led to stepped-up production and higher-priced, more lavishly produced books, both from independent and traditional comics publishers, as well as a handful of artists who published their own work. On the one hand, Marvel and DC took advantage of this new and growing appetite by publishing jazzed-up and revamped versions of their standard super-heroes, written and drawn by popular creators with a proven financial track record (Frank Miller's *Dark Knight*, John Byrne's *Superman*, Howard Chaykin's *Shadow*, Mike Grell's *Green Arrow*, etc.). On the other hand, an accessible market offered "alternative" cartoonists with richer perspectives and unique vision an opportunity to reach a wider, more attentive readership (best illustrated by the deserved success of art spiegelman's biographical *Maus,* but also including Jaime and Gilbert Hernandez's *Love & Rockets*, Harvey Pekar's *American Splendor*, and the work of Robert Crumb, as well as other, lesser-known cartoonists featured in this book).

The mass media, perennially subservient to economic trends and incompetent to report accurately on matters of merely artistic significance, have usually made no attempt to make qualitative distinctions among the new, popular comics, reporting on the trend with such juicy titles as "The Comic Book (Gulp!) Grows Up" (*Newsweek*, 1/18/88) or "The Passing of Pow! and Bam!" (*Time*, 1/25/88). Magazines as far afield as *Rolling Stone* and the *Atlantic* have run articles on comics, and there's no sign of surcease in the publicity. Comics are, for the moment, hip.

The hipness, the trendyness, the usually half-witted media attention aside, comics narrative is finally taking its place beside film and fiction as a medium capable of profundity, wit, humor, and drama. This book, an oral chronicle of the medium's most interesting practitioners, should help the curious reader separate the wheat from the chaff.

—Gary Groth, publisher
The Comics Journal

COMICS FOR BEGINNERS

SOME NOTES FOR THE NEWCOMER
BY ROBERT FIORE

MARVEL AND DC

THE COMMERCIAL COMIC BOOK INDUSTRY IS DOMINATED BY TWO COMPANIES: Marvel Comics Group and DC Comics Inc. Both trace their roots back to the earliest days of comic books; both are now owned by larger corporations, Marvel by New World Pictures, and DC by Warner Communications. Each publishes forty to fifty titles per month, almost all of them devoted to the adventures of costumed characters, or "super-heroes," as they are rather presumptuously known. Marvel's roster includes Spider-Man, the X-Men, the Fantastic Four, and the Incredible Hulk; DC's includes Superman, Batman, Wonder Woman, and the Teen Titans. It cannot be called the most dignified business in the world.

DC was the industry leader from the introduction of Superman in 1937 up to the late '60s, when Marvel began to catch up, thanks to a set of fresh, imaginative characters created by Jack Kirby, Steve Ditko, and Stan Lee. In the late '70s, Marvel developed a huge edge, rendering DC into little more than a weak sister. In the last few years, however, DC has begun to catch up, thanks largely to canny exploitation of the direct market (see below).

THE NEWSSTAND MARKET

Up until the late '70s, almost all comic books were sold on newsstands or in drug and convenience stores (in recent years, the newsstand market has become less significant than the direct market). Marvel and DC take up the lion's share of newsstand sales; about the only other newsstand comics are the children's humor comics published by *Archie*, Harvey (*Richie Rich*, *Casper the Friendly Ghost*), and Gladstone (the Walt Disney titles).

THE DIRECT MARKET AND THE INDEPENDENT COMICS COMPANIES

Throughout the '70s, the growing popularity of comic books as a collectible led to the proliferation of stores specializing in comic books. These comics shops came to be known in the industry as the direct market. By the early '80s this market had grown large enough to support comics companies that catered exclusively to comics shops. These companies are usually called independent'': First Comics, Eclipse Comics, and Comico. For the most and DC. At the top in terms of sales are what might be called the ''major independents:'' First Comics, Eclipse Comics, and Comico. For the most part, their product is virtually identical in style and content to that of Marvel and DC. First and Comico have even dabbled in newsstand distribution. There are any number of smaller companies doing Marvel and DC-type material, with results ranging from professional to wretched, emphasis on the latter. Several companies, such as Dark Horse and Renegade, cater to the more eccentric and offbeat tastes of comics fans. A few cartoonists, like Harvey Pekar and Dave Sim, publish themselves. On the fringes of the direct market are companies that aim for an adult audience, such as RAW Books and Graphics, Fantagraphics Books, and the hardy survivors of underground comics publishing: Rip Off Press, Last Gasp, and Kitchen Sink. Once the independent companies established the direct market's viability, Marvel and DC began slanting more and more of their product to it, and more than half of their profits now come from the direct market. Marvel and DC account for sixty to seventy percent of the direct market sales; First, Comico, and Eclipse another ten to fifteen; and the other companies scramble for what's left.

UNDERGROUND COMICS

Underground comics were iconoclastic, adult-oriented comics published outside the commercial comics industry, mostly from the late '60s to the mid-'70s.

THE PULPS

The "pulps" that are occasionally referred to in this book were cheap, garish adventure fiction magazines published from around the turn of the century through the '50s. Pulp magazines were named after the low-quality paper they were printed on; high-class magazines like the *New Yorker, Collier's*, and the *Saturday Evening Post* were (and still are) called "slicks." At their best, the pulps published authors like Raymond Chandler and Dashiell Hammett, but most pulp writers are quite deservedly forgotten. Nevertheless, the pulps created a violent, stripped-down, breakneck-paced style of fiction that strongly influenced comic books, not least because many pulp writers moved into comics when the pulps started to die out (comic books eroded the pulp readership in much the same way television would erode comic book readership twenty years later).

FANZINES

Fanzines are amateur magazines published by comics fans. A fanzine can be anything from a few photocopied sheets (mimeographed in the old days) to lavish productions that look far more professional than their subjects. Fanzines usually publish criticism or fan gush, though some are actually amateur comic books.

THE ASSEMBLY LINE

The high productivity demand of the comics industry necessitates an assembly-line approach to comics creation. Each step in the creative process is assigned to a different person: a penciller will draw the story in pencil; an inker will ink over and embellish the penciled artwork; a letterer will letter the captions and dialogue; and a colorist will make color guides for the color separator. There are basically two methods of writing comics stories. In one, the writer does a full script, setting out all action, captions and dialogue in advance. In the other, the writer and penciller will work out a rough plot, the penciller will draw the complete story from the plot and then return it to the writer, who fills in the captions and dialogue. This latter method was popularized in the '60s as the "Marvel Style," though it had been in use since the '30s. As inking is a vital part of comic art, many of the better cartoonists frown on the assembly-line process. It could also be argued that the best comics have been created by cartoonists who write their strips as well as draw them. Nevertheless, nearly all the comics published by Marvel, DC, and the major independents are done on the assembly line. As a rule, the higher up the artistic scale you go, the less prevalent the assembly line becomes. (It should be noted that many cartoonists have employed anonymous assistants to do inking, lettering, and sometimes even writing and penciling.)

Writers, pencillers, inkers, letterers, and so on are referred to collectively as "creators."

WORK-MADE-FOR-HIRE

Throughout most of the history of comic books, creators were required to surrender all rights to their creations to the publisher, without compensation. It was a condition of working in the industry. Jerry Siegel and Joe Shuster waged a long and ultimately unsuccessful legal battle over ownership of Superman, and since then no one has seriously challenged this precedent. In the '70s, changes in the copyright laws made this sort of larceny more difficult. Where once the creator would relinquish his rights simply by endorsing a check, now he had to surrender them more explicitly. Thus was born the work-made-for-hire contract. While it represented no real change in how business was done in the industry, creators were finally confronted with just what rights they had to give away, and some realized that only a fool would sign such a contract. No one expected to own a story featuring Superman, but many resented having to give away any other characters they might create themselves.

This discontentment coincided with the birth of the independent companies, who wooed big-name creators by allowing them to retain ownership of their creations, or at least receive royalties on them. Marvel and DC were eventually forced into offering royalty plans of their own, and Marvel set up a separate imprint, Epic Comics, for creator-owned titles. DC has yet to publish a creator-owned comic book, though this policy may change soon.

THE CODE

In the mid-'50s, widespread criticism of violence in comic books led publishers to establish the Comics Code, an extremely restrictive set of standards for comic book content. It was administered by an independent board called the Comics Code Authority. No comic book without the Code Authority's seal of approval stood a chance of being sold or distributed (the exception being Dell, then publishers of wholesome material like the Walt Disney titles, who stood aloof from the whole business). The Code was universally despised by comics fans, who quite rightly blamed it for retarding the development of the medium. Underground comics were in part a reaction against the Code and the sort of comics it had engendered. The last ten years have seen a steady erosion of the Code's hold over the industry. The independents never subscribed to it in the first place, and many of Marvel and DC's direct-market-only titles eschew it as well. While nearly all newsstand comics are Code-approved, the Code's provisions are enforced loosely, and occasionally Marvel and DC will simply drop the seal when a newsstand comic isn't approved. It is unlikely that very many people pay much attention to the Code seal at all these days.

GRAPHIC NOVELS

A "graphic novel" is a long comic book. The term is essentially a reflection of the industry's yearning for unearned status. Rather than improving the image of comics by improving comics themselves, it tries to enhance its status through semantic jiggery-pokery. Throughout most of the world, a comics story or collection of stories in book form is referred to as an album.

"CARTOONIST" VS. "ARTIST"

For comics purposes these two terms are basically synonymous. A cartoonist who draws adventure comics will generally be called an artist. To a certain extent this is, like "graphic novel," a bit of semantic self-aggrandizement. A cartoonist who draws humorous material will almost always be called a cartoonist. A cartoonist who both writes and draws his comics is more likely to be called a cartoonist. As we believe "cartooning" is the proper name of a distinct art form, "cartoonist" is the term of choice in this book. However, on some occasions the use of the term "artist" is so customary and natural that it is used instead.

PART I:

ORIGINATORS

PERHAPS YOU'VE HEARD THE STORY.

One day in 1933, a struggling novelty salesman named Max Gaines paused before throwing out some old Sunday newspapers to reread the funnies. It struck him that if he enjoyed reading old comic strips, others might, too. The idea had been tried a few times before, but it was Gaines's energy and persistence that made comic books a going concern. The first comic books were premiums issued free by businesses to their customers. Before long, comic books were being sold at newsstands. They were produced in the cheapest way possible and sold for the lowest price possible. It wasn't long before they ran out of newspaper strips to reprint, and had to commission original material. The comic book as we know it was born.

From there the story only gets longer. Suffice it to say that the fledgling industry developed a voracious appetite for new comic strips. This appetite would be filled by a combination of old pulp writers and young cartoonists fresh out of school (if they were schooled at all). Given the low rates and the crushing work load, the cartoonists *had* to be young. All the industry demanded was that pages be filled. From that day to this, the ones who made the comic book a creative medium were the writers and cartoonists themselves. Some wanted to make themselves good enough to break into newspaper strips or magazine illustration, some were motivated by a love of the medium itself, but the common denominator was a conviction that what their employers were willing to settle for wasn't good enough. Will Eisner, Harvey Kurtzman, and Robert Crumb, each in their own era, went far enough beyond expectations to reshape the medium itself. You could not find a comic book cartoonist today who is not influenced in some way by one or all of them, directly or indirectly.

Perhaps the final word for all creative cartoonists was said by the animation director Chuck Jones. When asked whether some of his cartoons might have been inappropriate for children, Jones replied, "They weren't made for children. They were made for me."

WILL EISNER

WILL EISNER'S CAREER SPANS THE ENTIRE HISTORY OF COMIC BOOKS, WHICH shows how young the medium is. When Eisner entered the business, comic books were still imitating the format of newspaper comics (one page episodes, a logo on each page), and Eisner is due a great deal of credit for developing comic book storytelling. An inveterate experimenter, he brought cinematic techniques and a more sophisticated sense of character to comic books. Eisner showed his fellow cartoonists how to use every element of the medium to further the story, from lettering to lighting to page composition.

Eisner started in comics in 1936, at the age of nineteen. In that year he and Jerry Iger started the Eisner-Iger studio, producing comic books and cartoon material for several companies and creating features like *Blackhawk* and *Sheena, Queen of the Jungle*. It was still a thriving business when Eisner left to supervise a weekly "comic book insert" for newspapers. The syndicate wanted a costumed character to cash in on the *Superman* craze. What Eisner gave them was *The Spirit,* a hard-boiled detective series with Runyonesque overtones. His "costume" consisted of a domino mask, which all the characters ignored. Eisner was drafted into the Signal Corps during World War II, where he pioneered the use of comic book techniques in training manuals. He returned to *The Spirit* from 1946 until 1950. Though the comic book insert was still successful, Eisner wanted to explore the educational uses of comics. Through the '50s and the '60s he created hundreds of training manuals for industry and the military. It was lucrative work, but Eisner and *The Spirit* were all but forgotten until his former assistant Jules Feiffer brought them back into the public eye in his book *The Great Comic Book Heroes. The Spirit* developed quite an

12

From *The Spirit*

From *The Spirit*

underground reputation, culminating in a magazine devoted to reprinting the series. In 1978 Eisner returned to comics with *A Contract With God*, a collection of stories about the residents of a New York tenement during the Depression, reminiscent of Frank Capra and O. Henry. He has done several other books in this vein, including *New York: The Big City*, *The Dreamer*, and *The Building*. It has been some career.

This is a transcription of an interview conducted by Cat Yronwode at the Multi-Media Convention.

YRONWODE: *I want to talk a little bit about what brought Will Eisner to where he is now, and to do that I've got to start at the beginning. Will, when you were growing up there were no comic books to read. Nowadays people who get into the business do so because they've been fans of comic books. You had only newspaper strips to read, and presumably it was through reading newspaper strips that you decided to become a cartoonist. What strips did you like?*

EISNER: Well, the major influences, as far as strips go, were the ones that were making the greatest changes in the medium. Milt Caniff, even Al Capp, but mostly strips like Herriman's *Krazy Kat*. The major drive that brought me into comics at the time was a lot different than it appears today. I think I'd like to say something about that, because I think it's an important insight. Comics have gone through at least three major stages. In the beginning, during the early '30s, when comic books came into being as the result of an accident, of a printing need, people who came into comics came from many other fields. They came from the illustration field, they came from the world of gallery painting, they came from book illustration. The artists that I hired at Eisner-Iger in the first production shop were people who had never had any comic book experience. There *was* no comic book experience before. The influences, then, came from early illustrators. Wyeth's illustrations of Stevenson's books were in themselves a kind of comic book illustration. When somebody asks me what got me into comics, I can only think of one word: malnutrition. All of us moved to comics because they were an outlet. Illustrators or artists who had the combination of storytelling ability and the drive for illustration and art could find no other outlet. I was very lucky. I was born at a moment when this medium was a-borning, too, which gave me an opportunity to employ two skills which I knew I had, the urge to tell stories, to write, and the ability to draw and illustrate them, to visualize them, if you will.

YRONWODE: *You were very young. How did you get a job, and where did you get one?*

EISNER: Well, there were *no* jobs. You wandered around trying to sell your work. The syndicates were the only form of opportunity. I wandered into a magazine called *Wow*, which was starting, and as a matter of fact, I asked Bob Kane [creator of Batman] one day what was around—Bob Kane was going to high school with me at the time—and Bob told me he had just sold some drawings to a thing called *Wow* magazine, which was going on somewhere downtown. I wandered in there, and I was able to sell them a story. The magazine lasted about two issues. I was able to successfully kill that. I have had great success in killing magazines. I killed the *Herald Tribune* in 1966. [*laughter*] But it opened up for me an opportunity because I realized that there was a need for so-called original story material, and a whole new kind of readership. From there on in, publishers were coming into the field, and changes were taking place, just as they are taking place today. Pulp magazines were dying, and pulp publishers were looking for other popular publishing ventures, and so comics represented that opportunity.

YRONWODE: *You added something to your career that many comic book artists and writers didn't do. You started your own packaging shop where you produced comics for these publishers who didn't have their own staff.*

EISNER: There again, it was a question of seizing an opportunity. There was a need, and I attempted to supply it. Most of the publishers had no way of knowing whether or not they could even produce this material; they didn't even understand how to produce it. So there was this marvelous opportunity to take this and deliver an entire package ready for camera, so that the printer could just run it off. We assembled a shop in late 1937–early '38. I had just been fired because this magazine had collapsed, I was out of work, on the street, so we formed a shop called Eisner and Iger. I put up the money. The entire financing of that came to fifteen dollars, which I advanced, and that's how my name was first, because I was the financial partner.

YRONWODE: *You supervised [the artists'] work?*

EISNER: The shop was run pretty much the way a Roman galley ship operates. I sat at the end of a long row of sweating artists. I created an idea, and then passed it down the side of a wall, and it came back. I would make a rough idea of what I wanted in the way of story. We would preprint the panels on big sheets of drawing paper. I'd rough out approximately the story and write in some of the balloons, and it would go down along the wall to a fellow named Jack Kurtzberg, who later changed his name to Jack Kirby—whatever became of him, I don't know. [*laughter*] And then it would go on down to the letterer, and then to a background man, and then it would come back and I would look at it. As we grew in size and prosperity, we had a whole staff of people. Bob Powell came along—by the way, no one in my shop used their right names— Bob Powell was Bob Powellowski, and we decided Bob Powell was a much better name. I was operating under four or five names, my favorite of which was "Spencer Steele," which I loved [*laughter*]. I always wanted to be called Spencer Steele, it seemed to me—

YRONWODE: *I always liked W. Morgan Thomas.*

EISNER: Well, that was good, but it sounded like a banker. Well, there was Fine, Lou, and there was Chuck Mazoujian—a number of people who found themselves a great career. All of them there, by the way, were there as a kind of stepping place, that was a first stop to either, hopefully, dreaming of becoming a syndicated cartoonist for the newspapers, or going on into book illustration. Those who started never dreamed, including myself, that there was a future there in that field, and they would grow up with their identity as a comic book artist. Comic book artists then were regarded both socially and in the profession as what the Germans called an *Untermensch*, a subhuman. It was not uncommon for those of us who were doing comic books not to say we were doing comic books; when we were at a cocktail party, we'd say we did illustrations. Cartoons. If you said comic books, some nice lady would stand there and say, "Oh, really?" This is in very small letters in a large balloon. And then she'd say, "How nice." Second pause. And go on somewhere else.

YRONWODE: *In 1940 you had the opportunity to stop doing costumed super-heroes, which you had been doing mostly up to this time, and start* The Spirit, *and you broke up your partnership with Jerry Iger at that point.*

EISNER: You want to hear about that?

YRONWODE: *The world wants to know.*

EISNER: Now it can be told. Due to the Freedom of Information Act, I think I might as well reveal it since you can find it out anyhow. Somewhere in the summer of 1939, one of our customers, for whom we had been producing some work, a guy named "Busy" Arnold, who himself was publishing several comic books, and the Register-Tribune syndicate, which was then owned by the Coles Brothers in Minneapolis, called me and asked me to come over and see them. Apparently they had no idea, and apparently it came about because newspapers asked for it, that there was the possibility to syndicate what we called in those days a "ready print." That is, a preprinted comic book which would be inserted into Sunday newspapers. And newspapers were beginning to feel the pressure of loss of circulation because by then *Superman* was a sensational success, *Batman* was doing well, and a whole bunch of other comic books were doing well, and they began to realize that maybe they were going to lose their newspaper readership. I would like to say they came to me because they thought I was the world's greatest genius, but I'm afraid I have to confess that they came to me because I apparently by then had a reputation of being able to deliver on a regular and reliable basis reasonably good comics, because when we were producing for publishers, we would deliver on time. I struck a very, very satisfactory deal. I would have, for the first time, my very own comic strip. But the most important thing was that for the first time, I would be able to address myself to an audience other than that ten-year-old cretin in Kansas City. Now, I had a corporation: Eisner and Iger was a corporation. We had a buy/sell agreement. I said to Iger, you can either buy me out or I'll buy you out, but I feel it would be unfair for me to go ahead and do this, where my entire aesthetic attention would be, and then remain your partner and turn out your stuff. I just couldn't be fair and so, we tossed a coin, but we talked about it for a few minutes, and then he said, I'd like to buy you out, because then I will have something and you can go on. Which he did. And I moved on, down the street to a little studio in Tudor City. One of the agreements we made was that I would not "raid" the shop. Since I was the creative partner, so to speak, the working partner in this partnership, I had a great deal of personal relationships with many of the artists in the shop as well as professional relationships. So there was a danger that I could empty the shop and leave him with nothing, and that wouldn't be fair, so we had kind of an election. I could only take five people with me. And so five people elected to come with me, and the rest of the people elected to stay. Lou Fine, Bob Powell, Chuck Mazoujian, Chuck Cuidera, and somebody else, elected to come with me, and we opened up a little shop and began producing this weekly newspaper strip, a daily, and two other comic books. Very exciting time. A very warm, studio kind of relationship.

YRONWODE: *And you did the lead feature,* The Spirit.

EISNER: I did *The Spirit.* It was a sixteen-page comic book at that time. The first one that appeared here in Philadelphia was a sixteen-pager with two other features, *Mr. Mystic* and *Lady Luck. Mr. Mystic* was done by Bob Powell, *Lady Luck* was done by Chuck Mazoujian. Later on, when Chuck went on to illustration, because he really didn't want to be a comic book artist, Klaus Nordling came along and took over and did it very well, and later on, another artist, Fred Schwab, came along, and we started a bunch of interesting features. I started a thing called *Blackhawk.* Very fascistic strip. As a matter of fact, the first *Blackhawk* was done by Dave Berg, who now works for *Mad* magazine.

YRONWODE: *So* The Spirit *was different from all the other things. It wasn't like* Blackhawk *or the heroic crime-fighters of that age. The Spirit was a crime-fighter on the surface, but the stories were more like human interest stories, or a little science fiction story here, a tragedy there, or a comedy. You varied them. There was no one format.*

EISNER: That's right. And the reason for that harks back to my perception of the medium when I started. As I said earlier, this was a great opportunity for me to address myself to an adult audience, adult in the sense that the Sunday newspaper audience was composed of a mix of adults, teenagers, and little kids, mothers, fathers, in the national demographic mix. So it opened up an opportunity for me, first of all, to do what I had always tried to do, which was, employ the medium for what it was. It was a literary form for me *always*; it was a form of literary expression, so I could address myself to this. Secondly, as I said earlier, I brought, as all my contemporaries did, some of my literary or cultural nutrition into the field. I grew up on short stories. I grew up on literary works of the Dickens magnitude, and so forth. I was a fan of Ambrose Bierce's stories, I loved O. Henry, so for me this was an opportunity to do short stories in the great, classic tradition. And in the late '20s these short story writers were writing short stories for newspapers, just as I was doing, so I saw myself as just doing this in my medium. That's a very important thing. I regarded it as *my* medium. I still see it today as a unique combination of words and pictures. Now, I was writing short stories. As far as *The Spirit* is concerned, the only reason *The Spirit* had a mask and wore gloves is because it was purely a spineless concession on my part to the syndicate. When we started, they said what are you going to do, and I said I'd like to do a series of short stories, and they said no, it has to be a recognizable, syndicatable character, and they said, do a costumed character. They didn't call them super-heroes in those days, it was "costumed characters." So, I just couldn't bring myself—I had my belly full of *Sheena, Wonder Man, The Flame,* all the other things I had done—I really wanted to do a human thing. I remember one rainy night—it always seems to be raining when I'm making big decisions—I got a call from "Busy" Arnold when I was just finalizing the character, and he said, "Has he got a costume?" And I put a mask and gloves on him, and I said, "Yes, he's got a costume." That was how the costume came about. But *The Spirit* himself was as confused about his role in society as I was. I could never figure how super-heroes—where they get the absolute, unmitigated gall to stand up and say, "Well, I will solve the world's problems." *I. The Spirit* was a very middle class kind of guy. Always has been.

YRONWODE: *You were drafted into the army. When you came back, after having done educational stuff for the military during the war,* The Spirit *continued. It was done by Lou Fine when you were gone, but when you came back, the whole quality of the strip changed again. You began using more black ink on the page; the backgrounds, the landscapes, became even more important in setting the mood.*

EISNER: Well, again, you must understand that the comic strip, the comic book in its finest form, in its most *honest* form, reflects the thinking, the culture, and the background of the artist and the writer who created it. My background, up until that time, was rather closeted. After four years in the army, I had a chance to get a new perspective. When I came back, I could see the city suddenly as it really was. Up until then, I'd only seen it from a curbstone view. Now I had the chance to see it as it was. It gave me a chance to develop with more confidence what I had really wanted to do. I had experimented during the year in Washington with using comics as a teaching tool, and came out filled with that idea. But still I felt that here was my medium, here was my literary medium. Now I want to interject something here: my real orientation is not film as much as people think it is. My real orientation is stage. My father was a scenery painter, painting stage sets in the Yiddish Theater down on Second Avenue. He had come from Europe, where he had been painting murals in churches. And his backdrops for sets [on stage] were very, very close to how I think. Thinking of panels as a stage is far different from thinking of them as a frame in a film. So the ambience, the mood of *The Spirit*, of course, took on that kind of background.

YRONWODE: *After the war, too, I remember* Spirit *stories where at the end The Spirit would even close the curtains.*

EISNER: You'll see that a lot in the lighting. Lighting is very revealing. Lighting, for an artist, generally depends on how he sees something, his sense of perspective. Those artists—if you look at comic books, you'll see them—those artists who come from the far west, or outside of major cities, think in terms of horizons. Their lighting generally is flat—maybe not flat so much as solid. They see lots of sky. I grew up in the city. Most of the light I saw came from a lamplight, vertically, or light coming through tall buildings. I either saw things sharply up or sharply down, coming down the stairwell in my apartment house, or walking up a stairwell in my apartment house, I saw light; I still do, even to this day, sharply and directly, and people coming from the West or from farms and places like that see light as diffused. This is an example of what I mean by cultural input.

YRONWODE: *Jules Feiffer, who worked for you at that time, said that what you were writing was a morality thing.*

EISNER: Well, he may be right. A lot of the things Jules has said in the past may very well be right. For example, he said *The Spirit* had no socks. I want to say here and now, if he had no socks, it was Jules's fault, because it was his job to color in *The Spirit* for a while, and he always neglected to color in the socks. [*laughter*]

YRONWODE: *You were also interested in the educational possibilities of comics. You stopped* The Spirit *simply—first you hired Wally Wood to ghost it, and then you brought it to a close and went into commercial work, and you did that for a long time. Most of your fans are unaware of the years and years and years you spent putting out educational reading material.*

EISNER: Well, Wally Wood came on as an assistant—I was really desperate at the time to keep *The Spirit* alive if I could, because I was no longer able to work on it. During World War II, as I said earlier, I discovered the technical and teaching possibilities of the comic medium, and I came out of the war and started a company called American Visuals Corporation, and to my astonishment and great pleasure, the company grew. Within six months, it was a going company. Our second customer was General Motors. I mean, people were just coming and buying this material. The use of this medium as a teaching tool was phenomenal. As the business grew, *The Spirit* became less and less—not less important—but I was less and less able to devote myself fully to it. You've got to keep in mind, too, that I was not at all ashamed—to this day—of that episode in my career. I believe what I was able to do then was demonstrate the viability of this literary form or this medium. The thing that has always attracted me personally and professionally is to be in the vanguard, to be experimental, to do new things, to be a mountain man, if you will, to be the first guy up the hill. It's not always financially rewarding, but it sure is very satisfying. So when you say commercial, I began applying comics, and sold to the Department of Defense in 1950 the use of comics, as a teaching tool which went into a magazine called *P.S. Magazine*, which was an instructional magazine in the whole area of preventive maintenance. Then, of course, Wally Wood's appearance was kind of a last gasp. Nobody wanted to continue *The Spirit*. *The Spirit* was running into trouble, anyway, because newsprint was getting more expensive and space was becoming short, so they were talking about cutting *The Spirit* down to an eight-pager, which we did, and we dropped the other two features. Then the newspapers were talking about reducing it to a four-pager, and I could see where it would ultimately—

YRONWODE: *After you left* The Spirit *to do this commercial work, comic book fandom really didn't know that you still existed. Then some reprints started of* The Spirit. *In 1966 you did that thing for* The Herald Tribune . . .

EISNER: *The Herald Tribune* had just discovered comics.

YRONWODE: *But that was during that whole explosion of pop interest in comics—the camp thing, the Batman craze—you did a new thing for them, and then Harvey Comics reprinted some* Spirit *stories, and you did a couple of new stories for them. You haven't worked very much on* The Spirit *since then. Most of it's been reprints, Warren publishing them, and now Kitchen Sink is reprinting* The Spirit. *I know people ask you when will you draw* The Spirit *again.*

EISNER: And I always answer, why? Why do it again? I feel the same way Sir Arthur Conan Doyle—to be presumptuous, putting myself in his company—felt about Sherlock Holmes. I've done it. I've done it well. As well as I could, anyhow. What's the point in going back and doing it again, when I have so many more other things to do and there are only so many miles to go, as the poet said, before I sleep. There's so much more to do. I see no reason to do it. I've been in this business long enough to say never say never, but I see no reason to do it. I have no objection to doing a cover for *The Spirit* once in a while, or doing *The Spirit* graffiti here and there.

YRONWODE: *Why did you decide to return to comics with* A Contract With God *in 1978, and why did you choose the autobiographical style?*

EISNER: Well, first of all, it's not easy being the 2,000-year-old cartoonist. And I came back largely to scotch the rumors of my death. As far as how I feel about what I'm doing now, it's not a hard question to answer. I really have no interest in showing two mutants dismembering each other, and spending thirteen to fourteen pages on that. I think there's something more to tell about, more to life than that. A fantasy world is fine, and it's a very easy world to write in and live in, and I think that somebody should supply that material, there's no question about it. I guess in that concept I'm for legalized drugs.

YRONWODE: *Is that how you see it, as an addiction?*

EISNER: Not as an addiction, but it's fantasy. It supplies a need for fantasy life that has nothing to do with reality, and I don't think we have time, or I'd go into the social implications, but I think there's a need. If you were just born ten, twelve, fifteen, eighteen years ago, and discovered that there's somebody, somewhere just sitting in front of a box with a red button that he can press at any time and wipe us all out, it's got to have an effect on your psyche and your thinking, and suddenly, things have a different meaning than to people who believed, in the '20s and '30s, that they had control over life and only if they worked hard, like Horatio Alger, you could marry the boss's daughter and get rich and live happily ever after. As far as working alone, it took me about a year to get used to the idea. I've spent most of my professional life working with a group of people whom I had working for a company, or doing all the things that are necessary to run a business. Now I found myself sitting in front of a board in a nice suburban setting in a nice, very comfortable studio, writing about the things that were very important to me. At first, I must say, I felt the same amount of fear. There's a need for a great deal of courage to go ahead and write about the kind of things I'm writing about, merely because there's no known audiences for it. Those of us who work in comics at least know that today comic artists can go to conventions and have an audience. But I grew up at a time when we never heard the applause. You don't hear it. I feel now that what I'm doing is merely an extension of what I started out doing, which is to move from a literary point and write on the subject of greater moment, greater importance, and greater value than the stuff from Krypton, or whatever.

From *Jungle Book*

HARVEY KURTZMAN

WHEN MAX GAINES DIED IN A BOATING ACCIDENT IN 1948 HIS NE'ER-DO-WELL son William took over the family business, an unprofitable company called Educational Comics. With enthusiasm, an affection for horror and science fiction stories, and no experience whatsoever, William Gaines turned EC (redubbed Entertaining Comics) into the dominant comics company of the '50s. He hired the cream of a brilliant new generation of cartoonists, including Jack Davis, Wally Wood, Al Feldstein, Johnny Craig, John Severin, Will Elder, and Bernard Krigstein. He paid them well and gave them an unprecedented amount of artistic freedom. EC's line of horror, science fiction, war, humor, and crime comics set standards in art and storytelling that in many ways have yet to be matched. They also set new standards in violence. Thanks in part to EC, comic books became the focus of a national scandal, culminating in a Senate investigation on a supposed link between comic books and juvenile delinquency. Though comic fans tend to characterize this as a witch-hunt equivalent to the Army-McCarthy hearings, given the standards of the times and the content of many of the books, it's not hard to see why parents became alarmed. Eventually Gaines called a meeting of comic book publishers to form a response to public pressure. The publishers' response was to turn on Gaines. They established the Comics Code Authority, which essentially banned everything Gaines was publishing.

Except for Harvey Kurtzman's *Mad*.

It could be said that in the great age of iconoclasm, Harvey Kurtzman was the first man to buy a hammer. He originally made his mark editing EC's war comics, *Two-Fisted Tales* and *Frontline Combat*. They were like no war comics ever before, tough-minded, deglamorized, and painstakingly researched. From Agincourt to the Changjin Reservoir, Kurtzman portrayed warfare as dirty, frightening, capricious, and absurd. In 1952 he created *Mad,* which was to become one of the biggest successes in the history of publishing (though not for Kurtzman). Starting out as a parody of other comics, *Mad* soon developed into a full-scale assault on the hypocrisy, sentimentality, and plain silliness of popular entertainment in general. As popular entertainment was the main repository of American ideology, *Mad* became a much deeper assault than Kurtzman might have at first imagined. In many ways, *Mad* set the tone for American humor for the next twenty years.

With the coming of the Comics Code, Kurtzman and Gaines converted *Mad* to magazine format, but Kurtzman would only edit a few more issues before a longstanding conflict with Gaines over ownership of his work came to a head. Ultimately Kurtzman demanded fifty-one percent of *Mad,* and ultimately Gaines refused. Kurtzman would start three more humor magazines after *Mad—Trump, Humbug,* and *Help!. Trump* and *Humbug* were artistic successes but financial failures. *Help!,* his longest running magazine after *Mad,* was more of a mixed bag, but contained some of Kurtzman and Will Elder's finest work. It also was the first magazine to publish soon-to-be underground cartoonists like Robert Crumb and Gilbert Shelton. *Help!* folded in 1965, and Kurtzman turned his energies to commercial art and producing *Little Annie Fanny* (with Elder) for *Playboy.*

Mad created in its young readers the desire to emulate Kurtzman. The demise of *Help!* left them no place to realize this desire. The end result was underground comics.

This interview was conducted by Kim Thompson and Gary Groth.

JOURNAL: *Could you talk about your peers during the EC days— what they were like, what their interests were, how passionate their interest in comics was . . .*

KURTZMAN: Well, we were all interested in comics at the time. We wanted to do nothing *but* comics back then, and the guys that I worked with—I'm talking mainly about Will Elder, Jack Davis, John Severin, and Wally Wood—we worked together and we played together. We were close professionally and socially. We were all about the same age, same circumstances. We'd all gotten out of the army or navy, we all got married during that same period.

Willie Elder went to school with me, so I knew him from way back. We had the Charles William Harvey Studio, so we had an almost uninterrupted continuity from high school on. He was always a zany cutup, particularly in high school; he was the class clown. Many years later Willie told me that he resented his clown period because he realized, as many clowns do, that they're clowns because they want desperately to be loved. Of course, that makes them the fall guy. Willie has quieted down a lot; you wouldn't recognize him for his sober approach to life right now.

But Willie was a bona fide clown in high school, a very funny man. I've told "Willie stories" time and time again, about when he was "absent" from class and a particularly nervous teacher opened up the coat closet and found Willie hanging by his neck, his face chalked white. Willie would hang in the coat room all period long just for that laugh—the fall guy.

We used to have study hall in the auditorium balcony and when the students would file into the balcony they'd fill in what was called a "Delaney Card" and leave it with the teacher and then he'd take attendance at the end of the period. Well, Willie would come in and fill out a Delaney Card, and then he'd secretly drop over the edge of the balcony some ten feet to the auditorium below, go around, get another Delaney Card, and another Delaney Card ... Later, the teacher would take attendance and he'd have these phony Delaney Cards. So he'd call out "Losophy? Is Phil Losophy here?" or "Tom Mato?" [*laughter*] Of course, nobody would answer. That was the kind of thing Willie was always doing.

He was a crazy, maniac kid. He told me this particular story, which is very distasteful but very funny, where he ran with a gang of kids in the rail yard in the Bronx, and they found an unsealed refrigerator car filled with joints of meat. So they borrowed some children's clothes from a local clothesline and they dressed the meat and spread the joints along the right of way and then stood on the overpass yelling, "Oh, Shloimie, what happened? Shloimie fell on the tracks!" And the police came and gingerly gathered up everything in baskets. They eventually came after Willie.

[general laughter]

KURTZMAN: All right, that was Willie. Now, Jack Davis is the Jimmy Stewart of cartooning. He's beloved. Everybody likes Jack, and if you can imagine Jack, he's practically a cliché of a moving-picture southerner. He speaks with a gentle Southern accent, although to hear him mimic people, he's like Peter Ustinov or Peter Sellers if he wants to make strange noises come out of his mouth: a truck driver, a German U-boat commander. He's probably the most stable cartoonist I've ever worked with. The word for Jack is "stability." Easy to work with, never complains, never gives you a hard time, compliant, and very talented. And an ideal guy from an editor's point of view to work with because very often cartoonists would get very edgy about your decisions and that was always a pain to deal with. But with Jack, if he had any complaints, he kept them to himself.

Jack is a very entertaining guy. He can entertain you face to face, and he can entertain you on paper. Jack's work is very much like his personality, easy-going—likeable. And whatever Jack did was pleasant-looking. I always used to argue with him over the speed he worked at—I wouldn't argue, I would berate and he wouldn't argue back because of his very stable, pleasant nature—but one fault I always found with Jack is, he worked too fast. I always tried to slow him down. When he really slows down he's capable of doing some incredible work. Whenever he worked fast I felt it was detrimental to his work.

Wally Wood was a workhorse and I feel that Wally devoted himself so intensely to his work that he burned himself out. He overworked his body. That's my own observation. Wally had a tension in him, an intensity that he locked away in an internal steam boiler, and I always had the feeling that Wally was capable of erupting—which he apparently did occasionally—but he had that quality of frustration and tension and I think it ate away his insides and the work really used him up. I think he delivered some of the finest work that was ever drawn, and I think it's to his credit that he put so much intensity into his work at great sacrifice to himself.

John Severin. I also knew John back at the High School of Music and Art. We corresponded before and during the War, and a remarkable thing about John—when he wrote letters, he would illustrate the outside of the envelope with a watercolor or a pen sketch—and I think he was as good then as he is today. He was born a remarkable draftsman. But another thing, I always had the feeling that he never knew what he was good at, which is why I don't think he ever *really* improved. He improved professionally in the sense that he knows more tricks today, he's probably faster, he's probably more resourceful, but the drawings he did when he was sixteen, seventeen, eighteen were as good as anything he's ever done.

I'll never forget, John once asked me to tell him, "What's the meaning of design?" And I tried to tell him back then when I was dumb. It was one of John's real problems, design. And design, of course, is the pure business of moving your graphics around. You move them this way, you try up, down, sideways—John was always weak in that department. His graphics were very conservative. He never really moved forward as I feel he should have. But he was so remarkable to begin with that if he never did another thing but his original envelopes, he'd be good. John and I drifted apart. We sometimes worked well together, and sometimes there was tension, and unhappily we did drift apart.

JOURNAL: *How do you compare the EC bunch to the rest of the cartoonists who were then working? Were they a different kind of people than the ones who were working in the other comic book companies at the time?*

KURTZMAN: Well, what happens in the cartoon business is, there are invisible magnetic lines of force the artists form themselves along into patterns. Artists who have similar "vibes" come together. Jack, Willie, Wally Wood, we were natural friends. We had similar attitudes that made us appeal to each other. With the subsequent success of *Mad* I really had the pick of the cartoon industry and our doors were open, so practically everybody who was important, artistically, came through the door. But it'd always come back to Jack and Willie and Wally, again and again. We tried people like Gene Colan, Dave Berg, Joe Kubert, even the house people like Johnny Craig, Reed Crandall, and they didn't work out! Bernie Krigstein, George Evans, they weren't quite right. God knows what the alchemy was. We not only enjoyed working together—I don't mean to imply that we were without problems—but we enjoyed each other's talent and we enjoyed each other's presence. We would picnic together, have outings together, have parties together, and like that.

JOURNAL: *Were you a student of history before the EC war books?*
KURTZMAN: No. I hated history. As a matter of fact there's some kind of lesson therein. When I had to do school book history, and

we'd get our assignments to read this and read that, it was the dullest, most boring exercise. Many years later, when I did the history and war books, and I *had* to find out about things—suddenly history became a fascinating subject. I could stay in the library forever and just read and read. The motivation to learn history was totally different, and motivation means so much, you know. In school the only motivation one had was to pass a school test. School history was just pale, dumb, and unbelievable.

But getting into library history books and finding out the real truth, finding out what the world was and had really been like, that was very exciting. Learning that Custer was an idiot and he was a disappointed presidential office-seeker, that he was *not* the last standing man in the circle of Indians. When I was a kid, the only thing I knew about Custer was the Budweiser Beer poster where you'd see this glamorous drawing of a guy heroically holding off the redskins. And that's the way it was in the movies, and that's the way it was in the school books—it was all phony! And then George Washington with his wooden teeth—and the way he'd almost given up in despair in his first battle with the British. Have I made the point?

JOURNAL: *You know, one of the complaints is that history textbooks are dull, unreadable, and blanderized, so that they aren't interesting to the students.*

KURTZMAN: I suspect that—I don't know if it's that way anymore, because some very interesting things are happening in education. They're full of all kinds of training aids now, but—I would imagine that the motivation behind the writing of school history books gets so confused that the end product that comes out of the censorship mill is dull and uninspiring, not because people want it that way but because there are uncontrollable, well-meaning forces at work.

JOURNAL: *And, of course, a textbook can never have a personal viewpoint. It's done by committee.*

KURTZMAN: For reasons that are essentially impure.

JOURNAL: *Maybe the difference is that textbooks are just giving you, instead of truth, a series of facts—*

KURTZMAN: No, they're doing worse than that. They're deliberately misleading you. They lie. The Custer thing—why was Custer pictured as a hero? That had no basis in fact. His last act was selfish, not heroic. There had been a time when he was a hero. He was very instrumental in the winning of the battle of Gettysburg, but for various reasons somebody—or a committee—decided that Custer should be a hero.

I was absolutely appalled by the lies in the war books that publishers were putting out. What they did when they produced a war book is they focused on what they thought the reader would like to read, which was, "Americans are good guys and anybody against us is the bad guys. We're human. They're not. And God is always on our side." This trash had nothing to do with the reality of life. Our *Two-Fisted Tales* was originally an adventure book and when the Korean war broke out we jumped on that particular bandwagon— some bandwagon!—and tried to tell about how war really was. Now to do that I felt a need to go into research and accuracy of detail.

JOURNAL: *It seems that much of your work is based on skepticism of what the media show us. On one side, the war books, where you were trying to tell the other side of the history books—*
KURTZMAN: Not the other side. The truth.

JOURNAL: *Right. Whereas* Mad *seemed to be founded on skepticism of the media.*
KURTZMAN: Again, truth. We'd say, "Hey, did you know that Mickey Mouse is a dressed-up, three-fingered rat and his friend Donald doesn't wear pants?" and that was funny. And it was true.

JOURNAL: *Essentially, what you did was take the fallacies and by parody inflate them so much that their fallaciousness was unmistakable.*
KURTZMAN: Yes. That's very good.

JOURNAL: *How do you think your perception of what was true was shaped? Was it through your experience in the army, or was it through reading books, or . . . ?*
KURTZMAN: All of that, and it was research and interviews. I think that a good piece of creative work is one that reflects the truth and is insightful, gives you a little bit of understanding; conversely, false work promotes ignorance. And when I talk of work that isn't true, I *don't* mean fiction or fantasy.

JOURNAL: *You're talking about moral truth as well as factual truth, then.*
KURTZMAN: Yes. *The Wizard of Oz* is probably my all-time favorite film; there's a moral truth in it and, of course, no factual truth at

all. What a nice lesson it teaches when it says, "There's no place like home" and "You should go back to Auntie Em" and things like that. I believe in *The Wizard of Oz* the way I believe in *King Kong*, which technically and factually has nothing to do with what's true, but at the same time has a moral truthfulness that I enjoyed enormously.

JOURNAL: *Yes, because I think there is an unfortunate tendency to focus on all the accurate factual details in your stories, but they don't really mean as much as the moral honesty behind it. You can construct a story with many many factual details and it might still be false or hollow.*

KURTZMAN: Of course. Factual truthfulness certainly isn't enough in this world, and I'd be the first to admit that. I like to think that I pursued moral truths, but I don't like to think that I was telling anybody what's wrong and right. I like to think that I'm a moral person, but the older I grow the more nervous that kind of thinking makes me, because I see so many people who are absolutely convinced that they're on the best moral ground while in actuality they believe in horrible things. "Everyone but thee and me . . ."

JOURNAL: *How was* Mad *created?*
KURTZMAN: Ever since *Mad* started I've heard twenty stories about who was responsible for *Mad*'s creation and to hear it I had very little to do with it. But as *I* remember it, I became desperate to do a quick comic. I wasn't making any money with the war books. There was too much research and laying out and authenticity involved, and I think I was averaging two weeks per story, as opposed to Al Feldstein who would write a story a day, or a minute, or a second. I just couldn't hack it. I was tired, I got sick, I went to the hospital with yellow jaundice. I was breaking down under the work load.

Gaines was accessible—we were always talking about troubles and problems—and I told him it was getting to me. I was always bitching to Gaines, because I was always working from that handicap that I imposed on myself—researching, writing, laying out . . . [*sighs*] It was a terrible handicap, but I couldn't work any other way. So I somehow convinced him that I should do something else that was easier. Gaines said, "Go ahead."

Now, I'd always been doing satire in school, in the streets; it was my kind of clowning. When I wanted to win popularity, I'd draw a cartoon. And in school everybody wanted me to sign and draw in their yearbooks because I could always say something funny. So I proposed the format *Mad*, I proposed the title, made little title sketches and showed it to Gaines, and he said, "Go ahead." The format would make fun of comic books as they were at that particular period. So I had a "horror" story and a "science fiction" story and so forth. We used the physical format of EC—four stories, with the legal text requirement in the center. I gathered in my favorite artists, I wrote the stories, laid them out, and that is the God's honest *truth* on how *Mad* started, goddamn it. [*laughter*]

JOURNAL: *I know* Panic *had at least one very major problem with censorship—the Santa Claus story—and I was wondering whether* Mad, *while it was a comic book, had any such conflicts?*

KURTZMAN: No, we didn't have any problems. Of course, we had the big problem: Could we ever live under the censorship of the Comics Code? We decided, absolutely *no*. We could not go on as a comic book.

JOURNAL: *How did you feel about the whole area of censorship?*

KURTZMAN: Well, I was bitter. I felt that the comics business had brought censorship down on its head because of the kind of thing the horror comics were doing. I always thought the horror comics were evil. At some certain point they'd turned sick, I thought, and I think they reached that point when EC was running short of classic book plots and had to turn inward; what came out was sheer grue—ideas that sniffed of necrophilia. (Of course, who am I to talk, with my own naked cartoons?) Back then I took issue with the horror stuff. When the investigation turned on EC, it was like, "I told you so! Look what you did to us!"

JOURNAL: *Did you think that comic books should have a censoring bureau like the Code to halt the kind of horror comics that were being done back then?*

KURTZMAN: I didn't like the horror comics and I felt that there should be some controlling system. See, comic books are essentially sold to children—or were—and children are second-class citizens. They *should* be. They don't have the vote, they're not responsible under the law for what a grown-up is, and for good reason. There's an unequal relationship between parent and child that's legitimate. A parent has certain responsibilities toward his child. The parent is responsible for the child's welfare and environment.

So here's the newsstand filled with horror comics that can be bought with lollipop money. How do you relate to that part of your child's environment? Do you keep your child off the streets? Do you censor the newsstand? Once you have a son or daughter, you clearly realize you have responsibilities! You can't say, "Okay, go out in the street and don't come back." You've got to feed the kid, you have responsibilities to teach your child as well as you can what's right, what's wrong, what's up, what's down. The horror comics were just bad.

JOURNAL: *How fast did it become apparent that* Mad *was going to become a huge success?*

KURTZMAN: Well, something was in the air with the first issues. We started getting letters. We got an avalanche of mail. I was very impressed by mail, and said, "Ooh, I've got to answer every letter." I actually asked Gaines to buy an office Dictaphone and he said, "Go ahead, I got you the Dictaphone." And I used to go on the subway and dictate answers to the letters for Marie Severin to write up. Marie was my then-assistant, she was of course John's sister, and I took her into the business as a colorist for the war comics. So when the mail started coming in, I knew that we had something hot.

JOURNAL: *How were the sales initially?*

KURTZMAN: They climbed. Just kept on climbing, climbing, climbing. Oh, we had our ups and downs. There were distributor problems, there was Gaines and the horror comics, and the Kefauver Committee and the inquiry and the court appearances.

JOURNAL: *Did you testify?*

KURTZMAN: No. Gaines and I always had a running battle over what we thought comic books should be. I look back at it now and it was all silly, but I never liked Gaines's horror comics, and I was always resentful of the fact that the horror comics were so profitable and all my carefully-researched stuff had to be a labor of love. And, of course, with the success of *Mad* now I wanted my reward.

Also, Gaines was a very paternalistic guy. Paternalism has its good and its bad sides—it gives you a certain kind of security, but at the same time you always have to go to poppa. And we had a series of ever-increasing arguments, and finally I decided to ask for as much as I dared, and if Gaines didn't give it to me I was going to quit. So we had a confrontation and I quit because he didn't give me what I wanted. And I certainly can't say that I blame him.

JOURNAL: *Was your demand unreasonable?*
KURTZMAN: Probably, yeah. I don't want to go into it because it's a very sensitive business.

JOURNAL: *Did you have any conflicts with Gaines over the editorial content of* Mad?
KURTZMAN: No. Gaines really left me alone.

JOURNAL: Mad *was initially a comic book parody that sort of branched out into other-media parodies . . .*
KURTZMAN: Yeah, we ran out of material! I mean, how long can you keep making fun of *Superman?* You do Plastic Man, you do Flash, and pretty soon you run out so you have to go on to other things, which is what we did.

JOURNAL: *What did you think of Marvel's later* Not Brand Echh?
KURTZMAN: There were so *many* imitations. The imitations were coming out of the woodwork. I've got an attic filled with *Mad* imitations, *Blechh, Echh, Ptui, Ergh, Blaugh, Blurp . . .*

JOURNAL: *I remember you built an ad around all those imitations, promoting EC's own* Panic *as the best imitation of* Mad.
KURTZMAN: *Panic* was another sore point. Gaines by some convoluted reasoning decided to double the profit of *Mad* by doing a Feldstein version of *Mad*, and he just plundered all of my techniques and artists. For me, there was a real conflict of interest.

JOURNAL: *When the decision was made to change* Mad *from a comic book into a magazine, what other magazines inspired you? How did you come up with the basic format of the magazine as opposed to the comic book?*
KURTZMAN: Well, I went to the biggest newsstand I could find— that was in the budget—and I bought a whole bunch of magazines. You have to understand, I had never been into the so-called slick magazine business . . . By the way, another one of the motivations that led to the new format of *Mad* was, I was offered a job by *Pageant*. A guy by the name of Harold Hayes—who subsequently became the editor of *Esquire*—came from *Pageant* to do an article on *Mad*, which he did. He then went with the story back to his

editor-in-chief Harris Shevelson, who then offered me a job as his assistant. So I went to Gaines and said, "Gee, I've got this chance to go into slick magazines, and I really want to do it." He said, "What can I offer you as an option?" and I said, "To do *Mad* as a slick magazine." That would be a dream fulfilled, because slick magazines were up *here*, you know, and comics were all the way down *here*, but to get into slick magazines . . . *wowee!*

So I ran around, and I designed a format on the basis of what was being done in magazines that year, and on the basis of what our production man George Daugherty told us that Gaines could afford. I chose the printer, the process, the package, and we were in business. It was a very brave step for Gaines to take, because he was stepping out into the void. We didn't have any idea of what the slick magazines business was all about or where we would wind up, and Gaines was in big trouble because of his failing comic book business, so he didn't have many shots in his pistol. And he had to borrow money for *Mad*. But it all worked out.

JOURNAL: *How many issues of the slick* Mad *did you do?*
KURTZMAN: Again, my memory . . . probably a half a dozen is all. I brought it up to Alfred Neuman and beyond Potrzebie.

Did I tell you about Alfred E. Neuman? He was picked off a friend's bulletin board, a guy named Bernard Shiv-Cliff, who worked for Ballantine Books. Bernie had this postcard on the wall with this "What—Me Worry?" photograph, so we took the face and we attached the name Alfred E. Neuman, which we borrowed from Henry Morgan, who borrowed the name from the musical arranger of the '50s Alfred Newman, who was credited with a thousand movies as musical arranger. We were originally using the Neuman name under a blank face as a forgettable name and a forgettable face. The *readers* brought the "Worry" kid and Neuman together by insisting on calling the kid Alfred E. Neuman. I got curious as to how the kid got started and I mentioned it in one of the issues. We got letters saying it started here, it started there. We got twenty versions of "What, Me Worry?," variously captioned: "What, Me Worry?," "Me What Worry?," "What, I Worry?," "Worry? Me?," "Who, Me Worry?," and we got drawings that dated back to World War I, 1918 Coca-Cola ads, Alfred E. Neuman drinking Coke. The most plausible version of where he came from and the one I accept today is that he originated in a medical text as an example of a person lacking in iodine. It was after Alfred E. Neuman's beginning that I left.

JOURNAL: *What did you think of the way* Mad *developed after you left it?*
KURTZMAN: Did they develop?
[general laughter]

KURTZMAN: They haven't had a new idea since—No, I shouldn't say that. They've done all right. Al Feldstein does a very efficient job. I think he's a lot better at making a profitable magazine than I was. Al's a real professional.

JOURNAL: *You've been linked with the underground in several different ways. EC was to a large extent an inspiration to many of the undergrounders; you gave a number of them their first break in* Help!; *how do you look at the underground movement, which is in a way almost your offspring?*
KURTZMAN: The underground was a remarkable phenomenon . . . Let me digress to make a point. Rick Meyerowitz—the guy who did the *Animal House* poster—talks about my work. The way he phrases it says something that may or may not answer your question. When he was a kid and got his first copy of *Mad*, he said, "All of a sudden I saw—you can do things this way! You didn't have to do it the old way!" It was a revelation to him that things could be done that "way," whatever the hell that meant.

The underground movement had the same kind of effect, on the Europeans in particular. The Frenchmen looked at Crumb, at S. Clay Wilson, and said, "Gee! *We* can do stuff like this! Why not? I mean, it's *possible!*" The underground was kind of a revelation to cartoondom. I've talked to Moebius, to Gotlib, to René Goscinny, and they talked about the revelation of the American underground. And also (ahem) the revelation of *Mad* magazine, and they were inspired. Inspiration really makes people go out and do new things. So I felt the underground was especially good in that it inspired so many new approaches to cartooning. It didn't solve the problem of the economics of cartooning. The underground was bankrupt as far as that goes, unfortunately.

JOURNAL: *What do your neighbors think of your career?*
KURTZMAN: It's like the time Hefner invited me to go from Chicago to his new mansion in California on the Bunnyplane, the big black jet. I never left air conditioning. You go from the air-conditioned house to the air-conditioned limo and out onto the field and into the air-conditioned jet, and it's full of showers and beds and luxuries.

The pilot came back to me and said, "We've got a new telephone system we're testing. Do you want to call home?" And I said [*gleefully*], "Ah, great idea!" The telephone was actually a radio-phone, it clicked on and off, talk-receive, talk-receive. And the radio signal beams into Bell telephone below feeding into the regular phone network. You call anywhere you want. The thing is, you're going 600 miles an hour at 30,000 feet and you've got to lock into a phone center fast before you get out of radio range. So the pilot is saying, "Okay, I think we've got it, we're over Phoenix, we've got a connection—quick, make your phone call." So I dial my number. My wife answers. "Hello," I say. "Adele? Guess where I am? Get this: I'm flying above the *Grand Canyon, 30,000 feet* in the *air*, flying *faster than sound, and I'm calling you on the telephone!*" She says, "What do you want?"
[**general laughter**]

KURTZMAN: So I say the only thing I can think of: "Were there any messages for me? Any letters, any phone calls?" And that's the way the neighbors are. *Nobody cares.* The neighbors get used to seeing you mowing the lawn and taking out the garbage.

But then you get to go to a comics convention and that's something else. All of a sudden I'm Frank Sinatra playing the Paramount in 1948 and everybody is asking for autographs.

JOURNAL: *How do you react to that kind of fan reaction? Do you enjoy it?*
KURTZMAN: After a particularly long spell in the attic, you get the feeling that nobody knows you're alive, and then you go to a convention and everybody loves you, so it's very good for your ego.

JOURNAL: *Well, we're going to make you famous with this interview.*
KURTZMAN: It's about time!

ROBERT CRUMB

ROBERT CRUMB BEGAN HIS CARTOONING CAREER IN THE PLAYPEN. A COMpulsive cartoonist from the age of three, Crumb spent his childhood drawing his own comic books, keeping monthly schedules, and "backdating" his issues like real comic books. His earliest influences were Walt Kelly's *Pogo,* Carl Barks's *Donald Duck* and *Uncle Scrooge,* John Stanley's *Little Lulu,* and, when he got into his teens, Harvey Kurtzman's *Mad* and *Humbug.* Like many another in the '50s, Crumb grew up thinking of comic books as a natural means of expression, only to see creative comics all but disappear with the introduction of the Comics Code and the collapse of *Humbug.* In 1963, convinced he could never fit into the commercial comics business, he took a job drawing greeting cards for the American Greetings Corporation in Cleveland, where he would work off and on until 1967. He continued drawing his comics and honing his skills, with no idea of how or when he'd ever get a chance to put them before the public. As it happened, he made the chance himself. In 1968, he and some friends published *Zap Comix.* It was like nothing ever seen before, going beyond Kurtzman's example to take on religion, sexual mores, and social assumptions in the most scatological ways imaginable. Most of all it was, as Bill Mauldin once put it, the funniest thing you could buy. Young cartoonists flocked to San Francisco to follow Crumb's example, and underground comics were born. Crumb went on to produce a dazzling array of comics, including titles like *Mr. Natural, Home Grown, Despair, Hytone, Uneeda, Motor City, Black and White* and *XYZ. Zap* became a forum for the cream of underground cartoonists, including Gilbert Shelton, Spain Rodriguez, S. Clay Wilson, Victor Moscoso, Rick Griffin, and Robert Williams. Crumb's

VOL. 3 NO. 47   OCTOBER 25, 1968

METROPOLITAN 15¢

Mr. Natural, disguised as a vacuum cleaner salesman, talks to the Housewives of America.

most popular comic, *Home Grown,* has sold over 140,000 copies, and the thirteen issues of *Zap* have collectively sold over a million. In the '70s, a series of financial and personal problems cut his output drastically, and he was considered by some to be a spent force. In the '80s, however, he came back with *Weirdo,* a magazine that revitalized comics in the '80s much as *Zap* did in the '60s, and entered into one of the most creative phases of his career. He is widely considered the foremost cartoonist of his day.

This interview, conducted by Gary Groth, picks up in 1965. It was an eventful year for Crumb. After returning to Cleveland from an extended trip to Europe, he began taking LSD. Harvey Kurtzman invited him to come to New York to take over from Terry Gilliam (who would later become a *Monty Python* member and film director) as assistant editor on *Help!*. When he reported for his first day of work with his idol, however, he found the furniture being removed. The publisher had suddenly pulled the plug. After a year of trying to make it in commercial art, Crumb returned to Cleveland . . .

JOURNAL: *Where did you go when you left New York?*
CRUMB: I went back to Cleveland. I gave up on New York. It was too fast for me. I decided it was better just to work at American Greetings, because the work there was fairly easy to do. It was a much more low-key kind of job. I stayed a year, and I couldn't stand that. That's when I was taking LSD. Everything then just looked like a big sham, the whole thing, fucking civilization all of a sudden just crumbled before my eyes into so much cardboard.

JOURNAL: *Why did you start taking LSD at that time?*
CRUMB: Nobody at American Greetings knew anything about it, but I knew these hipsters hanging around the university area in Cleveland who started taking it. It was just starting to come into circulation then. It was still legal, because you could get it from psychiatrists. That's where my first wife got it, from a psychiatrist. People were talking about it, Leary was talking about it. It was a kind of logical step from marijuana, which I also just started smoking around that time. People said it would give you visions and help

you understand the deeper cosmic significance of life. Well, that sounded good. I had no idea it would be as powerful an experience as it was. It just knocked me on my ass completely. It's taken me ten years to recover from it, basically. Ten years! What am I talking about? Twenty years it's been since I took it.

JOURNAL: *What were its effects?*
CRUMB: The experience itself is indescribable, but afterward you no longer feel a member of this accepted version of reality. Basically, you're coming from another planet. You're using the old language to communicate with people, but you're definitely seeing things as if you're coming from somewhere else. Going to work after a night of LSD was like coming from Mars back down to Earth. It was hard to do. People would stare at me, say, "Crumb, what's the matter with you? What's wrong? What's wrong?" I'd say, "Nothing, oh, nothing." "You look funny. What happened?" So, functioning in normal society became very strange: going to work, dealing with things that people were taking very seriously, which to you were obviously just a bunch of silly games that didn't mean anything.

JOURNAL: *Did this sense of distortion impair your working in the real world?*
CRUMB: In a certain way it made it easier, because you were no longer taking it seriously. But, of course, you were also just biding your time.

One day in January, 1967 . . . after work I used to go to this bar. There were a couple friends of mine, said they were on their way to San Francisco, and I got talking to them, and without even thinking about it I went with them. [Pause. Look of stunned disbelief on the interviewer's face.] I didn't go home. Left my wife, my job, didn't tell anybody anything.

JOURNAL: *Just like that?*
CRUMB: Yeah.

JOURNAL: *With the money in your pocket?*
CRUMB: Yeah, I think I had seven dollars.

JOURNAL: *Well . . . what prompted you to do that? Was it dissatisfaction at home, or was it the LSD . . . ?*
CRUMB: All of that. Also, I'd heard that interesting things were happening in San Francisco. About a month before that, somebody

brought some of the psychedelic posters back from San Francisco. When I saw those, I instantly knew there were artists taking LSD and that their artwork had been transformed by the experience. That was certainly not happening in Cleveland, so it was somewhat kindred spirits out there.

JOURNAL: *How did your wife hear about this?*
CRUMB: Three weeks later I called her up and told her where I was. She was pissed off, and then she came out.

JOURNAL: *How long did that last?*
CRUMB: I lived with her another several years after that, had a kid with her and everything . . . Jesus, what a mistake! But, in San Francisco I couldn't do any more cards. They were sending me cards to do and I just couldn't do them anymore. They'd send me the ideas in the mail and I'd look at them and just get sick to my stomach. I just didn't fit in any existing things that were set up. When I was in New York, underground newspapers were just starting, and they used some of my drawings, but they had just picked them up out of a coffeehouse where I had left them at a table. I saw them next week in the underground newspaper. In San Francisco, I went down to the guys who were doing the psychedelic posters for the dances, and they didn't want any more artists. That was the only thing I even tried to do as far as getting work doing art in San Francisco. Here and there I'd meet somebody who wanted a little drawing. I remember a couple of jobs I did. I did an outdoor enamel painting with psychedelic lettering. I did one for a guru church, and one for an antique store, and a couple of other ones. They paid me a few bucks. That's about it.

JOURNAL: *And you lived for three dollars a day in a dive on Mission Street?*
CRUMB: My wife got a job working in a home for unwed mothers. We lived on that for a while, then she got pregnant, and we lived on welfare for several years. I was still drawing, but I wasn't thinking about making a living or a career out of doing it. The LSD just knocked all that for a loop. You didn't think about careers or anything practical at all. You were walking around in a dream. All these other people were, too, so it seemed okay. [laughter] You didn't even ask anybody how he made a living, what do you survive on, where do you get your money. They would just look at you and say,

"You mean you still care about those things? Loosen up!" One guy said to me, "Survival's transcendental." "Oh, okay." [laughter] The government's paying for it. A lot of people lived on welfare, dealt drugs, some people got money from their parents, whatever. We kept things going. The rents were real low. It was real cheap to live in this town in those days. I had an apartment with two bedrooms for seventy dollars a month. It was nice. It was a nice life. I couldn't believe, after being in Cleveland and New York and Chicago and places like that, what a piece of cake this town was. It was so sweet, and everything was so fresh. There wasn't all this urban rot going on.

JOURNAL: *This was in '67 and '68?*
CRUMB: Yeah, in there. I was still drawing, filling up sketchbooks. Things were still spinning. I couldn't stop it, I didn't know what to do with it at all.

JOURNAL: *How could you afford LSD?*
CRUMB: Never bought it. It was just around. There was so much around that people were giving it away. I never bought it, never paid for any drugs ever. I never bought a goofy stick, nothing.

JOURNAL: *I think you've claimed that you've done some of your best work on LSD.*
CRUMB: Never *on* LSD. I could never work while *on* LSD.

JOURNAL: *Well, during the post-fog, then.*
CRUMB: All that stuff from the late '60s was inspired by LSD. The visions and attitudes I got out of taking that drug definitely altered my work drastically.

JOURNAL: *You told a story about how you took one very bad trip . . .*
CRUMB: One, or two, or three, or four . . .

JOURNAL: *No, this was one where someone actually warned you about the particular hit, but you took it anyway, and you described yourself as being in some "weird electric fog" which you had difficulty getting out of.*
CRUMB: Yeah, I took the drug in New York [in 1965], and I left New York and went to Chicago and stayed with my friend, Marty Pahls. That's when I thought up all those characters that dominated my comics from that period: Mr. Natural, Shuman the Human, the

Snoids, Flakey Foont . . . I was seeing Snoids everywhere. It was really weird. It was a state of grace in a way. I couldn't talk. Whenever I was riding a bus or sitting around my mind would just start to drift into this uncontrollable state. I would see ladies dancing, electronic figures in my brain, with no control over it. It was kind of a delirium, but it was visionary and it was kind of nice. I remember when it ended I thought, "Well, here I am, I'm back down to earth now. Too bad."

JOURNAL: *How long did that delirium last?*
CRUMB: For a couple of months. I would just drift in and out of it. But I was completely nonfunctional. I couldn't do anything. I could draw, but I could hardly talk to people, let alone hold down a job or anything.

JOURNAL: *So, you feel that you wouldn't have been able to create what you did without the drug?*
CRUMB: It would've been different, it definitely would've been different without that. Something happened in there. I could show you in my sketchbooks where that period starts, when I was in that fuzzy state, and how my art suddenly went through this change, this transformation in that couple of months. I don't know if it would've happened without that or not. I was free from any interference from that rational part of my brain. The frontal lobes were completely fuzzed. [laughter] It's like when you get interference on your TV and suddenly it all starts going fuzzy, that's what happened in my conscious mind. It was just fuzzy. If I tried to think rationally or focus my conscious mind, all I got was fuzz. If I wasn't doing that and I let it go, then all these dancing images would start up.

JOURNAL: *Do you find it at all unsettling that you needed LSD to push you into this particular creative state?*
CRUMB: No, not at all. I'm glad it happened.

JOURNAL: *But, are you glad that you couldn't engage your creative faculties without the use of LSD?*
CRUMB: I could, but they just would've been different. I was set on that path of doing that work from early childhood, but it just would've been different without it. It would've been more serious. I probably never would have gotten into that real ridiculous cartoony phase, where I was basically doing throwbacks to the Popeye/Basil Wolverton/Snuffy Smith style of cartooning. I did that as a joke. That

absurdity was such a deep part of the American consciousness, that way of seeing things, and I suddenly rediscovered that in that state. All the dancing images were in that grotesque, funny, cartoony style with big shoes and everything.

JOURNAL: *I find it interesting that you were in this delirious state, and yet you were still technically adroit.*

CRUMB: I lost a lot of technical skill. A lot of technical skill went by the board.

JOURNAL: *Is that evident in your art of the time?*

CRUMB: Very evident. In '64 I would do complicated drawings from life of buildings. I remember this one I did of a pier in Atlantic City with all the beams and everything just right, just drawn directly in pen, without even thinking about it. And I was amazed when I looked at those drawings recently and realized that for years I had lost that completely from being stoned all the time. Everything comes down to a very iconographic level when you're in that state.

JOURNAL: *Iconographic meaning rudimentary?*

CRUMB: Yeah, rudimentary, and iconic images rather than drafts-manship and technical things. It comes down to this simplistic, iconic level. It's the only way I can explain it. Technical stuff lost its importance. The whole thing became less serious, which was very good for me, because I tended to take myself so seriously. [laughs] And now I sometimes have problems because taking yourself so seriously as an artist can be a really inhibiting factor in terms of working. And I lost all of that in that period.

JOURNAL: *What do you do about becoming overly serious now?*

CRUMB: I just fight with it. LSD wouldn't work now. It stopped working. It was a free ride.

JOURNAL: *Do you think it's possible to have that change in perspective without taking LSD?*

CRUMB: Oh, sure. Lots of ways to do it.

JOURNAL: *But you needed the LSD.*

CRUMB: I don't know if I needed it, but I took it, and once you take it there's no turning back. You can't undo that. It's like once something's unraveled, it doesn't ever quite . . . that crack in the standard program of reality is never quite sealed up as tight again. Although confusing things happened later. The last few times I took

LSD, it wasn't the same anymore. It stopped working in that way. It became something else. I think like any other drug, it has a revelatory quality when you first do it, but after a while it just doesn't work anymore. I took it when I was very young, and I wasn't really sophisticated enough to know exactly what was happening with it. Although it was very magical and gave me certain understandings, as time went on it became difficult to sort those things out. Since then I've come back down to the old standard serious way of dealing with reality and sorting it out without the drugs, while trying to deal with reality in such a way that I don't get too seriously caught up in it or become self-conscious. I still deal with that, although having gone through that LSD experience, I know that my mind is permanently altered. I'll never be the person I would have been if I hadn't taken it.

JOURNAL: *Hmmm.*
CRUMB: Have you ever taken it?

JOURNAL: *No.*
CRUMB: Don't bother. [laughter]

JOURNAL: *But, it did succeed in changing your perception from that point on. It wasn't a temporary alteration.*
CRUMB: In certain ways it was temporary. To an extent, but not completely. The state I was in in 1967 and 1968 couldn't last. You can't be in that state of visionary grace forever. It's like a free ride . . . you can't spend your whole life on a roller coaster.

JOURNAL: *You hooked up with a guy named Brian Zahn, who published an underground newspaper called* Yarrowstalks *in Philadelphia. How did that come about?*
CRUMB: He saw some of my work somewhere. I guess I gave him some stuff out of my sketchbook for his underground newspaper. He said he really liked it and commissioned me to do a whole issue of the paper, all comics. So I did, and that went over great. Then he said he would publish comic books, so why didn't I just draw some comic books? This was in the summer of '67. I immediately set to work and turned out two issues of *Zap Comix,* and sent him all the stuff for #0, which was originally supposed to be #1. I never heard from him again. I called up the place and they said, "Oh yeah, man, he went to India on some kind of trip, man. I don't know," and that was it. I never got my artwork back.

JOURNAL: *But you made stats.*

CRUMB: For some reason I had made these Xeroxes to show somebody, something I never did as a rule, and I had forgotten about them. In the meantime, Don Donahue wanted to print the second issue, which became *Zap* #1. About a year later I remembered about the Xeroxes and I got them back from the guy. By that time #2 had gotten rolling with these other artists, so I called it *Zap* #0.

JOURNAL: *Why wasn't that* Zap *#3?*

CRUMB: Well, I sat around and talked about it with these other artists, because *Zap* had become a joint venture by that time. We decided it would be better to make it #0, since it had been drawn before. Calling it #3 would have confused the continuity or something.

JOURNAL: *How did you hook up with Rick Griffin and Victor Moscoso to do* Zap *#2?*

CRUMB: They were doing these psychedelic posters, they had played around with comic-type motifs, and they had been talking about doing a comic book. They saw *Zap* #1, I guess, and they said, well, that's the ticket right there. They contacted me about their interest in doing psychedelic comics. About the same time, S. Clay Wilson came out from Kansas, and he wanted to do crazy comics, too. So it seemed like a natural thing to put it all together. Then the Print Mint got involved. They were a publisher/distributor of psychedelic posters, and they thought they could handle comics as well.

JOURNAL: *Would you attribute this coming-together to the counterculture and the politicalization into different factions?*

CRUMB: All of that stuff, yeah.

JOURNAL: *Because today you just wouldn't see the kind of politicalization that would unite artists.*

CRUMB: Uh-uh. There are still some people trying to get together, but it's harder now.

JOURNAL: *But there's not a sense of community even among the more serious comics artists who should theoretically have similar goals in common.*

CRUMB: There never was that much. And before underground comics happened, there was no art comics community at all. Nothing. Now there is . . . of sorts. There was no such thing as a comics convention or anything like that in those days.

JOURNAL: *There was still a sense of shared attitudes among the underground cartoonists, wasn't there?*
CRUMB: Well, that still exists somewhat.

JOURNAL: *Actually, it's more like warring aesthetic factions.*
CRUMB: The next step after shared attitudes is warring factions.

JOURNAL: *You were propelled into the limelight in '68?*
CRUMB: Late '68, yeah. It happened real fast. Within six months it went from me, my wife, Donahue, and a couple other people hand-stapling comics and selling them on the street out of a baby carriage to having all these fast-talking lawyers fighting over the rights and sleazy guys offering big money contracts. It all happened within six months. It was a crazy time. All of a sudden my life was just turned completely upside down. By the end of '68 I didn't know what the hell was going on anymore. I couldn't think straight. I was young, I was like twenty-four when this whole thing happened, and all of a sudden the phone's ringing all the time, people want to talk to me. They want me to do work, this and that. The hippie thing was a happenin' thing and the vultures were descending to find out how they could shear the sheep. The comics thing was a part of that. These guys saw that the kids were going for this shit, so they tried to figure out how to market it and make a killing.

JOURNAL: *What was your first major confrontation with the money men?*
CRUMB: There was a series of them. Some guys would offer me free plane tickets to New York. They wanted to talk to me. "Oh boy! Free plane tickets to New York! Can't pass that up!" So I get to New York, and these three guys are there with their leather trench coats. They have a paper here they want me to sign. "Wait a minute, this is a five-year exclusive contract! You want complete control over everything I do for the next five years? What are you, nuts? I can't sign this!" There'd be drugs, there'd be women, there'd be alcohol, everything.

JOURNAL: *Did you take any of it?*
CRUMB: Sure. But I still didn't sign the fucking paper. The ones that finally got me were the *Fritz the Cat* people.

JOURNAL: *Ralph Bakshi?*
CRUMB: Bakshi, yeah.

JOURNAL: *You started drawing Fritz in Europe in 1965?*
CRUMB: No, I drew it in pencil in my notebooks for years, probably starting in 1959 or 1960. It was kind of an outgrowth of those funny animal comics that my brother and I drew all the time we were kids. We had this cat named Fritz, the family cat. I did these comic strips about our cat to amuse my little sister and younger brother. That's basically how it started. The earliest ones that are in print are from the sketchbooks I did in '64 and '65.

JOURNAL: *So you actually drew Fritz five or six years before that.*
CRUMB: Yeah, but the ones that are in print are definitely a lot better than the earlier ones.

JOURNAL: *So how did Bakshi get to you?*
CRUMB: Another free plane ticket to New York. He picks me up there, and he's like this seething, sweating, neurotic guy. He's already got all this work done before he'd even told me about it. He's got these pencil animation sequences of the *Fritz the Cat* movie already done. He was so desperate. He said, "Look, you've got to let me do this. My whole career is hinged on this thing. I love it so much." I said, "Well, I don't know, let me go home and think about it." I never did tell the guy he could do it. He was a schlock-meister, a no-talent bum, completely. He'd done these Saturday morning cartoons that were just terrible. The producer, Steve Krantz, was a complete Palm Springs sleazebag. He's sort of a Jewish character type, almost a Milton Berle kind of guy. I kind of liked that aspect of him. I had this meeting with Mr. Krantz, and I said, "I worry about my work and I don't know what's going to happen with it. I'm young, and I don't have enough savvy to know how to control these things." He puts his arm around me and says, "Robert, if I had it in my power, I would take you in my arms and protect and shelter you from any harm that could possibly come to you in this business." He was gushing with sincerity. What a shark!

JOURNAL: *So you eventually gave them permission to do the film?*
CRUMB: No, I never gave them permission.

JOURNAL: *Didn't you get paid?*
CRUMB: Well, what happened was that Bakshi finally came to San Francisco desperate for me to sign this contract. He'd already done half the film, and I still hadn't signed. I didn't tell him no, I just said, "I don't know, I don't know." I just couldn't confront the guy. He was such a desperate neurotic, so aggressive. He was just sweating, beads popping off with desperation. Finally, he came to my house to get me to sign this thing, and I said, "Okay, but look, I've got to go see some people. I told them I'd be over at their house at one o'clock. I'll be back a little later." I left and didn't come back for a week. [laughter] In the meantime, he finds out that my wife had my power of attorney. He told her, "You sign this paper, you get a check for $10,000 right now." She signed it, no problem. [laughter] He gave her the ten grand. She took it and bought a house immediately.

The thing about it is that these lawyers who were supposed to be representing me said, "What's your problem with this? These guys are going to put you on the map with this fully animated *Fritz the Cat* movie. What are you quibbling over your precious creation for? You're going to get money, you're going to get fame." I knew they'd louse it up. There was no way they could make a quality product.

JOURNAL: *You hated the movie?*
CRUMB: It was terrible.

JOURNAL: *Hated it enough to put an ice pick in Fritz's head?*
CRUMB: He needed killing bad. [laughter] Then they did that *Nine Lives of Fritz the Cat.*

JOURNAL: *How and why did you grant them permission again?*
CRUMB: I didn't. They had permission. It was all in the contract my lawyers wrote up. They owned *Fritz the Cat.*

JOURNAL: *So they could've done as many Fritz movies as they wanted to.*
CRUMB: Yeah, *Fritz Goes Hawaiian,* whatever.

JOURNAL: *What were some of the other schemes that were offered you?*
CRUMB: Oh, God. One guy in New York had this whole merchandising package for *Fritz the Cat.* He wanted to do this even before Krantz. He wanted to push it for all it was worth. A lot of

schemers were just hippie guys with big ideas about stuff. There was one group called Prodigious Productions—I'll never forget it—which was this whole group of hippies, I think they were from the upper class, real idealistic. They had all kinds of schemes: films, music, multimedia, everything. Nothing ever came out of that. It just evaporated. We lived on welfare. I didn't start making any money off comics until '71, '72, when it started paying enough to actually get me off welfare.

JOURNAL: *These were your most prolific times.*

CRUMB: Yeah, just nickle and dime stuff until then. So many sharpies and fast-talking guys. Jesus. Up until I got well-known, I'd never seen this side of life. I was a simple guy.

JOURNAL: *Do you consciously look for new ways of stretching yourself as an artist?*

CRUMB: No, not consciously. I don't think you can consciously contrive to do that, really. I think it's actually better for me not to look for that. I have no formula for coming up with ideas. They come all different kinds of ways, you know. Biographies of people whose lives are real gripping to me somehow, like Jelly Roll Morton or Boswell. I seem to be getting more and more in-depth in my own autobiographical stuff. As you get older you find your early life more and more fascinating. You get a more detached angle on your life.

I'm amazed that I still enjoy drawing. I'm so lucky. I'm just thankful that I still love to draw. How many people can say that when they're forty-three, that they still love what they do? I enjoy drawing in my sketchbook as much as I did when I was nineteen.

JOURNAL: *Are you compelled to draw?*

CRUMB: Yeah. If I don't do it for a few days I get really depressed. Life becomes completely meaningless. I'm so tied up with the drawing thing. I'm nothing if I'm not drawing. I like playing my musical instrument sometimes, too, but it's not the same thing. It's a diversion. Art is my life, Gary, what can I tell you? [laughter]

JOURNAL: *You're an artiste.*

CRUMB: Part of the benefit of LSD in the '60s was that it enabled me to separate my ego from the drawing a little bit, which allowed this whole flood of inspiration. If you have a heavy ego involvement which makes you worry about what you're doing all the time, it stiffens you up and causes a loss of spontaneity. Taking all that acid made my work very spontaneous. I spent all those years of struggle before that, so I had the ability. Acid separated me from it, so that I became real loose with it, casual, which is something that I don't think I'll ever have again. When I became disillusioned with drugs and stopped taking them, I thought I would never have another source of inspiration. But as you get older just the accumulation of your life becomes an inspiration.

JOURNAL: *Just life experience?*
CRUMB: Yeah. An accumulation of your vision of life. It's so rich and interesting in itself that you don't need anything else as inspiration except that.

JOURNAL: *Is there a sense when you do autobiographical work that you're trying to resolve something? Trying to make order out of your life?*
CRUMB: Oh, sure. It's therapy, whattaya tawkin' about! Make sense of it all. Probe it and understand it.

JOURNAL: *But does this actually work or does it only raise more questions?*
CRUMB: Well, everything that works creates more questions, but the questions become more interesting and more sharply defined. There's no end to questions. It's like peeling layers off. It becomes more and more interesting. Like I said, my big problem now that I have to struggle with is just clearing the deck so I can work and concentrate on it. It becomes more and more gripping and interesting as I get older. Expressing my life in my work becomes such an interesting, complete, self-contained drama that I could spend three-quarters of my life doing it if I'm allowed to.

PART II:

MEN IN TIGHTS

IN DECEMBER OF 1937 SHELDON MAYER, MAX GAINES'S EDITOR AND
production chief, ran across a much-rejected proposal for a newspaper
strip called *Superman*. Gaines sold it to one of his clients, Harry Donenfeld,
who, with the prophetic words ''Nobody's going to believe this,'' made
it the cover feature of *Action Comics* #1. From that day on the costumed
character or ''super-hero'' genre would become synonymous with comic
books. Even so, in their heyday comic books covered every imaginable
genre, from crime and westerns to sports and romance. However, the
anti-comics hysteria of the '50s and the growing popularity of television
reduced the medium to its two hardiest genres, costumed characters and
children's humor (such as the Walt Disney titles and *Archie*).

The costumed character comics of the '60s and after were not aimed at
children so much as adolescents. Jack Kirby, Steve Ditko, and Stan Lee of
Marvel Comics ingeniously tapped into the adolescent distemper of the
day; Spider-Man's alter ego Peter Parker was essentially Clark Kent
in high school. They also hit on the idea of having all the company's
characters live in one coherent ''universe,'' thus building the sales of
the whole line instead of this or that character. DC would eventually
follow Marvel's lead. As the '60s turned into the '70s, comic books
drew their writers and artists more and more from the ranks of comics
fans. Early comic book creators like Will Eisner took their lead from
pulp fiction, newspaper comics, and movies. The comic book creators
of the '70s and '80s more often than not take their lead from other comic
books. The costumed character comics of the '30s and '40s, by virtue
of their immense popularity, were an ubiquitous part of American culture.

The costumed character comics of today are, though profitable, insular and self-limiting.

There are, however, a handful of creators in this genre with wider horizons than their peers, whose interests are closer to those of the general audience than the comics cult, and who are getting broader recognition as a result. Foremost among them are Frank Miller, Bill Sienkiewicz, Howard Chaykin, and Alan Moore.

FRANK MILLER

FRANK MILLER WAS ALREADY MAKING A NAME FOR HIMSELF AS AN ARTIST ON Marvel's *Daredevil* when he took over writing the series as well in 1981. Left to his own devices, Miller created a crime comic that combined the social attitude of '30s gangster pictures, the plotting of '70s action pictures, and the visual style of *film noir*. While it was not, strictly speaking, anything new, it was a breath of fresh air in a decidedly uninspiring era for adventure comics. *Daredevil*, a perennial low seller, suddenly became one of the most popular titles in the industry. In 1982 Miller left *Daredevil* to work on a more personal project for DC, a lavishly produced six-issue series called *Ronin*. *Ronin* was a rather uneasy combination of science fiction and fantasy elements, exhibiting the strong and not yet fully digested influence of the French cartoonist Moebius (Jean Giraud) and the Japanese cartoonist Goseki Kojima. Though it garnered enthusiastic praise from Miller's fellow professionals, the public response was disappointing. He spent the next couple of years woodshedding.

In 1986 Miller roared back, dominating the field as no one has since Jack Kirby in the '60s. As writer, Miller did a five-issue return to *Daredevil* (art by Dave Mazzucchelli), a four-issue stint on *Batman* (also with Mazzucchelli), an eight-issue series called *Elektra: Assassin* (art by Bill Sienkiewicz), and a *Daredevil* graphic album (Sienkiewicz again). But the real blockbuster was *The Dark Knight*. His goal was to make Batman a living character in the public mind, and there can be little doubt that he succeeded. The sensibility of *The Dark Knight* might best be described as "mugged liberal"; it mixes a hard line conservative view of criminology with a radical view of politics, and can be criticized as demagogic on

#4 IN AN EIGHT-ISSUE LIMITED SERIES

·ELEKTRA·
Assassin

EPIC COMICS

ELEKTRA 4
NOVEMBER 1986

$1.50 $1.75 CANADA

MARVEL

PRELIMINARY TESTS ON THE ALLOYS THAT COMPOSED PERRY'S *SKELETON* LEFT US LITTLE HOPE OF DOING DIRECT STRUCTURAL DAMAGE--

--BUT WE WERE ASSURED THAT HIS PLASTIC *SKIN* WOULD BE VULNERABLE TO SUSTAINED *LASER* FIRE.

PERRY'S *OWN* LASER CAPABILITY WAS COUNTERED WITH *BODY ARMOR.* NO DEFENSE AGAINST HIS *PHYSICAL* STRENGTH COULD BE PREPARED.

MOST IMPORTANT OF OUR EQUIPMENT WAS OUR *PARTICLE CANNON,* DESIGNED TO CANCEL OUT PERRY'S *INTERNAL GENERATOR* WITH A CONCENTRATED STREAM OF *PROTONS.*

From *Elektra: Assassin*

either count. Still, its impact on the public perception of comics is undeniable. Frank Miller has established himself as a superior creator of thrillers in comics form.

This interview was conducted by Kim Thompson, just before the storm broke.

JOURNAL: *In the* Journal's *previous interview with you, you started off by talking about your reasons for moving to New York City. Now you're here in L.A.; why?*

FRANK MILLER: When I left New York, I had come to regard it as an emotional, psychological, and spiritual dead end. It simply costs so much in terms of aggravation and frustration. After eight years it became clear to me that the normal human response to the crime and unending hostility of the city would be to become as ungentlemanly and uncivilized as the city's customs demand. One Bernhard Goetz is enough, though I'm amazed there aren't more people doing what he did. Also, moving to California exposes me to a whole new world, very different from New England, where I was raised, or New York. And the weather is great here.

JOURNAL: *Your work always had a very strong urban, specifically New York sensibility. Do you think this will change? It's odd that you've moved just as you're embarking on two major projects, both of which are going to be extremely New York-oriented.*

MILLER: There is a delay built into how any life experience shapes my work. I'm a long way from completely assimilating what I lived through in New York. I am taking notes constantly about California. It's *much* stranger than I expected. And there's a lot more material here than I ever thought there'd be. Still, I would say that the only way that California is being applied to my present work is that, because I run into a lot more children out here, it's helped me to put the notes together on the new Robin. The speech patterns of California children are very, very peculiar. I've been keeping a notebook of odd little phrases I hear, to help me put together her way of speaking. She's the hardest character I can ever remember having written. And the more material I can get, the better. That's much more available out here. I don't know, maybe the weather will affect me and my stories will get a lot more pleasant.

JOURNAL: *[laughter].*
MILLER: That hasn't happened yet.

JOURNAL: *Is it possible also that the radically different environment will throw into even sharper focus your perception of New York? That in some ways you might not even be able to understand it while you're living there, but once you're somewhere else you can see it for what it is?*
MILLER: Absolutely. I'm already seeing a clearer, more accurate picture of the city in my new stuff. I came to New York with very specific expectations, all based on movies made before I was born, episodes of *Kojak*, and the warped impressions created by TV news. My first year demolished those expectations, but they still had more to do with the New York that I wrote in my *Daredevil* stories than the reality of the city did. In the *Dark Knight* series, there's a much more direct use of my real life experiences in New York, particularly my experiences with crime, my awareness of the horrible pressure that crime exerted on my life, and the fury of the fact that crime is so much taken for granted that people live in fortresses and walk around looking and acting like victims, carrying money to bribe muggers, acting as if it's all a numbers game, all up to chance, whether or not some monster can rob, rape, or kill them, for all intents and purposes giving total power over their lives to anyone who's savage enough to take it. I have found that my five months away from New York have given me a much better idea of what I was dealing with. I'm angrier about it now than I was when I was in the thick of it. I don't regret moving. Not often.

JOURNAL: *It's interesting that you're going to incorporate a more realistic view of New York into your* Batman *series, since* Batman *has always presented a stylized, more iconic vision of the city (here a.k.a. Gotham City), and the character. In this context, do you plan to go more with Batman as an icon?*
MILLER: Oh, much more. Much more. As a matter of fact, it feels as if this is the first super-hero strip I've ever done. I guess getting away from them for a while has given me a better perspective on what the super-hero is a response to, and what can be done with

the idea. Also, Batman is as good and pure a super-hero as you can find. He wasn't created to fill pages or meet the assumed expectations of an audience. He's actually a good character, as compromised as the idea has become, as corrupted by shifting political attitudes and fifty years of monthly publication. True, he has his roots in the pulp magazines, particularly *The Shadow*, but that material and at least a part of the Batman come from somebody's reaction to real life, which puts him closer to artistic legitimacy than almost any other super-hero, with the exception of Superman. What I'm trying to demonstrate in the *Dark Knight* series is that super-heroes do come from a good idea. By portraying the city in somewhat more realistic terms, and showing much more than I ever have of the way I think things actually happen in society, and why they happen, I want to show that the idea is good and strong and valuable.

JOURNAL: *I know that toward the end of your run on* Daredevil, *you were giving some serious thought to the fascistic implications of super-heroes. Have you since come to terms with that?*

MILLER: Well, I've gotta split your question in two. First off, what is implied by the super-hero stories that are being written now has become so muddled that it's very hard to apply any of it to reality. If you take the idea of a host of heroes out there seriously, you're pretty soon going to end up with a story where the entire world is radically transformed. If you really take seriously the idea of Superman, a character with the power of God, there's really no reason why he wouldn't completely transform the world. They can only continue publishing comics so long as they don't take the ideas that they've got the distance. I think Alan Moore's working on something that *does* take the idea the distance [this turned out to be *Watchmen*], but I stay away from the hosts of super-heroes stuff. As far as fascistic implications of a character like Batman, that's one of the things I'm really having fun with in the series. I think that in order for the character to work, he has to be a force that in certain ways is beyond good and evil. It can't be judged by the terms we would use to describe something a man would do because we can't think of him as a man. I'm doing this series at a very good time for me, because it's very clear to me that our society is committing suicide by lack of a force like that. A lack of being able to deal with the problems that are making everything we've got crumble to pieces. As far as being a fascist, my feeling is . . . only if he assumed political office. [*laughter*] If there were a bunch of these guys running about and beating up criminals, we'd have a serious problem.

JOURNAL: *Essentially, because he's an abstraction, it's not really a moral situation?*

MILLER: It's still a moral situation, but he's not the one being judged. He can't be judged the way humans are. Here we get into another important aspect of the *Dark Knight* series, and another quality of the super-hero that's been lost—the hero as a moral force, as a judge, as plainly bigger and greater than normal men, and perfectly willing to pass judgment and administer punishment and make things right. This idea, which I believe is a crucial part of what makes super-heroes worth doing, rarely pops up anymore. I've seen it in Michael Fleisher's *Spectre.* In some of what Mike Barr's done with *Batman*, and, most notably, in Steve Ditko's *Mr. A*, whose every adventure is a morality play. While I go for work that doesn't explain itself in such great detail, *Mr. A* is a real favorite of mine. Ditko's ability to construct a tight, simple, direct morality play is another demonstration of the man's astonishing mastery of the form. Crediting Ditko simply as a brilliant cartoonist is not giving him enough credit, nor is just describing him as a powerful storyteller. What I feel is most exceptional about Ditko's work is his ability to cartoon a character or situation from an emotion, from an intellectual or moral abstraction. *Mr. A* is a character who, visually, could not be improved on. Given the "judge not that ye be judged" mentality that dominates modern fiction and entertainment, it's no surprise that his work is notoriously unhip. And, as in Ayn Rand's case, he explains his thinking in such detail that he leaves himself open to endless attack. I feel that *Mr. A* is Ditko's most advanced and evolved work. But, in a time when the super-hero is constantly apologizing for himself, when the righteous "wrath of God" quality of the super-hero has largely been displaced by the screaming of a rebellious child, personal viewpoint is bound to be unpopular.

Back to *Dark Knight*—the closest parallel to what I've got in mind, the closest example in my own work is the *Daredevil* story I recently did with John Buscema, "Badlands." Batman, in my series, does not apologize or question what he does, or its effects. There's a whole world out there who can argue about that, and they do, constantly, throughout the series. And the effects of what he does are tremendous. He changes the quality of life in Gotham City, the way everyone there thinks and lives. Now, presenting a vigilante as such a powerful, positive force is bound to draw some flak, but it's the force I'm concerned with, more as a symbol of the reaction that I hope is waiting in us, the will to overcome our moral impotence and fight, if only in our own emotions, the deterioration of society. Not just some guy who puts on a cape and fights crime. That's a great thing about super-heroes, the substance of what makes them "larger than life." Not that they can fly or eat planets, but that they can, or should, manifest the qualities that make it possible for us to struggle through day-to-day life. The success of the first *Superman* movie demonstrates that, now that the world is good and fucked, the super-hero could be revitalized, could encourage us on a fantasy level to find the strengths we need. The dwindling box office at its two sequels demonstrates that Hollywood has no idea what to do with it, quickly turning it into ingenuous self-parody, focusing on all the parts of the character that are sentimental and outdated. It's as if the weak spots in the first movie were cracks in a dam, and by the third, the dam had completely crumbled.

I think Clint Eastwood is more in touch with what we should do with super-heroes than virtually anybody in comics. Dirty Harry is clearly larger than life; his behavior would certainly land him in jail. But that's irrelevant. What is relevant is that, through all his hostility, and despite his dirty language, Harry is a profoundly, consistently moral force, administering the "wrath of God" on murderers who society treats as victims. The sudden critical acclaim for Eastwood is, I think, less a sign of a political shift to the right than a reluctant acknowledgment by critics who really can't understand what he's doing, that his is a major talent and presence, that his work has more to do with what's happening in society than any dozen of the more hip filmmakers, even though he's making heroic adventure movies, something that neither Hollywood nor Hollywood critics can understand. What makes me nuts is that we, in comics, have the opportunity, if we can drop our bad habits, our concessions to the '60s generation along with the no longer appropriate view of the world, the view of the '30s and '40s that gave birth to the super-hero, if we can redefine the super-hero and make him a response to the insanity of our own times, we will have something to offer the world. And, incidentally, our chance at selling millions of comics.

But as far as actually putting on a cape and jumping across roofs and fighting crime, I would say, "Maybe, if it could be made to work." But . . .

JOURNAL: *[laughter] Seems somehow doubtful.*
MILLER: Yeah. And everything *Batman* does is in fact illegal. One of the fun things I do is explore the consequences of that. That is, there's a warrant issued for his arrest, and I follow that to its logical conclusion.

JOURNAL: *So you're taking the Batman to his limits?*
MILLER: I think so.

JOURNAL: *Do you think this series will affect the way* Batman's *been done for the last twenty or thirty years? Or is it just going to be regarded as an anomaly?*
MILLER: Oh, I have no idea what the effect'll be. I'm having a great time with the story, and that's really all that I'm concerned about. I'm doing some things with the character that have taken a great deal of thought to put together, other things that are so painfully obvious that I'm amazed they haven't been done.

JOURNAL: *You mentioned your working relationship with Jo Duffy on the* Elektra *material. Tell me about your creative relationship with Bill Sienkiewicz.*
MILLER: Working with Bill has opened up a whole new section of my career for me. I had no idea it would be anything like this. It started with a couple of fill-in issues of *Daredevil* that I'd been asked to write. Now, I have regarded Bill for several years as a talent who was a little too big for the material he was drawing, and had seen across *Moon Knight* and *New Mutants* pieces of work that stood out like a piece of Technicolor film on a black-and-white video screen. Moments where he showed an alarming perception, and an ability to take an unusual idea and make it into a picture. I could see him illustrating internal drama. So when I wrote these *Daredevil* stories, I tried to play into that, I wrote a psycho-drama. It was like a dam breaking when Bill got to work; he immediately produced pages that Marvel couldn't publish in a regular comic. Because they were so unfamiliar, so . . . strange, by comparison. It became a graphic novel because the work needed to be published, and then the situation started escalating. Every time the story would bounce back and forth between me and Bill, he would receive my

script pages, and we would talk and I would bounce back onto them again. It escalated like a war, and in a way, what goes on between me and Bill is; it's almost like we're shooting at each other. It's a volleyball game or a game of mumblety-peg. A lot of challenges flowing back and forth. Well, to put it simply, I'm having to reevaluate the way I approach my work. I've always had my own pictures to work with, and always regarded the pictures as providing a particular kind of information, and the words another kind. With Bill it's very different, a lot of the things that I would think would go into dialogue, or into a caption, are in the picture, and in fact my captions are covering what I usually use pictures for. The *Elektra* series we're doing is turning out to be an extraordinary piece of work on Bill's part. It's unlike anything he's ever done. He's using more techniques to greater effect than I would have thought possible. It's invigorating to work with him, because I generally don't collaborate much. I do sometimes feel like I'm in limbo, and this is very refreshing, to work with somebody whose method and whose thinking is so different than mine. I feel that Bill is one of the very few artists I know of who should be pushing the form forward. Bill's one of the people who should be doing graphic novels and Epic Comics and such, because he's got the talent, and he's got the perceptions, and his work is fresh and original, and he's dropping his comic book habits one by one.

JOURNAL: *What particularly impresses you about Bill's work?*
MILLER: The fact that in spite of all the disparate elements, it all pulls together and coalesces and makes sense. But if I was going to nail down a particular aspect of his work, I'd say it's the way that Bill cartoons human expression, the way he takes illustration techniques and uses them as well as the illustrators, but to greater purpose. He also draws like hell; I mean, he draws great. But I think it all boils down to emotion. I think he's a natural-born dramatist, and that's something that's going to become more evident. One of the things that he and I share, that's really enjoyable, is both of us have gone from a position in our careers where our clients and colleagues regarded us as kind of established, having arrived, and we both plunged into a very uncertain, scary, thrilling time, of discovery. Like the old saw, everything old is new again. Because of the work I've done, I'm now approaching the idea of the superheroes almost as if I'd never heard of it—almost.

JOURNAL: *As Patti Smith put it, "plunge into the sea of possibilities."*
MILLER: [*laughter*] Yeah. Bill and I are both enjoying the fact that we're young cartoonists facing a big open field that has hardly been explored. Both of us are enjoying testing and playing and throwing things against the wall and seeing if they stick.

JOURNAL: *Bill is more trained as a commercial illustrator, which I guess you aren't.*
MILLER: No, no, I've done very little commercial art. I hated every minute of it.

JOURNAL: *About the* Elektra *series . . . you know, on virtually every other comics project I can think of, the central responsibility for the narrative is lodged with one of the parties. For instance, in the case of Kurtzman-Elder, Kurtzman was in control; in the case of Kirby-Lee, Kirby was in control. Even when it gets a little harder to nail down, as with the current* Swamp Thing, *you can usually tell that one person (here, Alan Moore) is the main guiding intelligence.*
MILLER: Clearly.

JOURNAL: *But the* Elektra *material seems very evenly split between you and Bill as far as control goes.*
MILLER: Well, the way it works is that I write the story, anticipating what I think Bill would do with it, trying to play into his strengths and throw things at him. I believe he's been waiting to get problems along the line of those I'm throwing at him. So I come up with the story, and I structure it, and I give him the words and descriptions that really amount to suggestions for pictures. Then he proceeds to throw back at me his response to what I've written. And then I respond to that, rewriting. In every case, there's rewriting required, because of possibilities that are opened up, or redundancies that need to be removed. But it bounces back and forth. We relate very much as equals.

JOURNAL: Dark Knight, Elektra, Daredevil . . . *any plans after that?*
MILLER: Yikes. I got tons of plans. I've got lots of work I want to do. None of it at this point involves using Marvel or DC heroes or any characters that I've used before. I'm impatient to get on to some new stuff. I'm having a real good time on the various things I'm doing now, but in certain ways, this stage feels like it represents kind of an endpoint.

JOURNAL: *Yes. It strikes me that, not necessarily in terms of quality, the* Batman *and* Daredevil/Elektra *material is in some ways a regression compared to* Ronin.

MILLER: Yeah, it is.

JOURNAL: *I would tend to guess that probably once this sequence of stuff is over, you're going to venture into the big unknown again?*

MILLER: Yeah, yeah. What it all boils down to is what story I really won't be able to live without doing. That's what my decision will be based on. I'm continuously making notes for different story ideas. Most of them go nowhere, some of them go somewhere, and then every once in a while, enough pulls together and I realize that I've got something that I've *got* to do. The only reason I did the couple of issues of *Daredevil* that are turning into the Sienkiewicz graphic novel, besides helping Denny [O'Neil] and Ralph [Macchio] out of a bind, was that the story had been stuck in my head since I left the series. It had to be let out. And with the *Elektra* graphic novel, I was perfectly content to leave everything as ambiguous, as spacy as it was, in the series. Except as this idea grew on me, it grew on me in a big way. It became something that I wanted to do. But it's a lot of work to actually execute a big story, and the story has to be pretty good to be worth doing. I can't be more specific than that about what I'm going to do next.

One thing I find really fascinating right now is that there are very few middle-aged people in comics. The companies didn't hire anybody for about twenty years. The position that generation would have occupied has been assumed by people my age. And the best of us are very young, and are exploring. It's fascinating to be in the position of being an authority in my field at the age of twenty-eight. [*laughter*] One of the things that *Ronin* did was to dynamite my own and anybody else's expectations of me. And now, I feel like playing around a lot. [*pause*] It's very weird, standing at the beginning of a possible history and not at the end of one, because there's nothing left of the road behind me.

BILL SIENKIEWICZ

AT THE START OF HIS CAREER, BILL SIENKIEWICZ (PRONOUNCED SING-KE-vitch) was haunted by Neal Adams, a cartoonist who influenced comic art in the '70s in much the same way that Jack Kirby did in the '60s. Though he was only one of many, Sienkiewicz became the most notorious of "Adams imitators." It has taken him many years and a radical change in style to break the stigma. Still, Sienkiewicz became quite popular in his own right on Marvel comics like *Moon Knight* and *New Mutants*. It was during the latter stint that his art began to get, well, weird. The influence of decidedly non-comic book cartoonists like Ralph Steadman and Ronald Searle began to show itself, and his artwork became more and more stylized and less and less representational. It has also become less and less appropriate for costumed character comics. Unfortunately, in the comics industry that's where the money is. The only project Sienkiewicz has gotten ahold of that matches his talent is *Elektra: Assassin*, written by Frank Miller. Since then he's devoted most of his time to covers, illustrations, and the occasional offbeat comic like DC's *Shadow* (not to be confused with the Howard Chaykin limited series) and Epic's *Doctor Zero*. Among his more recent work is a strip on the history of CIA covert operations written by Alan Moore in *Brought to Light*, a comic sponsored by the Christic Institute.

This interview was conducted by Peter Sanderson.

FROM *BROUGHT TO LIGHT*

ASHORE, THE QUAYSIDE UNDERFOOT IS SICKENINGLY STILL. YOU WATCH MEN, LOADING CRATES OF SHRIMP WITH CROSSHAIRS ON THEIR BLACK GLASS EYES. YOU TRY TO VISUALIZE AN OCEAN BED WHERE SUCH MONSTROSITIES MIGHT THRIVE, BUT FAIL.

CRANES SWEEP ABOVE, UNLOAD CONTAINERS LEAKING CRYSTAL SNOW UPON THE SUMMER WHARFS BELOW. THIS IS NOT AMERICA. IT HAS A DIFFERENT TRADEBASE AND ECONOMY.

SHRIMP

A DIFFERENT GOVERNMENT.

ABOVE THE LIGHTLESS ANT-FARM STREETS HE STANDS. A HUMAN ROCKWELL PAINTING, RIBBONS SPILLING FROM HIS BREAST AS IF HIS HEART HAD BURST, DISGORGING SHREDDED FOREIGN FLAGS, AND SILVER COINS.

TOWARDS THE CENTER, MAFIA DONS AND P-2 MASONS SHARE A COTTON CANDY UNDER COLORED LIGHTS, WHILE EXILED TYRANTS IN THEIR EPAULLETTES QUEUE FOR THE RIFLE RANGE WITH S.S.GENERALS.

THE SHADOW POPULATION SWAYS. THE DISTANT BAR-LIGHTS SHINE AND YOU COULD USE A DRINK, A GLASS OF WATER.

THIS IS NOT A DREAM.

- the News -

AROUND THE BAR, STREETS ANKLE-DEEP IN MONEY HAVE A FRESHLY LAUNDERED SMELL. THERE'S NOTHING SMALLER THAN A MILLION DOLLAR BILL, AND NEWSBOYS IN DEPRESSION CLOTHING SELL YOU BLANK AND EMPTY PAGES. NOTHING 'ROUND HERE EVER SEEMS TO MAKE THE NEWS.

BEHIND THE FROSTED GLASS THE LIGHTS ARE DIM. YOU PLACE YOUR PALM AGAINST COLD, THUMB-SMEARED BRASS, AND PUSH

BAR

...AND STEP WITHIN.

© 1988 BILL SIENKIEWICZ

FROM *BROUGHT TO LIGHT*

JOURNAL: *How did your collaboration with Frank Miller start? The first project you started doing together was the* Daredevil *graphic novel, which was originally intended to be a two-part fill-in story in the regular* Daredevil *comic.*

BILL SIENKIEWICZ: It started as a gleam in [Marvel editor] Ralph Macchio's eye. Frank and I had known each other and liked each other's work. I think we both thought in the backs of our minds that it'd be interesting to work with each other on a project. But things never seemed to be headed in that direction. But then Frank was going to write a couple of issues of *Daredevil* dealing with the Kingpin and his wife Vanessa, and Ralph (who edits *Daredevil*) asked me to draw them. I jumped at the chance to work with Frank. It's now the *Daredevil* graphic novel. I feel it's a true, true collaboration. It's so much fun.

JOURNAL: *You work from full scripts with him, not just from plots. His scripts could be illustrated very realistically, but you take quite a different approach to them.*

SIENKIEWICZ: When I see Frank's scripts, I get a point-counterpoint thing going on. Frank and I know what's going on here, but I don't want to show that. I want to show something that's the opposite to that. His words are so powerful, why be redundant?

JOURNAL: *So the picture acts as a counterpoint to the words?*

SIENKIEWICZ: Yes, and there's been a lot of that going on.

JOURNAL: *Could you give any examples?*

SIENKIEWICZ: In the first issue of *Elektra*, when things become realistic in the script, I give them a storybook treatment; where things get more like a storybook, I point up the more realistic elements. The scenes with the most brutal stuff are shown in very childlike drawings. During one scene Elektra is being hosed down with other, starved women by this sadistic bastard. I do the scene in muted grays, and it's a pretty horrendous scene. And she remembers *Alice in Wonderland* and tells herself the story the way her father used to. She's trying to remember something pleasant from her childhood.

JOURNAL: *You even put the Cheshire Cat into one panel of that first issue.*

SIENKIEWICZ: Some of these pictures counterpoint what's going on. In the scene in the asylum in the first issue, the Cheshire Cat's saying, "We're all mad here," in *Alice in Wonderland* kept running through my head. It emphasized what's going on.

Often when Frank and I get together now, it's like a tennis game. We're volleying ideas back and forth. We're always considered so dark and serious, but when we get together, we end up laughing like crazy.

JOURNAL: *So do you mean* Elektra *is a kind of black comedy?*

SIENKIEWICZ: Yes. In the second issue of *Elektra*, Garrett, who's *Elektra*'s main antagonist, doesn't quite look real because he's comedic.

For fans Elektra became a sex symbol. I think at one point Frank wanted to show her as a death symbol, with nothing sexual about her. Now I think she's both. It's like what Frank's doing with *Batman*: she's become mythic. You can't really know her. You can't ever know what she's thinking, although you may think that you do. Her motivations are elusive. The more we show about Elektra ultimately the less you'll really know about her. I've handled her very coldly, very cartoonly, very super-heroey, very realistically—all different ways and, after the first issue, I've started to put a lot of that sexual element back into her.

A lot of what I did with the first issue came from a process of assimilating my artistic influences. It was a reflection of what I was as an artist that bounced into the story.

JOURNAL: *You portrayed the flashback of the murder of her father in a self-consciously childlike style.*

SIENKIEWICZ: It was pretty brutal. I didn't want to make it a pretty picture. I couldn't reconcile myself to doing it literally. The equivalent to what I wanted to do was to get a shotgun full of buckshot, hold it up to that panel, and pull the trigger. That would have been the effect I wanted. I tried to describe it with paints as viscerally and immediately as I felt it.

JOURNAL: *The depiction of her father's corpse spattered with blood certainly makes it visceral, but the childlike scrawls in the scene suggest that the memory of the murder forces Elektra to regress mentally into a helpless child who needs her father.*

SIENKIEWICZ: In that first issue as her memory becomes more lucid and the flashbacks get closer to her present, there is less of a difference in style between the flashbacks and her present time.

I did the sequences in which Stick is teaching her in cold colors. It's like Elektra's blue period, a combination of Picasso and Keane. She's got large doe eyes. You want to pick her up and cuddle her. But it's like taking in a viper.

JOURNAL: *Why do those flashbacks in blues?*
SIENKIEWICZ: It was a very cold period for her. For one thing, the temperature: it took place in the snow. It was also a cold period for her emotionally. She felt alienated. She wanted to be accepted.

I also give the earlier flashbacks a childlike style because I want to treat her feelings when she was younger more viscerally (there's that word again). More like a child would draw them. Because for a kid, drawing is naturally a means of expression. After that you start wanting to make things look like what they're supposed to look like. That's usually the point where most people give up drawing, the point where they feel frustrated because they can't make something look like it's supposed to. But if they stick with it, they usually give up drawing realistically by the time they're fifteen. Like Picasso, they move through exact representationalism for its own sake to experimenting with shape and pattern.

JOURNAL: *You once said you don't draw what things look like; you draw what they feel like.*
SIENKIEWICZ: Yeah, I get bored drawing representational stuff. I've gone to art exhibits and seen pictures done with very exacting and belabored rendering technique, and in a lot of ways they're very pretty, but my initial reaction is "So what?" this person isn't telling me anything; isn't adding anything. It's pointless. There are artists who show me pictures they've done and they're worse than bad. They're half good. No *joie de vivre*, no sense of playing around at all. It's as if they're trying so hard not to have their own point of view. It's like reportage, with them removed, uninvolved.

JOURNAL: *You think cartooning is a particularly good medium for showing how the artist feels.*
SIENKIEWICZ: Cartooning cuts through all the shit, if it's done well.

JOURNAL: *To show a personal point of view.*
SIENKIEWICZ: Oh, yeah. Look at [Ralph] Steadman's stuff. Look at Gerald Scarfe's work.

JOURNAL: *But when you started out doing comics, you wanted to be very representationalist.*
SIENKIEWICZ: Yes, I was.

JOURNAL: *So your more recent work has surprised people.*
SIENKIEWICZ: The question I keep getting is "Why did your style change?" It frustrates me. They've got a right to ask it, but I think their question points up a complete ignorance of art as process, of art as means of moving through life.

What artists are called upon to do in this business is to immediately have an identifiable style. And then thou shalt deviate not. Most artists don't hit their maturity, their stride until their forties. In this business you're supposed to hit the ground running.

My stuff doesn't look like anybody's else's now, at all, least of all Neal [Adams]'s. That may have been true at one time, but not any longer.

JOURNAL: *How did you become influenced by Ralph Steadman's work?*
SIENKIEWICZ: I saw someone on the train reading Hunter Thompson's *The Curse of the Lono*, which Steadman illustrated, and laughing hysterically. I bought the book, read it, saw the visuals, and also read Thompson's descriptions of Steadman, who's a character in the book, and they're hilarious. I didn't feel consciously influenced by him at the time, particularly, but I seemed to fall into it when I started doing the Bear. [In *New Mutants* #18–20] After that I started to work with it more and more. I noticed my work starting to get more geometric. I started to use more circles and right angles and a straight edge, for godsake.

JOURNAL: *Such as he does.*
SIENKIEWICZ: Yeah. His work's very loose, but it's also very rigid in some ways, which interested me. I never set out to *do* a Steadman, per se, but I enjoyed it so much it just manifested itself in my work.

JOURNAL: *Why do you so admire the work of Gerald Scarfe?*
SIENKIEWICZ: Scarfe, I feel, is a lot like Steadman, but even more political and gutsy. His stuff is a lot less representational than Steadman's stuff. Steadman's figures are grotesque, but still recognizably human. The things Scarfe uses to do his caricatures may not even be human, like using bombs as Richard Nixon's cheeks.

It's a statement about his political leanings as well as their physical shape.

JOURNAL: *In your comic work you don't do anything that blatant.*
SIENKIEWICZ: No.

JOURNAL: *So how does Scarfe's work affect what you do?*
SIENKIEWICZ: Well, it's frustrating, because I would like to know how much I would push it. It's almost like I'd like to be given the opportunity to find out, to really push it. A lot of the stuff that I do in my sketchbooks is more personal stuff. It's difficult, regardless of the quality of the writer I'm working with, to find a particularly apropos place to throw that kind of stuff in. I'm doing it more now with Frank [Miller] than I've done with anyone else. I did it a *lot* with Chris [Claremont]. The problem was that I could only push it so far because *The New Mutants* isn't that kind of book, although I regard my year with Chris as some of the best work either of us has done. Just read this Bear trilogy or *Legion*. Just beautiful writing. Elektra is a different animal. Completely.

JOURNAL: *She's not a role model or hero.*
SIENKIEWICZ: Yeah. *Elektra* is more of an ongoing psychodrama. But much as I like doing psychologically-oriented stories, I don't want to be typecast as somebody who draws only psychotic people, or people with square heads.

JOURNAL: *What do you feel about working for Marvel and DC nowadays?*
SIENKIEWICZ: I have been told by various sources that for me to do a regular book with my style the way it is now would be inviting trouble. I think it's probably true. Not so much at DC right now. Marvel has said they will find a format for me to do my work. I think it will be outside the regular comics line. I think the pressure is really on to be commercial, which I think means to draw like John Byrne or George Perez.

JOURNAL: *So you feel there's less and less room for you at the major companies?*
SIENKIEWICZ: Yeah. I'm changing my style, and it's always easier, instead of facing the fact that I'm moving away from mainstream comics style, to start feeling pushed out; and blame it on the Other Guy. I think I'm moving away, but I also think I am being pushed

out. At least out of the mainstream. And part of me is sad and part of me is excited by the new possibilities.

But I've made my decision to move in this direction, to play around with it as much as I can, to explore comics as a means of expression rather than a something you do by rote. The companies have every right, because it is a commercial art—those two words don't even really belong together, unless the remuneration's really fucking high, to warrant your wanting to give up part of your art by selling it—the companies have every right to want the usual styles. They're paying for that. I don't happen to like it. So I do different projects.

I find myself in a constant battle. I know the standard styles are what sells. I want to make a decent living. Now I could do *x* and *x* would sell. But there's also part of me that wants to follow this other drummer inside me and see how much I can push that envelope. And that doesn't sell as well. At least that's the crap they've tried to foist on me. So on one end of the scale there's monetary considerations. I'm not starving by any means. But I've become an adjective and an example and an oddity. "Bill Sienkiewicz's art is weird." I feel my work requires a little bit of work on the part of the reader and his involvement. I like to presume intellect and involvement on the part of the readers. A lot of what is being done presumes idiocy.

JOURNAL: *So will you stick it out at Marvel and DC or do you foresee yourself leaving?*
SIENKIEWICZ: I don't know. I think I'll be in them for awhile. I'd like to think if I were to leave it was not because I was pushed out but because I decided to try something else.

JOURNAL: *How would you describe your current work overall?*
SIENKIEWICZ: I think I'd describe most of my stuff right now as embryonic. All my stuff right now is a sapling. It's growing, coming up through the soil. I've got to be really careful that nothing steps on it. It's got to grow. It's the same with my writing, my painting, the illustration, the gallery work, and even my comics stuff. My comics work is going through a change, because it's being affected by all these other things I'm doing.

It's odd that when I first came into the business, artistically I was everybody else but me. Actually, it's not odd. It's pretty normal artistic development. Other people do it as well. I was Neal [Adams]; I came under the Bob Peak influence for a while. Steadman. I was very much wearing my influences on my sleeve. Now I feel that all the influences are coalescing, if they haven't already coalesced. And I'm sure they'll continue to do so.

I'll always be experimenting, trying to figure out who I am artistically. Every time I do a piece it surprises me, because invariably along the way it assumed a life and direction of its own and led me in another direction.

So when I first got into the business, I was drawing like Neal and got slammed for it. Then I went through the whole change and growth period, and now people say, "Well, we like your old stuff better." My reaction to that is basically, "Fuck that!"

JOURNAL: *You would like to see far more acceptance of greater artistic stylization, then.*

SIENKIEWICZ: My biggest dissatisfaction isn't with the companies, but with the majority of the people out there reading this stuff.

JOURNAL: *So are you hoping that the readers' tastes in art will mature? Or that people who would appreciate such stylization will come in from outside the current comics audience?*

SIENKIEWICZ: What Frank and I are trying to do in *Elektra* is latch onto new readers, both people who have given up comics and people who always looked down on them, as well as grab the regular readers. Hopefully, if such people become aware of the kind of work we're doing, it'll usher in a whole new age of acceptability of work done in the comics medium among the public. Frank and I are busting our asses to do just that. My fingers are crossed, and I'm giving it my best shot. Time will tell.

[*to waitress*] I'll have a cup of coffee, black. I don't know whether or not I'll drink it. I might ink with it. [*laughter*]

HOWARD CHAYKIN

THOUGH HE'D BECOME SOMETHING OF A STAR, BY THE LATE '70S HOWARD
Chaykin was completely disenchanted with the comics industry as it was.
His taste in stories run more to pulp adventure than super-hero punchouts,
his artwork leaned more toward classic magazine illustration than the
currently popular comic book styles, and the major companies were loath
to let artists write their own material. He became so disenchanted that he
left comics behind for a time, turning to book illustration and commercial
art. The rise of independent comics companies in the '80s and the subsequent loosening of comics formulae brought Chaykin back to the field, and
he found that his time had come. His *American Flagg* (from First Comics)
was one of the first direct-market hits. Chaykin's stories combine spectacu-
lar stylistic fireworks with a sometimes devil-may-care attitude toward
substance. They all revolve around the Chaykin hero, who, whether his
name is Reuben Flagg, Maxim Glory, or Cody Starbuck, is a hedonist with
a moral sense, a cynical idealist in a corrupt world. In the last few years
he's found himself welcome at the major companies. His three-issue
Blackhawk series for DC was one of the most popular comics of 1988. His
Black Kiss series for Vortex Comics is bound to be one of the most
controversial.

This interview was conducted by Gary Groth.

FIRST COMICS™

SEPT. $1.00
NO. 12
$1.25 CANADA

AMERICAN FLAGG!™

THE REVOLUTION WILL BE TELEVISED!

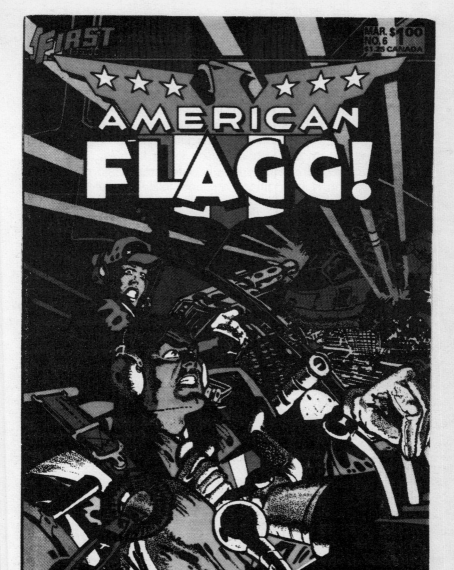

JOURNAL: *Can you summarize your career—where you are now, and where you intend to go? I know that you see your career as a series of stages.*

HOWARD CHAYKIN: Yeah. I mean, I'm thirty-five now. I've been a working professional for about fifteen years, and I'm a lot more restrained about self-expression or any kind of expression, self or otherwise, than I was when I first started in comics. I had a lot more youthful enthusiasm and exuberance. I feel if I were to look back, my career could be artificially divided into three basic parts. First, enthusiasm; then, numbing boredom; and, following that, a renewed interest, resulting from having been out of comics for a number of years and then returning in '83.

JOURNAL: *What prompted your boredom and what period was this?*

CHAYKIN: I think the great connective of comics is a really hysteric enthusiasm when you're very young—you're shaking your head and I'm hoping there's a certain amount of recognition.

JOURNAL: *Sure.*

CHAYKIN: For example, as much as you as an adult or I as an adult rail against the twelve-year-olds who can't turn away from one kind of comic to examine another, we have to take into account that we were doing precisely the same when we were twelve. I had exactly the same sort of aversion to newness that a twelve-year-old has today. Once that enthusiasm is tampered with by either professional or commercial realities of existence . . . face it—talking about doing comics and doing comics are nowhere near the same thing. And actually having to do the material without all that heat and passion you had when you were sixteen, seventeen, and eighteen becomes sort of enervating and numbing. I found it very difficult to maintain my enthusiasm for comics through the '70s. Most of that talk in those days was about what we would be doing for a living now—expectations were that comics would not survive the 1970s. I know this may be a little hard for people who are reading comics now to accept, but this was the major professional discussion. I found myself rather bored by the work that was being done around me and by the work I was doing, and I couldn't quite put my finger on it, because I couldn't honestly say, beyond juvenile lashing out and screaming and losing my temper, what was really wrong with the material. I hit my nadir of interest in the late '70s, and found myself purged through a series of trip-wire coincidences and circumstances which made it necessary to leave comics to make my living in another business, i.e., editorial and book illustration, where my personality had nothing to do with my getting work. It gave me a very, very different set of self-images. And when I came back to comics in '83 to do *American Flagg!*, I was much more capable of investing an enormous amount of energy and drive—focusing a lot of that energy that had been dispersed by over-enthusiasm.

JOURNAL: *Your career prior to* Flagg *was actually very erratic.*
CHAYKIN: Yes.

JOURNAL: *You said you lost a certain amount of passion for comics in the late '70s, but you never answered the question as to why that was.*
CHAYKIN: Well . . .

JOURNAL: *What were you doing in the late '70s? You were just doing jobs hither and yon, weren't you?*
CHAYKIN: I was never able to maintain my interests in a single project for particularly long. I didn't know then why, and I have an aversion to self-flattery. People who regard me as an egocentric look askance when I say I don't want to flatter myself, but the fact is, while my ego is huge, it's also tempered with the recognition of my own value seen from a reasonably objective point of view.

JOURNAL: *Which is what?*
CHAYKIN: I'm not sure at this point if I'm in any position to decide how valuable I am. Time will judge my work and its value.

JOURNAL: *You just said your ego was tempered by your own evaluation of yourself, which presupposes that you have an evaluation of yourself.*
CHAYKIN: I think I'm okay. I think I do good work, I'm reasonably witty. I'm finally able to channel some of my own personal charm into my work. I think those who know me well know that reading my work is a reasonably personal experience. I'm no longer afraid, ashamed, or uninterested enough in my personal background to keep it out of the work. I'm no longer a Jew masquerading as a Gentile through comics. From reading my stuff you can get a pretty good picture of what I sound like conversationally—obviously within a certain range.

JOURNAL: *That segues well into something I wanted to ask you: How much of you is in your work?*

CHAYKIN: More than ever. Whether in a direct sense of characters speaking language that I speak, or sort of testing my own reaction to attitudes. Right now I'm doing *The Shadow*, and the characterization I'm playing on *The Shadow* has absolutely nothing to do with my own particular political and moral attitudes. I couldn't in good faith impose my political and moral attitudes—let's face it, I'm a bit of a bleeding heart—on a character like *The Shadow*. I didn't refashion and restructure the character to suit my own particular political discipline. Instead, I wanted to see how I could handle writing a character who, although he perceives his own stance as a form of justice, is really anathema to my way of behavior.

JOURNAL: *So, how did you handle that incongruity?*

CHAYKIN: Um . . . by walking a fine wire. It's an exercise, an exercise in this case, to speak through secondary characters. I'm doing a job of work and I'm cutting yard goods. I'm trying to deliver a strong set of yard goods. And I'm intrigued by the incongruity as I'm hoping my reader will be. I told your interviewer from *Amazing Heroes* that the character of the Shadow would not be in any way be mistaken for the character of Reuben Flagg. I believe I'm doing some sort of myth-debunking in my reinterpretation of the Shadow. On the other hand, there are certain constants, without which, the character would not be the Shadow.

JOURNAL: *Do you think you're writing an immoral character?*

CHAYKIN: That's a difficult question. Immoral is a difficult word to apply here.

JOURNAL: *You said the character was anathema to your political and moral beliefs.*

CHAYKIN: Well, I have a hard time with vigilantes. I don't go to those kind of movies, either. On the other hand, there is a certain humped-back beast, at least in me, and I would assume everybody, who, recognizes that, although it may not be a long-term solution to the problem, that the idea of taking a bunch of terrorists and putting them into a big ditch, filling it with oil, and then throwing some phosphorus grenades and a submachine gun in there, is like Circus Maximus, and a hell of an idea.

JOURNAL: *Are you indulging in those fantasies in doing* The Shadow?

CHAYKIN: I wouldn't go so far as to say that. I would say, rather, that I'm being fairly pragmatic, and I'm doing a crime comic book, because it's time to practice doing other things. It's an opportunity to draw stuff and write stuff that I haven't been called upon to draw or write before, from a point of view I haven't been asked to deal with before. I feel I have a responsibility to keep part of my audience confused at any given time.

JOURNAL: *Are you serious?*

CHAYKIN: Yes.

JOURNAL: *Why do you feel that compunction?*

CHAYKIN: Because one of the problems that I see in comics is a phenomenal sameness and a house-style mentality that transcends companies. I believe that I was asked to do *The Shadow* because of my identification with 1930s characters. Unfortunately that identification is five years old. Comics professionals, as talent or creative people, are rarely allowed to move past any particular point at which we hit.

JOURNAL: *Wouldn't it be safe to say that you moved past* The Shadow *with* Flagg?

CHAYKIN: I would think.

JOURNAL: *So you're regressing.*

CHAYKIN: I think that's what was asked of me [by DC]. And I wasn't particularly interested. But, with the offer of carte blanche, which I answered with a letter of intent, which nobody seemed to be particularly upset about, I then felt I could take the character and do with it what I felt was right commercially. I regard it as an exercise in commercial behavior to see whether I could take a character as moribund as this and give it some impetus to sell.

JOURNAL: *You referred to* The Shadow *as a pragmatic job; did you mean taking the job as a whole or writing the character itself— solving this incongruity in how you feel and how the character must behave?*

CHAYKIN: In both senses. In *Flagg*, I was basically building it from the ground up. My rules. That was both the success and failure factor of the material. I'm a structuralist—this is something else I share with Gil [Kane]—I believe in organization and structure in the creation of a life, and I think those pictures of me as a child would indicate that I'm my favorite creation. *Flagg* basically became a demanding proposition because I had to live up to the dogma that I had created, which is not to say that I couldn't go back to it now with a completely fresh eye and say, "Damn you, dogma, I can play around you." *The Shadow* was an opportunity to work within more confines, to do something that took place *now*, within the confines of accepted society with real people, behaving in the ways that characters in crime fiction behave. The great connective of comic book people is a universal nerddom, and in childhood all of us grew up reading fantasy fiction of one kind or another, and I've outgrown science fiction. I'm not particularly interested in science fiction very much, and what I read for relaxation and entertainment is crime fiction. I read the work of Jim Thompson, Horace McCoy, W.R. Burnett.

JOURNAL: *Do you find crime fiction qualitatively superior to science fiction?*
CHAYKIN: Yeah, I do.

JOURNAL: *Really?*
CHAYKIN: Yes. This is going to get me in trouble with all these science fiction fans that I'm going to run into, but I do believe it is.

JOURNAL: *In what way?*
CHAYKIN: Well, I think the cliche situations have a greater resonance of truth than those in science fiction. Cliches need a source of birth as well as anything else. Crime fiction deals with the better stuff, with the more familiar, darker aspects of human greed, and I'm more interested in human greed than in galaxy-spanning adventure. What it comes down to is that I'm getting back to what first inspired me to even think about the idea of making a living as a storyteller in comics, which was cowboy pictures, and crime movies.

JOURNAL: *What kind of cowboy movies?*
CHAYKIN: Monogram and Republic westerns. When I was a kid, channel thirteen in New York City, which is now WNET Public Broadcasting Station, was a syndicated station out of New Jersey. It showed nonstop sixty to seventy minute long Johnny Mack Brown formula westerns, Johnny Mack Brown and Wild Bill Elliott and Don Red Barry, broken up with onslaughts of fairly cheesy black-and-

white cartoons. And until recently the staff announcer at NET-PBS was the same guy who was the host of *Cartoon Town*. It was just great.

JOURNAL: *In order to be more commercial, would you have to make what you would consider compromises?*

CHAYKIN: I believe I would. Based on what seems to be commercially successful, it's pretty clear that I would have to make some kind of concessions. What they'd be I don't know, and how those concessions would manifest themselves as compromises I don't know. I have a bleaker outlook than most people who read teenage mutant comic books would prefer. I'm not a cynic, but I perceive most teenage mutant product as fairly cynical in that it plays off coziness that we know isn't real, a bedtime story coziness.

JOURNAL: *By saying it's cynical, are you indicting the motivations behind it?*

CHAYKIN: No, not especially. I'm envious of it because I'm not capable—

JOURNAL: *Then, how is it cynical?*

CHAYKIN: Well, it's cynical in the sense that . . . well . . .

JOURNAL: *Spielberg produces that same gingerbread view of the world. Would you characterize him as cynical, too?*

CHAYKIN: Look, we're living in the 1980s, and as a generation are regurgitating a lot of our childhood fantasies and toy games, and I think if we're going to do that professionally, we have a responsibility to bring more to it than gloss and sheen. What I was trying to do with *Flagg* was to do a high-tech version of *Gunsmoke* and it got out of hand. What I did in *Flagg* for twenty-six, twenty-seven issues, was an extended run of a reasonably literate comic book that didn't take itself seriously, that played with a lot of familiar themes in different ways and tried to introduce a different kind of character speech than had been seen in comics before, at least in my time. But, it's still a blip, I recognize that.

JOURNAL: *A blip?*

CHAYKIN: It'll disappear. It's irrelevant. Considering its sales in the greater scheme of things, if First went under tomorrow and *Flagg* reverted to me as a property, and I took Flagg as a body to Marvel Comics, for example, and said to them, "Let's print this as

American Flagg! #1—Marvel Comics," we'd be reaching four times the audience. That's what I mean when I say it's a blip. There is a good possibility that three out of six people who happen to thumb through this magazine on the racks before they put it down and don't buy it are going to be wondering who the fuck I am. I'm worth interviewing, apparently, but probably half the people who buy comic books out there don't know who I am. [*pause*]

JOURNAL: *Does it disturb you that you consider* Flagg! *a blip, a throwaway product?*

CHAYKIN: No, not really. It disturbs me more that there are people around who are doing work of similar quality who are beating their breasts and just walking around like it's the be-all, end-all, like the second coming. I do the work . . . let other people tell you how wonderful it is.

JOURNAL: *You've referred in print to* American Flagg! *as a "piece of shit." Is it in any way disturbing to think of your creation in those terms?*

CHAYKIN: No. It's trying to bring the hyperbole all down to a more discussable level. I also think at the same time that it was the best book of its kind in the mainstream form, which is to say that by calling it a piece of shit, I've been damning the rest of the shit to purgatory. It certainly had more work per square foot, more thinking, and simple, backbreaking, sweaty labor. And, at the same time, it remained a reasonably enjoying, compelling product. I'm very proud of the work I did.

JOURNAL: *What did you mean when you referred to* Flagg *as a piece of shit"?*

CHAYKIN: I said it was a piece of shit by comparison to something outside comics, to the real world. The whole line was, I produced one of the five best comics of the past five years and I still think it's a piece of shit. What I meant was I'm going to be better next year and the year after that and that I'm not ready to have an *Art of Howard Chaykin* published, and I'm uncomfortable with the fact that we're living in a time when self-congratulation is taken as journalism. Where it is perfectly acceptable behavior to express opinion as fact without even the qualification of "I would like to think that you believe this."

JOURNAL: *Are you disturbed merely by the semantics of this condition?*

CHAYKIN: No, if I were merely disturbed by the semantics I could shrug it off and say to hell with this. Unfortunately, we live in a time where semantics are everything and people believe everything, too. The fact that I am perceived as a big-mouthed egocentric disturbs me a great deal because there are people out there who I know to be at least as egomaniacal as I am but because they don't follow through with the right kinds of egocentric behavior their egos aren't perceived.

JOURNAL: *Why would you be so disturbed at the general atmosphere of hyperbole and monomaniacal bragging and not at your own assessment of your work as a "piece of shit"? Are you more concerned with other people's propensity to brag than with your work?*

CHAYKIN: No . . . well, I would like to think that I'm going to improve. I also referred to *Flagg!* as my first mature work, and I'd like to think it is my first piece of work that acknowledges my growth. I'm thirty-five years old. Comic books are a business where you're an old man by the time you're twenty-five. I married Leslie eight years ago. I would take her to a convention and these chuckleheads would come over to her with these attitudes of concern and condescension that she'd married this complete, washed-out fucking loser. And I was twenty-seven years old! It's a business where, if you're not a pistol by the time you're twenty-three, you're dead by the time you're twenty-seven. How many illustrators do you know who have made any kind of inroad with their work before they were thirty? I mean, Christ! It drives me nuts. I'm delighted to see guys at twenty-two doing extraordinary work, but I also feel that they're nipping at my heels. The good part is that these guys are going to burn out by the time they're twenty-five, too. It's a business that devours talent. It certainly devours skill. What I would like to think is that I'm going to get better from now. That the thirteen years that existed before *Flagg* was practice, was school.

JOURNAL: *How are you going to avoid the industry devouring your talent, your skill?*

CHAYKIN: Sooner or later, and I hope sooner, I'm going to segue out.

JOURNAL: *Out of comics entirely?*

CHAYKIN: That, and also I don't think the field is welcome to me. As you said, I *do* sit on a fence. And ultimately, I'm not particularly welcome. It seems to me comics are divided into three classes, an upper class, a lower class, and me. I'm a middling guy. I'm not as much of an elitist as I used to be, I'm a bit more of a democrat.

JOURNAL: *Explain what the format of* Time^2 *will be. I understand it will be published as a series of graphic albums.*

CHAYKIN: The special issue [of *Flagg*] will actually be a deluxe comic book in the First deluxe style. The actual format of *Time^2* will be the European-style forty-four-page trade paper graphic novel—blue line, painted color, aimed at a mature reader.

JOURNAL: *Published how frequently?*

CHAYKIN: We're talking about every six, seven months. Each story will be complete unto itself, readable without the previous one, and, of course, I'd be delighted if you bought all of them in sequence because we like that kind of reader.

JOURNAL: *You said, in an interview published in* Mile High Futures *[a comics wholesaler newsletter], "The stories in* Time^2 . . . *will be a bit more morally ambivalent than* Flagg *has been." You also say, "The book is about the quest for more money, getting by in an enclosed environment, an environment of scum."*

CHAYKIN: Yeah!

JOURNAL: *You also said—*

CHAYKIN: Bear in mind that the characters and concepts have gone through a lot of development since then; that's nearly a year old.

JOURNAL: *I'll ask you to alter or add to this. You also say, "Most of his friends"—him being the protagonist, presumably—"are either musicians, actors, or thieves, or criminals, or murderers, and they let him be because he used to be the best shit-heel around, and he's not anymore. No talking cats, no ray guns, no cute robots." Can you add to that, clarify it? Has it changed?*

CHAYKIN: Not a lot. The moral ambivalence stays. The hero is an ex-criminal who has gone through an undescribed epiphany, undetailed, no particular explanation, no particular physical change. He's been away for approximately five years when he returns. He is a night club owner, a saloon keeper. The milieu he functions in—I've often described it as what you'd get if Philip K. Dick and Damon Runyon collaborated on a prime-time soap and that about covers it.

JOURNAL: *An existential crime comic.*

CHAYKIN: An existential crime comic book in which nobody gives a fuck who did it. In a milieu that looks a lot like Times Square with aspects of the Ginza and Picadilly Circus thrown in. It's a sideshow world. I am not going to acknowledge it as science fiction or fantasy, although you will see Bix Beiderbicke, Bunny Berigan, and Charlie Parker playing on the same stage.

JOURNAL: *How is it going to be more morally ambivalent?*

CHAYKIN: It's a world in which the only presence of an authoritative force, i.e., the police, will be through a corrupt . . . fairly irrational presence. The least defined character so far is the police officer, Bon Ton MacHoot.

JOURNAL: *Is the protagonist less self-righteous than Flagg?*

CHAYKIN: Oh, yes, considerably so. Well . . . actually, I shouldn't jump to that. He's less self-righteous in an official sense, but more apt to call shit shit when he sees it, less cynical. The characters in the strip are thieves and musicians and actors. I was on the phone, about a week ago, talking to Rick Oliver, telling him the basic plot of the second volume of *Time*^{2}, the blocking note that I've got, the story is about an attempt to mount a big-budget musical comedy based on Stagolee and Billy doing a backstage story. As I'm sitting talking to Oliver, I happen to glance down at that day's *Reporter* and there's a whole column about Phillip Michael Thomas and the fact that he's in the process of raising money to do a musical based on Stagolee. I was so pissed! Because a) he was doing it, and b) it was him.

The [*Time*^{2}] stories are going to be inspired by Philip K. Dick and Damon Runyon. They're not continued stories. Runyon's pieces ran 5,000 words almost to the word. Talk about your structure. I want to do a very pretty book. That's what I'm looking for.

ALAN MOORE AND DAVE GIBBONS

THE MAINSTREAM COMICS WRITER IS SOMETHING OF AN ALCHEMIST. HIS TASK IS to make something worthwhile out of what can be very base material. The usual approach is to introduce elements from outside the genre. Alan Moore works differently. He will examine a genre and try to bring its best elements out of it, while staying, for the most part, within its conventions. For example, when given a comic about a swamp monster, rather than fight against the absurdities of such a concept, he tried to make the most intelligent swamp monster comic possible. He succeeds more often than not.

Moore and his *Watchmen* collaborator Dave Gibbons are part of a whole generation of creators that came out of the British science fiction comic *2000 A.D.* Most British comics are weeklies, and the shorter installments and continued stories have given rise to a style that is tougher and more plot oriented than their American counterparts. In 1983 Moore made his American debut with the aforementioned monster comic, DC's *Swamp Thing* (in collaboration with Steve Bissette and John Totleben). It became one of the most acclaimed comics of the time. His real breakthrough came when Gibbons joined him to create *Watchmen*. *Watchmen* (based loosely on characters DC acquired from Charlton Comics) uses a set of forlorn and outlawed super-heroes to build a portrait of a society in collapse. Beneath it all, it's actually a fable about the dangers of getting what you want. Gibbons has filled it with visual allusions, puns, and telling detail. *Watchmen* is likely to be as close as costumed character comics will ever get to literature, and it comes closer than anyone might have expected. As such, the question is, where do you go with the genre from here? Moore him-

From *Watchmen*

From *Watchmen*

self has come up with one answer: For the time being, at least, he's left it behind.

This is a transcription of a panel moderated by Neil Gaiman at the UK Comic Art Convention.

GAIMAN: *I thought I'd start off by asking Alan and Dave a couple of questions about the genesis of* Watchmen—*how it started out way back when Alan was asked to do something with some Charlton superheroes, and how it evolved into the rather remarkable comic it is now. [Charlton is a minor comic book publisher whose characters were bought by DC.]*

ALAN MOORE: We weren't asked to do anything with the Charlton super-heroes. I just thought that they were all lying around, up for grabs, and I hadn't heard of anything else that was being done with them. They were just a nice, innocent little bunch of characters, which is always fair game, really, and there was a self-contained universe with four or five characters, and I thought it'd be nice to just take that and do whatever you wanted with it. So I started mapping out a few ideas, and originally it was just a murder mystery. "Who killed the Peacemaker," and that was it. We sent all this stuff to Dick Giordano and some of it was extreme. We were going to treat the Question as a lot more extreme than he'd been treated before. Dick loved the stuff, but having a paternal affection for these characters from his time at Charlton, he really didn't want to give his babies to the butchers, and make no mistake about it, that's what it would have been. He said, "Can you change the characters around and come up with some new ones?" At first I wasn't sure whether that would work, but when Dave and I got together and started just planning these things out, it all really snapped into place and worked fine. I'm much happier now doing it with original characters. It's worked out much better than it would have done if we had used Captain Atom, Blue Beetle, and all the others, and I'm pleased with it.

Me and Dave have been wanting to do something together for a long time, so when this came up I said I'd be happy to work with Dave and Dave said he'd be happy to work with me and that's it.

DAVE GIBBONS: Yeah, I'll go along with that. People ask me how I got involved in it, and I can't really remember. I remember Alan sending me a synopsis. We'd done quite a lot of things that we'd tried to get done with DC—we were going to do *Martian Manhunter* and *Challengers of the Unknown*, and some of the aspects of that led into *Watchmen.*

MOORE: Some of them, yeah. There were projects that we'd talked up that we both wanted to do, and it all just came out. The thing was that with *Watchmen* if you read that original synopsis it's the bare skeleton. There's the plot there, but it's what's happened since then that's the real surprise because there's all this other stuff that's crept into it, all this deep stuff, the intellectual stuff. [laughs] That wasn't planned. The thing seems to have taken on an identity of its own since we kicked it off, which is always nice.

GAIMAN: *What was DC's reaction to a book that didn't have people fighting on the cover and a plot with people dripping blood and so forth?*

MOORE: There's bound to be a certain amount of nervousness, but to DC's credit they backed us all the way on it. It could be said that it's commercial suicide just having a badge on one cover, a statue on the next cover, a radiation symbol on the third one and so on, and it was a new title with no known super-heroes in it. You're going to sell a few copies on me and Dave's names I suppose, but there's nothing else there that's going to grab the reader. You've got the title on sideways so that it's not always easy to see it on the racks if they don't have flat displays, but DC could see what we were doing, that we were trying to produce a package that looked radical, that was maybe going to interest people who weren't interested in comics, that you could put out in Waldenbooks or something like that and people would say, "Oh, this doesn't look like a comic, I'll buy it." DC backed us all the way on that and have been really supportive about even the most grotesque excesses.

GIBBONS: I remember the covers in particular. We hemmed and hawed for a long time about what would be on them, and we knew that whatever it was, it wasn't going to be fight scenes or full-figure super-heroes. After drawing the first issue I thought, "Perhaps we could have the smiley face on the cover," and drawing it and immediately having a really good idea of where the series was going, another six cover designs popped into my head. I think the fact that what was sent to DC wasn't, "Here's this smiley face, the cover of the first issue," but six or seven covers that all worked as bits of graphic design, was what really sold them on it. Subsequently, it was Alan's idea to take it a bit further and make each cover the first panel of the story, and that's a really strong idea as well. The way that we rationalize it to ourselves is that it's a crossover. The cover of the *Watchmen* is in the real world and looks quite real, but it's starting to turn into a comic book, a portal to another dimension. This is the kind of thing we think about while we're doing it.

This might come up when you're asking questions later, but it's where we really ought to have the *Twilight Zone* theme in the background because there've been some really spooky coincidences. For example, the issue that's just out, #5, is about symmetry and there's a scene in it where the two detectives we feature are called to this apartment where an aging hippie . . . [looks at Alan; laughter from the audience] . . . has just butchered his children rather than have them killed in a nuclear war. Alan, as he usually does, made lots of suggestions for the decor of the apartment and I thought, "What they really need is a '60s rock poster," and I don't know anything about '60s rock groups . . .

MOORE: [disbelieving] Oh ho ho.

GIBBONS: Well, I know lots about '50s rock groups. I thought that it could be a Grateful Dead poster, because that ties in as these kids are dead, and they ought to be grateful . . . [laughter from the audience] . . . so I'd like to stress that not possessing any Grateful Dead albums, I got a book called *The Album Cover Album* and looked up Grateful Dead in the index for a cover, and it's an album called *Aoxomoxoa*, which is a symmetrical word.

MOORE: It's a Rick Griffin cover as well, which is absolutely symmetrical.

GIBBONS: And it's got a skull on it, and throughout issue #5, there's the skull and crossbones of the pirate ship. Also, this skull has an egg in its hands, and the book starts with Rorschach breaking an egg. And also on the facing page of the book there's an album called *Tales of the Rum Runners* and I forget who it's by but at the beginning of issue #5 we have the Rumrunner Club. [*Tales of the Rum Runners* is by Robert Hunter with the cover also designed by Rick Griffin]

FROM THE AUDIENCE: *In Alan's interview in* Q *Magazine there was a quote pertaining to* Swamp Thing *saying that if ever a country needed scaring it's America. Do you feel* Watchmen *is taking this further?*

MOORE: Yes. This is not antiAmericanism, it's antiReaganism, and these are only personal opinions, not necessarily shared by Dave or John. My personal feelings, because I'm the writer and can do anything that I want, is that at the moment a certain part of Reagan's America isn't scared. They think they're invulnerable. There's this incredible up mood that leads at its worst excesses to things like the Libyan bombing and things like that, and they worry me and frighten me. The power elite in America and an awful lot of the people who vote for them seem to have this . . . I think the best example is a quote that Clive Barker dredged up for one of his books, *The Damnation Game*, from an explorer called Freya Stark, a wonderful old woman who went everywhere in the world, an incredible pioneer, and she wrote an awful lot of travel books and said some really bright things, and one of the things she said is, "The society that knows fear is not the society that's faced with extinction. It is the society that has forgotten fear that is faced with extinction." The society that just thinks that they can do whatever they want because they're invulnerable, they're not afraid, and they can gloss over the terror of the nuclear stockpiles, the world situation and all that and just think, "Hey, we're doing all right, we're okay."

That's unhealthy. I know it's only a tiny little comic book that goes over there every month and gets seen by a relatively small number of people, many of whom perhaps agree with us anyway, so it's difficult to see what it's doing, but I was consciously trying to do something that would make people feel uneasy. In issue #3 I wanted to communicate that feeling of "When's it going to happen?" Everyone felt it. You hear a plane going overhead really loud, and just for a second before you realize it's a plane you look up. I'm sure that everybody in this room's done that at least once. It's something over everybody's head, but nobody talks about it. At the risk of doing a depressing comic book we thought that it would be nice to try and . . . yeah, try and scare a little bit so that people would just stop and think about their country and their politics. It's not that America's worse than England, that we're any better than them, because we have our fair share of strange political leaders as well. When I'm doing *V for Vendetta* it's aimed at England, and

Watchmen is aimed at an American audience and the intention was to try and make people feel a little bit uneasy about it.

FROM THE AUDIENCE: *Is it possible to handle the super-heroes realistically without the fascist overtones creeping in?*

MOORE: I think that when *Watchmen* was first announced everybody assumed that it was going to be *Squadron Supreme*, the super-heroes take over. We never said that. We said that we were going to try to treat them realistically. I think that because there've been a lot of fascist overtones in *Marvelman* [*Miracleman*] people assumed that the super-heroes had taken over. There aren't really any fascist super-heroes in *Watchmen*. Rorschach's not a fascist, he's a nut case. The Comedian's not a fascist, he's a psychopath. Dr. Manhattan's not a fascist, he's a space cadet. They're not fascists. They're not in control of their world. Dr. Manhattan's not in control of the world—he doesn't even care about the world. I think that while people expected that, we've not investigated the idea of super-heroes as fascists the same way that Frank [Miller] has in *Dark Knight*, or the same thing they've done in *Squadron Supreme*. It wasn't really our intention. Our intention was to show how super-heroes could deform the world just by being there, not that they'd have to take it over, just their presence there would make the difference. It's what we try to show in *Watchmen* #4. From the point where Dr. Manhattan appears, it slowly starts to go downhill from there—everything starts to change. He doesn't take over the country or make people subservient to him, but just his presence there makes everything begin to change. Yet on another level, if you equate Dr. Manhattan with the atom bomb, the atom bomb doesn't take over the world, but by being there it changes everything. That was more the idea that I was trying to explore. I'd say it's possible to do super-hero stories that are realistic without getting into that Nazi mode.

FROM THE AUDIENCE: *How did you actually conceive and put together the universe of the* Watchmen? *And question two is, "Who watches the* Watchmen?"

GIBBONS: As Alan said, it's a universal world that's deformed by the presence of super-heroes, and I think Alan is more concerned with the social implications of that and I've gotten involved in the technical implications of it. You've got electric cars and airships because of the technological breakthrough. Dr. Manhattan could transmute metals and create supplies of rare metals and so there probably wouldn't be as much need for the petrochemical industry because you'd have clean electric cars. I'm not putting this very well. They can't make electric cars here because the batteries are too heavy, and there's a thing called polyacetyline something, but you need lithium to make this, and lithium is a very rare metal. Of course, Dr. Manhattan can actually form lithium, so there's as much lithium as you want, so that's why you've got electric cars.

GAIMAN: *What about the cigarettes?*
GIBBONS: They were just to give a small element of strangeness. It's something they obviously smoke, but doesn't look like anything people here smoke.
MOORE: It's like a water-cooled pipe or something like that, something to cool the smoke. It's a slightly different sort of cigarette, and there's the Gunga Diners. It was Dave's idea to have Indian restaurants instead of McDonalds, and that made sense because there's a different political situation in this world, there's going to be wars in different places. In our story, some sort of conflict in Asia has caused a massive famine in India, so there's been a massive amount of Indian and Asian refugees teeming into America, and consequently you've got Indian food catching on, and you've got this stream of Gunga Diners stretching across the country. There's a lot of little things like that and all of them are semilogical, they all follow from the idea of super-heroes. The comics are different because people are fed up with super-heroes, there wasn't a big super-hero boom like there has been here, and so all the little details are worked in. That's how we came up with the world. We took a central premise and worked it from there.

As for "Who watches the Watchmen?" we didn't know where the quote came from until I had a phone call from Harlan Ellison, who phoned up just to tell me because he'd seen us expressing our ignorance in *Amazing Heroes*, and wanted to put us out of our misery. Apparently the original quote is "Quis custodiet custodies?" which means "who guards the guardians," "who watches the watchmen," and it was said originally by the satirist Juvenal, and it was the quote that got him slung out of Rome and placed in exile. It's a dangerous political quote. Who's watching the people who're watching after us? In the context of *Watchmen*, that fits. "They're watching out for us, who's watching out for them?" That's where the title comes from. It's also a nice bit of graffiti, so you get little snatches of it in the background.

FROM THE AUDIENCE: *What's the quote for the third comic?*

MOORE: It's "Shall not the judge of all the earth do right?" The quote from issue #1's "At midnight all the agents" is from a Bob Dylan song: "At midnight all the agents and the superhuman crew go out and round up everyone who knows more than they do," from "Desolation Row," which fits pretty nicely with the first issue. The second one is "Absent friends," from "The Comedians" by Elvis Costello: "I should be drinking a toast to absent friends instead of these comedians," which with the second issue being about the Comedian fits in nicely. The third one is from the Bible and it's from that bit in Genesis where God's going to nuke Sodom and Gomorrah, and one of the prophets goes out and tries to barter with him and says, "If there's a couple of good people there, perhaps you could spare it," and God says, "Yeah, all right." So he says, "What if there's one good person there? Is it okay?" And God says, "Shall not the judge of all the earth do right?" So that also fits in nicely. It fit in very nicely with the story because there's an awful lot of judges of the earth there: the news vendor who is giving his judgment of the earth earlier on, the president and the people in the war room at the Pentagon who're obviously judges of the earth in a very real sense, because they're the ones who're going to decide when to set the nukes flying and there's Dr. Manhattan. At the end with that last panel where he's sitting there on Mars looking up at the sky it should have said, "Shall not the judge of all the earth do right?" So that's where that one comes from. The rest of the issues will all have the proper quote at the end.

FROM THE AUDIENCE: *Is there any chance of turning* Under the Hood *into a book?*

MOORE: No, because there's only three chapters of it. It's not a real book, you see.

GIBBONS: Ooohhh.

MOORE: If you opened it up, most of the pages are blank. Originally we thought, "Okay, we've got twenty-eight pages of comic strip in here and what are we going to do with the rest of them? We thought; "letters page. But there's no letters coming until issue #3, so what shall we do to fill the first three issues? Shall we do something self-congratulatory that tells all the readers how wonderful and clever we all are for thinking up all that?" And we thought, "No, because that should be obvious, shouldn't it?" So we thought we'd do something that tied in with the story and threw this *Under the Hood* stuff in because it was mentioned in the book. By the time we got around to issue #3, #4, and so on, we thought that the book looked nice without a letters page. It looks less like a comic book, so we stuck with it.

PART III:

UP FROM UNDERGROUND

WHEN ROBERT CRUMB PUBLISHED ZAP #1 IN 1968, A WHOLE MOVEMENT WAS waiting to happen. Crumb was only one of many cartoonists who had been biding their time, not knowing when or if they'd ever get the chance to do the kind of comics they imagined. They honed their skills in college humor magazines, fanzines (which also helped put them in contact with each other), second-banana humor magazines like *Cracked* and *Help!*, and later in the underground newspapers which were popping up in major cities. In fact, *Zap* was not really the first underground comic; that honor goes either to Jack Jackson's *God Nose,* Frank "Foolbert Sturgeon" Stack's *The New Adventures of Jesus,* or Joel Beck's *Lenny of Laredo*. It was *Zap,* however, that set the format of underground comics and established that there was an audience for them. Beyond that, Crumb set the tone for the movement: no limits, no restrictions, no compromise. The result was a period of creativity unlike anything since the earliest days of comic strips. Like the pioneers of the medium, the underground cartoonists could treat the comics as a blank slate. Unlike the pioneers, they didn't have to struggle to develop the grammar of the medium (not that some of them didn't try to make a new one). The styles of underground comics ranged from the anachronistic imagery of Kim Deitch and Jay Lynch to the antic social satire of Gilbert Shelton and Bill Griffith to the jacked-up acid visions of Robert Williams. They are among the least dated of all products of the '60s counterculture, not least because the skepticism they inherited from Harvey Kurtzman kept them from falling into many idiocies of the day.

Underground comics flourished for a brief period from 1968 to 1973.

San Francisco quickly became the undisputed center of the movement, partly because Crumb was there and partly because the publishers were there. The publishers were hippie print shops which had previously been devoted to producing psychedelic concert posters. The comics were sold mostly through head shops, record stores, and other counterculture-oriented outlets. The sales could be phenomenal: Crumb's most popular comic, *Home Grown,* sold over 140,000 copies; the twelve issues of *Zap* have sold over a million; and the ten issues of Gilbert Shelton's *Freak Brothers* have sold over two million. But even as the movement was reaching its peak, its foundations were beginning to crumble. Underground comics had always been the target of obscenity prosecutions, but in 1973 a new Supreme Court ruling making the definition of obscenity subject to local community standards made them increasingly vulnerable. A paper shortage pushed printing costs sky-high. Antiparaphernalia laws were shutting down head shops. Most of all, the counterculture that supported them was beginning to melt into the mainstream. By the late '70s, underground comics had slowed down to a trickle. Some of the more popular cartoonists, like Crumb and Shelton, could continue as they had. Some of them melted into the mainstream themselves. And some of them found new ways to publish alternative comics, paving the way for the comics of the '80s.

JAY LYNCH

CHICAGO WAS THE SECOND CITY OF UNDERGROUND COMICS, THANKS LARGELY TO
Jay Lynch and Skip Williamson, founders of *Bijou Funnies*. *Bijou* more or
less published the cartoonists who couldn't fit into *Zap*. Aside from Lynch and
Williamson, *Bijou* regulars included Justin Green, Kim Deitch, Jay Kinney,
and art spiegelman. *Bijou* ran for eight issues, the eighth being an underground version of Kurtzman's *Mad,* with underground cartoonists lampooning
each other's styles and a cover by Kurtzman himself. Lynch was one of the
more conventional (and consistent) underground cartoonists. His main
feature was *Nard 'N Pat.* Drawn in a "bigfoot" style reminiscent of '30s
strips like *Mutt & Jeff* and *Barney Google,* it centered on the suburban
guerrilla warfare between a conservative wallflower and his bohemian-outlaw
cat. Currently Lynch divides his time between commercial art and collaborating with Gary Whitney on *Phoebe and the Pigeon People,* a weekly
strip in the *Chicago Reader*. In this interview, conducted by Richard Green
and Craig Yoe, Lynch talks about the roots of underground comics.

JOURNAL: *You got involved with fandom in the early '60s, didn't
you?*
LYNCH: In about 1961 there was a letter column of *Cracked*
magazine from Joe Pilati. Pilati was publishing a little fanzine called

Smudge, which was about humor/satire fandom. *Smudge* contained articles about the men behind *Mad, Cracked, Help!, Sick,* and other big-time newsstand satire mags that existed at the time. Pilati's *Smudge* had a circulation of under 100 copies. It was printed in purple ink on a ditto machine. Anyway, Pilato sent an issue of *Smudge* to *Cracked*, and the *Cracked* editors printed his letter about *Smudge* along with his address. I spotted this *Smudge* plug, as did artie spiegelman in Rego Park, Long Island, Don Dohler in Baltimore; Phil Roberts in Michigan; Jay Kinney in Ohio; and a whole group of other young kids who had an interest in this sort of thing. We all got our copies of *Smudge*, and in the pages of *Smudge* we learned of other little humor/satire fanzines. Eventually we all sent for copies of Don Dohler's fanzine, *Wild*. Skip, artie, and I all wound up drawing cartoons for *Wild* when we were kids. It was through this humor/satire fanzine network that we all got in contact with each other initially. So when you look at the big picture, *Cracked* was responsible for linking us all up into contact with one another very early in the game.

JOURNAL: *Later you were a writer for* Cracked?
LYNCH: In the years between 1963 and 1966 I wrote for *Cracked*. Especially during '63. I wrote a great deal of stuff for *Cracked* in '63. I had moved to Chicago by then, but most of my writing was done through the mails. Once in '62 I went to Manhattan and visited Bob Sproul, who edited and published *Cracked* at the time. I guess it was around '62 that I started writing for *Cracked*. When Sproul and Betty Martin were on the mag, they bought lots of my stuff. Then Joe Kiernan became editor, and I think there may have been budget cuts—or maybe he didn't like my stuff. I don't know. All of a sudden I wasn't writing for *Cracked* all that much, and I was writing for *Sick* instead. Then I went to New York and met with Dee Carusoe, who was doing *Sick* at the time. I liked the fact that when I wrote for *Cracked* it was mostly drawn by Bill Ward, an artist whose style I liked. *Sick* would give my stuff to guys like Bob Powell to illustrate, and this didn't turn me on. Powell was a good artist, but only for the super-hero type stuff. His satire stuff didn't impress me. *Cracked* and *Sick* paid about the same at the time.

JOURNAL: *What did they pay writers then?*
LYNCH: In 1963 I got fifteen dollars a page. I know that sounds unbelievable by today's standards—but in 1963 my rent was thirty

dollars a month for a two bedroom apartment. Cigarettes were like thirty-five cents. *Playboy* cost fifty cents then. Now what is it? Four bucks? In '63 you could eat for a week on four bucks.

JOURNAL: *How did all of this lead into the underground comics scene? How did your involvement with that start?*

LYNCH: I was doing cartoons for Harvey Kurtzman's *Help!* magazine in '62 and '63, and in *Help!* I first saw the adult work of Crumb. Now a few years earlier I had seen Crumb's fanzine *Foo*, but I kind of dismissed it as being too Disney-like. I mean, Skip and artie and I were doing cartoons for fanzines like *Wild* and *Jack-High* (Phil Roberts' fanzine). artie was doing a fanzine called *Blase*, and Skip Williamson was doing a fanzine called *Squire.* So the 'zines that Skip, artie, and I were involved with were all kind of like teenage imitations of *Mad* magazine. Crumb was doing *Foo* which was kind of a cross between *Mad* and Disney. So it wasn't until Crumb's work started appearing in *Help!* that I really got interested in his stuff. Also in '63 I was doing cartoons for *Aardvark* in Chicago and a magazine called *Charlatan* in Tallahassee. Both of these started out as college humor mags, and both were kicked off the campus as soon as the first issue came out. *Charlatan* was published by Bill Killeen, a Kerouacian type guy, originally from Lowell, Mass. At this time, [Gilbert] Shelton was editing the *Texas Ranger*, a college mag out of the University of Texas in Austin, Jack Jackson had just published *God Nose*, and he was working on his own off-campus college mag in Austin called *The Austin Iconoclast.* I lived in a cheap hotel room in Chicago. I went to Roosevelt University for night courses, got involved with *Aardvark* mag, took a bus to Tallahassee to meet Killeen, hitchhiked to Miami—where I set up a radio appearance for Killeen on the then fledgling Larry King radio show. *Charlatan* was running reprints of Gilbert Shelton's *Wonder Wart-Hog* strip from the *Texas Ranger. Help!* was also running *Wart-Hog* reprints at this time. Killeen's girl friend posed nude in *Charlatan*, and it got the magazine big national publicity—but when she appeared on Johnny Carson's show, she forgot to mention the title of the magazine. Anyway, a lot happened during the college humor mag days. And this is when I got in touch with Shelton and Jackson and a lot of other guys who later became the pioneers of underground comics. Then during this same period, I'd go to Manhattan and hang out with spiegelman, who later went to Harpur College at

Binghamton, New York and started a little college humor mag there called *Mother*. And I'd go to Missouri and hang out with Skip Williamson. And those guys would come to Chicago, and we'd have lots of hip artistic fun.

JOURNAL: *This is when spiegelman and you started leafletting.*
LYNCH: Well, that was in late 1965. artie and I used to do these wacky projects when we'd get together. This leaflet project may sound pretty trite today, in lieu of the fact that two years later the hippies came along and did lots of similar inane things. But anyway, we thought that since whenever somebody handed you a leaflet on the street in those days it was always an ad, or a political tract, or a religious tract . . . We decided to make and pass out totally guileless leaflets. We cut out the dictionary definition of the world "love," and drew a surreal picture around it. We printed it up and passed it out on the streets of Chicago in the middle of winter. It was years before people were conditioned to expect such things from the hippies, who came later. So we had a lot of fun grooving on the confusion of people trying to figure out what the point of our leaflet was. Also—it was a good way to meet chicks. Later, artie made lots of great leaflets himself. Some were in comic strip form. He became known across the land as the mad leafleteer. It was around this time, too, that artie and Skip and I were experimenting with surreal comic strips. These were printed in various literary mags of the day. I did a few for *Nexus*, a San Francisco-based literary mag.

JOURNAL: *And how did your involvement with underground comics evolve from all of this?*
LYNCH: Well, by '67 I was editing and publishing a mag called *The Chicago Mirror* with Skip Williamson. This was a satire mag for hippies—which was like a contradiction in terms, since the hippies en masse seemed, by this time, to totally lack a sense of humor. By '67 hippiedom had become a national fad and converts to it were predictably humorless. So we were doing *The Chicago Mirror*, and Crumb sent me a copy of the first *Zap*. Skip and I were impressed by *Zap* #1, which was the first underground comic, I guess you might say. So we changed the *Mirror* to *Bijou Funnies*—since we wanted to do comics anyway, and since our readers really couldn't tell where we were coming from with *The Mirror*. As we were putting together *Bijou* #1, Shelton was out in Austin putting together *Feds 'N Heads* comics. In the beginning, I guess we figured

that these things would only be locally distributed—so some of the same material of Gilbert's is in *Bijou* #1 and also in *Feds 'N Heads* #1. Then the whole yippie thing started, and Crumb came to town to check out the yippie scene at the '68 Democratic National Convention in Chicago. He stayed at my pad, and he drew some stuff for *Bijou* #1. I was working at a commercial art studio doing diarrhea suppressant ads then. I spent a week's pay to print *Bijou* #1. We got a guy named Lenny on the southside to print the book. Lenny had a four-color press. We bound it ourselves in Lenny's print shop. The rest is history.

JOURNAL: *So there was* Zap, Feds 'N Heads, Bijou, *and from there it just grew.*

LYNCH: Yeah. Within a year there were a hundred titles. Within two years 300 titles, and so on until it peaked. Then the proliferation of titles began to dwindle, and ultimately it stabilized. Today it's a viable industry. So where's *my* cut?

JOURNAL: *You sound bitter.*

LYNCH: No. I'm just kidding. We all learned a lot about the business end of it during those years. We gained valuable knowledge, and we got to communicate with our peers. Also I made many a lifetime friend. It was through this underground comics thing that I met Denis Kitchen. When *Bijou* got big, we joined forces with Denis's company. Just last month I went out to Kitchen's farm in Wisconsin to celebrate his fortieth birthday with him and all the cartoonists from around the area. I got to talk at length with Reed Waller there. To me, this guy is one of the best guys working in the field today.

JOURNAL: *How do you think some of the original underground comics material stands up by today's standards?*

LYNCH: Well, when we first saw Crumb's early stuff . . . I really liked *Zap* at the time it came out, because it was a thing where Crumb would be taking images from the '30s, '40s, and '50s—images from our youth—and he'd put them in a modern context. He'd put these images in contemporary situations. You know. Jokes about hippies and drugs and sex and things of the late '60s. There was something extremely haunting about it at the time, because nobody *but* Crumb was doing it. Red Grooms was doing a similar type of thing then. Grooms made a film called *Fat Feet*, which was very much in the same vein as Crumb's late '60s stuff. Grooms was doing this for an effete art gallery-type of audience, though. Crumb was speaking to the masses through the comics he did, so to me Robert's stuff was more interesting, because he had the potential to influence society more.

JOURNAL: *Bijou Publishing Empire is still in business, isn't it?*
LYNCH: Yeah. Today we sell reprints of *Foo*, the 1959 fanzine put out by Robert Crumb and his brother Charles. These are individually numbered sets. Part of a limited edition. They cost eighteen dollars postpaid from, Bijou Publishing Empire, Inc., 3516 Merchandise Mart Station, Chicago, Illinois 60654. Yeah. We gotta get in some plugs for stuff in this interview. Otherwise, I feel guilty about wallowing in my own thoughts on the printed page without any profit motivation to it. Such self-indulgence only invites negative vibes from people who read this. We must sell stuff to justify all of this.

JOURNAL: *Your* Phoebe and the Pigeon People *books are currently available.*
LYNCH: Yeah. There are three issues. They're available at fine comic book stores throughout the nation.

JOURNAL: *In the underground comics you wrote and drew the adventures of the characters* Phoebe and the Pigeon People, *which appears weekly in the* Chicago Reader *newspaper. How does the writing of a weekly strip differ from the writing of comic book stories?*
LYNCH: Well, *Phoebe* has to be a joke a week. It's a different thing than *Nard 'N Pat* in that *Nard 'N Pat* was long stories with a lot of dialogue, and those stories didn't necessarily have to have punch lines. *Phoebe* pretty much has to have a punch line every week. Even if we get involved in a continuity situation in *Phoebe*, there still has to be a gag a week in addition to the continuity. Gary Whitney draws *Phoebe*. I just write it. With *Nard 'N Pat*, I drew many hundreds of panels of a man, a cat, and a chair. When I had the idea for *Phoebe* about nine years ago, I didn't want the tedious task of drawing it because originally—for the first year or so—it was just a woman, a bench and some pigeons. Then I met Gary, and we combined forces. After the first year, Phoebe got up off the bench, and now the strip has evolved, and there are dozens of regular characters in it. It's a whole little universe unto itself.

JOURNAL: *Do you find doing this weekly strip in a 150,000 mass-circulation newspaper a lot different from doing underground comics? I mean, it's a different audience that you have for* Phoebe, *isn't it?*

LYNCH: Well, when we were doing the underground comics we felt that we were communicating with our peers. Now when we do *Phoebe* we feel the same thing. Everyone I know in Chicago reads the *Reader*, the paper that runs *Phoebe*. Today, though—I don't think I know very many people in this town who read underground comics.

JOURNAL: *Why is that?*

LYNCH: Because they're sold only in comic collector shops, for one thing. The *Chicago Reader* is available on every street corner. Underground comics, you've gotta search 'em out. There are maybe four or five stores in the whole city that sell them. In the '60s they were in head shops, and there were lots of head shops. People didn't make a special trip just to buy the comics.

JOURNAL: *Was this the reason for the demise of the underground comics craze—the transition from head shop distribution to comic shop distribution? Or is it partially tied in to the fact that the hippies became yuppies? Why didn't underground comics make a transition to the '80s?*

LYNCH: Who knows? Maybe the comics themselves could have made the transition if the distribution system had made the transition. They went from head shops to comic collector shops, rather than going from head shops to supermarkets. The people who went to head shops in the '60s now go to supermarkets. They *don't* go to comic collector shops.

JOURNAL: *Who* does *go to comic collector shops?*

LYNCH: Comic book collectors. Usually males between twelve and thirty who can afford to spend a lot of money on these things. They want super-hero stuff. They're not shopping for heavy satire. It's a more specialized crowd than you'd get in the supermarket check-out lane.

JOURNAL: *Which you'd prefer?*

LYNCH: Well, I'd prefer a more cosmopolitan audience. An audience of *both* sexes. What I mean is that the readers whom I wanted to read what I was doing are not . . . I didn't want what I was doing in my comics to be the most important thing in their lives. I wanted it to be something casual, something to read for fun without thinking all that much about it. The reason we started doing underground comics when there were no underground comics in the first place was that there was nothing to read—and there was nothing good on TV. So we decided to do it ourselves in the form of comic books. If readers have to make a special trip to go to a comic collector shop to buy these books, it gives the books a role of importance that they don't deserve.

JOURNAL: *So—comic books should be the servant rather than the master?*
LYNCH: Comic books should be something that you read on the toilet and not worry too much about. So should everything else.

GILBERT SHELTON, FRED TODD, AND RON BAUMGART

HARVEY KURTZMAN ONCE CALLED GILBERT SHELTON "THE PRO OF THE GROUP," and Shelton has borne that out in more ways than one. Among underground cartoonists he was second only to Crumb in popularity and esteem. His main characters are Wonder Wart-Hog, the definitive parody of costumed characters, and the Fabulous Furry Freak Brothers, the three-headed apotheosis of longhaired freakdom. With the help of his collaborators Dave Sheridan and Paul Mavrides, Shelton has had an uncanny knack for keeping his characters fresh and up-to-date over the years. Rather than becoming anachronisms, the Freak Brothers came to symbolize a consistent set of values in a wildly shifting culture. Meanwhile, in *Wonder Wart-Hog and the Nurds of November*, the Hog's alter ego Philbert Desanex became an Everyman enduring all the slings and arrows of the '70s, including unemployment, the swine flu vaccine, self-help cults, political assassinations, and professional sports worship.

As mentioned in the Jay Lynch interview, Shelton was one of several underground cartoonists who came out of the University of Texas. In 1968 he made the trek to San Francisco, and in 1969 he helped found the Rip Off Press, which was to become one of the most important and enduring underground publishers. As the underground market started to wither away in the mid-70s, Rip Off branched out into the Rip Off Syndicate, providing underground comics to alternative newspapers. It was ahead of its time, but it helped create an alternative comics market that would become very important in the '80s. Shelton presently lives in Paris, where he collaborates with Mavrides on further Freak Brothers adventures and edits and

translates foreign material for *Rip Off Comix*. Even as an expatriate, he remains one of America's most acute satirists.

In this interview, conducted by Diana Schutz, Shelton is joined by his Rip Off Press cohorts Fred Todd and Don Baumgart (Baumgart has since left the company) and cartoonist Hal Robins as they talk about the high times of underground publishing.

JOURNAL: *To start off, maybe you can tell me a little something about the history of Rip Off Press.*

FRED TODD: Well, the business started in January '69 when four of us, Gilbert Shelton, Jack Jackson, Dave Moriarty, and me, Fred Todd, went together and bought a Davidson printing press at Printer's Exchange down in Hayward, and we took that printing press and moved it into Don Donahue's loft, which was the upstairs of Mowrey's Opera House—which had been the city hall right after the earthquake. It was a real neat old building.

DON BAUMGART: Until it burned down.

TODD: Yeah, until it burned down . . . Don Donahue was printing *Snatch Comix* on his little printing press, and the deal was that for twenty-five dollars a month or so you got a key to the loft space, and you were able to go in there and do as much stuff as you could get away with, without the other people with keys complaining too much about it. So we set up a print shop, and Donahue had a print shop, and Ben Van Meter was producing pornographic movies, and there were at least two hippies and dogs living off in different corners of the place, and several other enterprises. Not to mention a *huge* pile of garbage. It was a terrible neighborhood, too. You couldn't take a picture of the outside of the building, because the girls that worked outside would think you were taking pictures of them. [*laughter*] Then, if you walked up and took your time, you would probably be robbed, or propositioned, or something like that! It was a really terrible neighborhood.

JOURNAL: *So why did you get the printing press in the first place? You wanted to do comics, but were there other reasons?*

GILBERT SHELTON: Well, there were rock posters, too. The Avalon Ballroom at that time was being managed by Texas people.

JOURNAL: *All four of you came out here from Texas?*
EVERYONE: Yes.
TODD: Essentially at the same time, or spread over a couple of years.

JOURNAL: *Was it a "Go west, young man" kind of thing, to make your fame and fortune?*
SHELTON: Well, there was an awful lot of fame and fortune being made in the music business at the time, from Texas people: Janis Joplin, Boz Scaggs, Steve Miller. Chet Helms had the Avalon Ballroom. So there was a big Texas clique rakin' in the bucks, and I figured I could get a job doing posters, like Mouse and Kelly, Rick Griffin, Victor Moscoso, and those guys.

JOURNAL: *So at that time you had no actual plans to do comics?*
TODD: There was probably that in the hearts of Jackson and—
SHELTON: It's just that it had been done before. Robert Crumb kinda started the underground comics movement with *Zap Comix*, although there was actually some earlier stuff, Jack Jackson's *God Nose* and stuff.

JOURNAL: *So how did Rip Off evolve from having one printing press in a loft to today's more professional setup?*
TODD: Gee, it took lots of turns in the process of going off that way. We discovered, after we got started, that a print shop was a reasonable way to spend your time and make some money. And although Gilbert never really got involved in it, Rip Off Press was actually a print shop. Low price and moderate quality [*laughter*] for . . . oh, gee, five years. And that was the main part of how we earned our money, as it paid a payroll and everything. And while we were doing it, we would take extra paper and publish the comic books that we were able to come up with. I guess we started up with Robert Crumb's little comic [*R. Crumb's Comics and Stories*] and *Big Ass* and *Motor City Comics* and a new edition of Jackson's *God Nose*. We published a batch of comics, including the first *Adventures of Jesus* comic [by Frank Stack]. And that was fairly profitable, but the thing was that we didn't have a distribution system, and we had to figure out how to do all that, and we didn't have a whole lot of capital. And so we kind of stayed that way for

five years or so, as a print shop and a publishing company: twelve printers and two or three cartoonists.

JOURNAL: *So printing was your primary source of income then, and publishing was just more of a sideline?*
TODD: At that point it probably was.

JOURNAL: *Okay, how did you come up with the name "Rip Off"?*
TODD: Ask Gilbert.
SHELTON: Gee, I don't even remember!
TODD: You're the one that picked it out! In fact, he picked it out while my back was turned. I was out of town or something. I came back and I discovered that "Oh, the name's 'Rip Off,' man. That's it, we've already started doing business. Too much trouble to change it." And then I had to go down to PG&E and pay a damned electric bill. "Uhh, hey, who you tryin' to kid with a name like that?!"
SHELTON: Well, it's easy to remember, isn't it?
TODD: That's right. It's easy to remember, I'm telling you, man.

JOURNAL: *And you didn't think it would frighten people away?*
BAUMGART: Well, that was the spirit of the '60s.
TODD: It was an interesting thing about the time and the location. Like I say, it was a terrible neighborhood—most of the time what we were talking about when we were down there was who got ripped off on the way to work. And in our printing qualities the notion of ripping off was really apparent when we tried to rip the posters off the printing press, since we used too much ink and they stuck together.

JOURNAL: *Yeah. That's one of the things when you're learning how to print: If you get too much ink on the machine, the paper sticks to it. The machine doesn't stop though, so it's . . .*
TODD: Naturally we had to start out doing the hardest kind of work, too, just because we were confident of our abilities.
SHELTON: A couple of guys got their long hair caught in the printing press while it was going, too.
HAL ROBINS: That really happened?
TODD: Oh yeah.
SHELTON: Twice.
TODD: Yeah. Not to mention the time the actresses were running around without any clothes on.

JOURNAL: *Do go on!*

TODD: Well, I was working in the darkroom, and was actually going to the art institute at the time and was really desensitized to naked female flesh. I'd been drawing naked women all day, and when I came in, there were naked women running around. Who cares? But Moriarty was beside himself!

It was an awful place though. The thing about it was: It's pretty rainy here in San Francisco, and this was a real rainy year and the roof leaked like a sieve, so the only way we could keep the printing area dry was to go up in the attic and spread out a tent of plastic so we'd have water running down the walls instead of through the roof of this one room. There was still water on the floor, loose electric cords . . . oh, it was terrifying.

Oh, the story of how the thing burned down is kind of interesting and I'd like to tell it. We were trimming comic books with a paper cutter and putting the trash into plastic bags, and, not me, but others there would take the trash and deposit it in the neighborhood. Now, this was kind of a bombed-out redevelopment area and half the houses didn't belong to anybody, but there were still lots of people living around the area, and some of the things that got put into these trash bags, besides little slips of paper that would catch fire real easily, were wasted sheets of *Snatch Comix*. And kids would just grab onto that, and if they happened to be playing with matches, too, well, that's not real surprising, is it? Especially hanging around with comics like that! And, sure enough, the house next door caught fire at the worst possible moment: while the rock and roll band was practicing its brain-wave-generator light show and getting instruments tuned—and the other band that was waiting to practice was coming up the elevator. It was great. We had a press run of comic books spread out in there, and sure enough it all went up. Ruined everything. We had to dismantle our printing press and carry it down three flights of stairs over this rubble.

SHELTON: The firemen wisely came in and prohibited anyone from using the elevator in our building—or else they *would* have and they might have died in the process, because that's what happens in a fire, the air current gets sucked up or down the elevator shaft. They got their expensive electric organ loaded in the elevator—we had about fifteen minutes after the building next door was on fire before the firemen made us leave our own place— the band loaded their instruments in the elevator, and then were ordered out of the building, so they roasted their instruments in the elevator.

TODD: Ahh, they would have been ruined anyway.

JOURNAL: *So you all just stayed outside and watched your building burn down?*

SHELTON: Yup.

TODD: Well, the roof was still on it when we went back to empty it out.

SHELTON: I was standing there watching it burning, and the hose popped off the fire hydrant next to me and drenched me and threw me against the brick wall! [*laughter*]

JOURNAL: *And when did all this happen?*

TODD: Oh, that was in April of '69.

JOURNAL: *Was it then that you moved here?*

TODD: No, we moved then to the Family Dog office. All the buildings around there were part of the San Francisco Redevelopment Agency, and the redevelopment people said, "Well, we'll put you in a place. You can have a spot in this building down the street." We went down the street and looked at it and said, "Wow, this is terrible, I don't like this." But the Family Dog people were in the process of being evicted. There was a little note on the door with a gold seal from the sheriff's department and everything, so we just went in and said, "You guys said we could have a place. We pick this one!" And they said, "Oh, yeah, gosh!" So we took over that office and set up our printing press, until they came back and said, "No, we're really gonna tear this building down. You can have this other place over here." It turned out to be on the seventh busiest intersection in town. We set up our printing press, and we had an apartment in the back and a basement, and above it was the ex-hotel that all the people were out of, and next door was a print shop. After we were there awhile, we opened little holes into the other parts of the building and expanded—took over the hotel and had a bunch of people living there. It was a real circus! The redevelopment people kept saying, "Well, we're gonna tear this building down week after next, so you guys better find a new place." Well, finally after a year, we decided, "Well, we can't stand this anymore. We'll find a new place." By searching around we found our present location and moved. It's real interesting: It took them another eight years to get around to tearing that place down and to build something new! But when we moved in here, it was a wonderful opportunity. To get cheated. [*laughter*]

SHELTON: Our rent has increased a thousand percent since we moved in here thirteen years ago.

TODD: What a drag.

JOURNAL: *But you're here now and you have an established business. Gilbert is Editor-in-Chief and—*

TODD: Gilbert is editor-in-chief and I'm president. Don [Baumgart] is vice-president.

JOURNAL: *So what does that involve? I mean, those are impressive titles and all, but what do you actually do?*

SHELTON: Basically, I pay myself to read comic books.

JOURNAL: *That's convenient!*

TODD: And I write the checks.

SHELTON: I travel around the world reading comic books.

TODD: Well, he does more than that. Everybody knows that.

JOURNAL: *Well, on to the Freak Brothers: How did they come about?*

ROBINS: They started as Commie seeds, man.

SHELTON: Commie sinsemilla seeds.

ROBINS: But organically grown.

SHELTON: The first Freak Brothers strip was an advertisement for a little film that I did, a 16mm black-and-white called "Texas Hippies March on the Capitol"—the only print of which we later lost. Anyway, the advertisement for the film featuring the Freak Brothers was better received than the film itself, so I just kept doing the comic strip and forgot about being a film director.

JOURNAL: *When was that?*

SHELTON: In '68? '67, maybe.

JOURNAL: *You were still in Texas then?*

SHELTON: Yeah. I moved to California in '68.

JOURNAL: *And you brought the Freaks with you.*

SHELTON: Yeah, I published *Feds 'N Heads* comics then, and that had a Freak Brothers story in it. I think. Yeah.

BAUMGART: Was that their first published story?

SHELTON: The one about the giant magic marijuana seed: "Jack and the Beanstalk." Yeah, that was the first—after the advertisement.

JOURNAL: *Do the Freak Brothers have real-life counterparts? Did you have specific people in mind when you created them?*
SHELTON: No, not three specific people. In fact, there are hundreds, thousands, millions of 'em out there. People keep coming up to me, saying, "I know Fat Freddy! You must know so-and-so who lives down the street from me in St. Petersburg, Florida. He's the original Fat Freddy; he's been telling everybody that. And he looks like him!" But no.

JOURNAL: *Given that the Freaks sprang from the '60s and encompass that whole era, why do you think they're still so popular in the '80s? More than other undergrounds.* Freak Brothers *comics continue to sell like crazy. It's a whole different generation now, but they're still tuned in to Freak Brothers. Why? What's happening there?*
SHELTON: Gee, I don't know. We're lucky, I guess.
TODD: They're good! They're funny! I mean, I've read the damn things several hundred times and I still laugh!
ROBINS: Well, the stories take place today. They're not in the '60s, they're not frozen in time. That's their starting-point but they're not bound to those times.
TODD: Even from the '60s . . . *Freak Brothers* #1—I still laugh every time I read that thing!
BAUMGART: An essential element of the Freak Brothers is that they're disobedient of the rules of society, and I think that's not anything that's locked in time; it's something that's—
SHELTON: Yeah, they're traditional literary characters just doing the same things that people have always done, in more or less contemporary garb. The comic books today are into this fake fantasy and mythology stuff, like Tolkien started. But the traditional human is still around here and there. It's like "Punch and Judy" stuff. It's well disguised from its contemporary garb, but "Punch and Judy" is still alive down there: the San Francisco Mime Troupe and theater groups like that.

JOURNAL: *Gilbert, do you intend to keep on doing* Freak Brothers? *I mean, is this sort of a lifelong commitment?*
SHELTON: Well, I don't know. This current story, "The Idiots

Abroad," which I'm committed to, is going to be close to 100 pages long and might take me the rest of my life! Couple of years, anyway.

JOURNAL: *So they're still very much alive for you as characters?*
SHELTON: Oh yes!

JOURNAL: *Other than some of the coloring, which you've already mentioned, what does Paul Mavrides contribute to the* Freak Brothers *strips?*
BAUMGART: Whining, complaining . . . [*laughter*]
TODD: Don't tell her [Schutz] that. Paul's a valuable and creative individual. Too bad he isn't here right now because he'd tell you so! [*laughter*]
SHELTON: No. He probably does the majority of the work on the thing. His drawing style is like mine would be if I could draw as well as I wanted to. It's hard even for me to tell who drew what.

JOURNAL: *But you do the writing?*
SHELTON: Paul does some of the writing, too. There's no clear delineation or division of labor there.

JOURNAL: *So the strip has become more of a joint effort?*
SHELTON: Yeah. Basically we spend the same amount of time on it.

JOURNAL: *There's been a big cat craze going on for the last few years. Has* Fat Freddy's Cat *benefited from that at all?*
SHELTON: I don't think the sales of *Fat Freddy's Cat* have changed any in the last few years, although I think that cat craze has been going on longer than that. I think it's more like the last *six* years: Kliban's *Cat, Fritz the Cat* . . . It started reaching bad proportions about six or eight years ago, and now with things like *Garfield*, it's going downhill rapidly. [*laughter*]

JOURNAL: *Well, all right, but your cat has now been published twice in trade paperback format—like these other cats.*
SHELTON: Yeah. That's kind of a matter of experimenting on our case, to see if we printed the same book in two different formats how the sales would compare.

JOURNAL: *Not that* Freak Brothers *doesn't have that kind of wide acceptance, but* Fat Freddy's Cat *has even more. It's the kind of* *thing I could show to my grandmother—without her being quite as shocked as she would be were she to read* Freak Brothers.

ROBINS: Are you sure?!

SHELTON: Yeah, the cat's just shit jokes, no drug jokes!

JOURNAL: *Right!*

TODD: Usually.

JOURNAL: *Undergrounds in general seem to be on the decline these days and the market seems to be drying up. Do you think that we're now seeing the death of underground comics—and if so, what accounts for that?*

TODD: I've always wondered what undergrounds were. It seems to be whatever the small batch of people who were doing underground comics back in 1970 to '73 care to do. It doesn't really have anything to do with the content, the theme, the format of the production, the production values, or any damn thing like that. It's just whatever Gilbert or Robert Crumb or Rip Off or Last Gasp happens to do—that's underground. It is by definition.

ROBINS: Of course, that classification comes after the fact. And now with the small press, the alternative press . . .

JOURNAL: *But there is a difference between the kind of stuff that Rip Off tends to publish and the sort of material that, say, Eclipse would publish. It's not that easy to pinpoint, but—*

TODD: The thing that I gripe about is *The Cartoon History of the Universe*. That whole series has been labeled as "underground" comics and the artist is *not* an underground cartoonist. The only thing that's underground about it is the fact that *we* published it. We didn't have any editorial input into it—I mean that's all straight history. He's very talented . . .

ROBINS: Highly opinionated.

TODD: Well, any version of history is opinionated.

BAUMGART: Well, when undergrounds first started, the initial impact was shock: "My god, here are people doing something that nobody's done before! Here's sex! Here's violence! Here's anti-Americanism! Here's what we're into, the against-the-war movement, against politicians! Here are vagrants smoking marijuana!" It's like somebody jumping out of a closet and scaring you. It only works once or twice, and then you have to find something of real substance if you're going to continue to publish. We've found our core of what we do through *Freak Brothers, Wonder Wart-Hog, Fat Freddy's Cat*, and *Cartoon History*. Everybody kind of started the same and had to find out what handhold they were going to hang onto. We were very lucky because we had a very, very talented person who was doing a lot of really good stuff.

SHELTON: There's another thing about so-called "underground" comics—the fact that they emphasized a *regional* aspect of whatever it was. They were personal and regional—whereas before everything had been published in New York, the center of the publishing industry.

ROBINS: And because of that, all the work started resembling itself.

SHELTON: Yeah, it got inbred, in the sense that a "style" and tradition of comic books prevailed in the stuff that was all published in New York.

ROBINS: Except for rare cases like Basil Wolverton, who came out of Montana or someplace like that, and he would always mail in his stuff and it would always look different.

JOURNAL: *New York publishers also had the Comics Code to contend with, which you guys don't.*

SHELTON: That didn't have anything to do with regionalism.

TODD: Well, also, the Comics Code is saying that this stuff is for a different audience than what we're really aiming at. We've always aimed, I thought, at our own audience, which was folks of our own age and type. There's millions of us who are satisfied with ourselves, so we've never really gone after the Comics Code audience, who have to be protected.

JOURNAL: *Although* Freak Brothers *comics aren't under restricted sales.*

TODD: Well, it depends on the local whatever. There's really not much that's objectionable, except for their antiestablishment voice of anarchy.

JOURNAL: *Yes, we've got to protect the youth of today from that!*

TODD: Not me!

SHELTON: The youth of today know all about that.

ROBINS: That is one thing about undergrounds that does definitely click in young people's minds: constant antiauthoritarianism.

JOURNAL: *So you don't feel, then, that there's any cause to worry about an untimely death of undergrounds?*

SHELTON: Oh, I don't think Robert Crumb's gonna have any trouble.

ROBINS: It's really drawing comics from a different impulse—and whoever prints them, there'll always be comics.

TODD: There aren't really as many different titles as there used to be. Gee, for a while anybody who could scrape together $1,000 could produce himself a comic book. They were terrible.

BAUMGART: For a long time distributors published a bunch of terrible comics so they could trade them for good comics.

TODD: Boy, there were some that were gross.

JOURNAL: *Okay, on to the punk movement: There have been more and more punks appearing in* Freak Brothers, *there's Paranoid Punk-Pig—*

ROBINS: That was precognition.

JOURNAL: *—and I'm wondering what you think of the movement, and how or if it has any affect on comics.*

SHELTON: Well, basically, there's "Punk" and "New Wave" graphics. You see more of it in European comics. Here, it's more fashion and music. It doesn't have a lot of meaning except for that. Seeing someone with green and purple and orange hair, I think I'm in England. Nobody in Europe does that but the English. Maybe the Germans and the Dutch a little bit, but the Spaniards, French, and Italians don't do that. And they're just as advanced, if not more advanced, in graphics and comics and everything else than the English.

JOURNAL: *And yet, that movement has translated into comics?*

SHELTON: Yeah. This is a Spanish "New Wave" comic [*Displays a copy of* El Vibora.] You see what I mean about the style.

JOURNAL: *You must have a certain affinity for this style because you've been publishing this kind of material.*

SHELTON: For me, the story's more important. If there was a good story writer who happened to draw in that style, sure, and in fact there are some, but in the majority of cases what you see is just an excuse for the drawing; and the words and the literal content of the thing are zilch. That sort of thing should be hung on a wall, and not published as a comic book, basically. Or, that is to say, there should be plenty of good stories without having to print something that is totally devoid of literal meaning, that is totally visual. Also, I mean, if it's all pictorial, it should just be hanging on the wall, unless it's an art book or something which lets you see reproductions of pictures that carry no emotional baggage.

TODD: Well, maybe you should say—

SHELTON: Literary baggage.

TODD: —literary baggage.

ROBINS: Well, of course, literary quality can exist in a story that doesn't have a bit of words in it, if the pictures delineate well enough a strong narrative action and do tell a story.

SHELTON: Uh-huh. And then it's not pictorial anymore, but narrative. They used to teach us in art school that you had to rid yourself completely of any meaning in your visual work, or else you couldn't be "pure."

ROBINS: Oh, that's so pernicious! Or else you get accused of being an "illustrator"!

SHELTON: Yeah, right, you were an "illustrator."

TODD: We're obviously on the side of illustration in this part of the world.

SHELTON: Yeah.

JOURNAL: *Do you see yourselves, essentially, as continuing with the comics, or are you into exploring other forms of entertainment?*

TODD: Well, Rip Off Press will probably remain a publisher of printed somethings, instead of movies, or computer programs, or a used-car dealer! [*laughter*] We'll continue being a comic book publisher for as long as we continue being in business. We may actually produce an eight-and-a-half-by-eleven-inch something-or-other instead of a comic book. And we may produce paperback books, postcards, and other things like that, but basically we're sellers of printed images.

JOURNAL: *Okay gentlemen, I have one last question for you: Who—please tell me—who is Frappington Wildebeest?*

TODD: Wildebeest!

JOURNAL: *Wildebeest?*

TODD: Wildebeest!

SHELTON: Well, uh . . . Wildebeest . . . uh, yeah, he's a live person. It's kind of mysterious. Sounds like a pseudonym, doesn't it?

JOURNAL: *Yes indeed! [laughter]*

ROBINS: You mean people are actually curious about him?

SHELTON: Well, it might be an acronym. I haven't tried to figure it out.

JOURNAL: *So he's just someone draped in mystery, then? Right. For convenient purposes.*
BAUMGART: He gets fired or something, doesn't he?
SHELTON: He's a traveling contributing editor right now. Of his own volition.

JOURNAL: *Oh. So he's no longer Managing Editor?*
SHELTON: No. There isn't any Managing Editor right now. I guess I'm Managing Editor.
TODD: Right, it's all out of control! It's like the weather.

MANUEL "SPAIN" RODRIGUEZ

ONE OF THE IRONIES OF UNDERGROUND COMICS IS THAT WHILE BY THE MID-'70S the underground comic book was all but dead, the comics themselves were better than ever. Indeed, it could be said that with the possible exception of Justin Green, all the cartoonists in this section did their best work after the movement had peaked. Though underground comics slowed down to a trickle, what comics there were—*Arcade, Zap, Rip Off Comix, Young Lust, Anarchy*—were of very high quality.

A case in point is Manuel "Spain" Rodriguez. Spain was one of the movement's earliest stars. He was the most overtly political of underground cartoonists, and his main character, *Trashman*, was a revolutionary super-hero fighting "the shadow of tyranny that has covered the land" in a near-future America (or Amerika, if you're sentimental). In the '70s and '80s he turned to autobiography and history. In his autobiographical stories he told of his days in motorcycle gangs and his sexual experiences with a mordant humor that had always been under the surface in his earlier work. His historical stories about war and revolution combine the powerful imagery of the Trashman stories with a more compassionate, politically sophisticated world view. His work still appears regularly in magazines like *Weirdo* and *Prime Cuts*.

This interview was conducted by Gary Groth in front of an audience. Robert Crumb was present and chimed in occasionally.

THEY HAD MARCHED AND DEMONSTRATED FOR YEARS BUT THE WAR STILL RAGED ON. NOW THEY HAD COME TO THE NATIONAL CONVENTION OF THE DEMOCRATIC PARTY....

CHICAGO, '68

PART I

© 1972 SPAIN

JOURNAL: *The first thing I'd like to ask Spain to do is to chronicle his political education and tell us why, considering the history of comics, which is that of an innocuous and politically trivial form, he felt comics is an appropriate forum for his political views. [laughter from audience]*

SPAIN: That's a long question. Do you want the—

JOURNAL: *It's a 120-minute tape.*

SPAIN: Do you want the chronicling of my own political development? Actually, being kind of a comic book person when I was a teenager I was attracted to more fascistic types of things, as kids are today. Characters had neat outfits and stuff and I wasn't too sophisticated about what was going on.

I went through a phase where I thought Nazis and fascists were neat guys—you know, they kicked ass. When you look close you see the difference between the visual factor and performance. At a certain point it became clear to me that the ideal that you're taught wasn't really occurring in the real world. As a kid growing up—especially as a kid growing up during World War II—I was kind of bombarded with heroic World War II stuff, and grew up with a certain feeling of idealism. As you grow up you quickly get that knocked out of you. I was looking for something to replace it when I thought I saw things as they really were. I figured, "Well, the world really sucks," and these guys kind of see the world for what it really is, and everyone basically eats it, and these guys are just honest about it—basically, the fascistic view of the world.

JOURNAL: *What kind of fascistic view of the world are you talking about?*

SPAIN: Well, a view of the world in which the strong take what they want and victimize whoever they can. That seems to be the way it really is.

JOURNAL: *Was there anything in particular that caused you to notice this?*

SPAIN: I remember the first thing that shattered my youthful idealism. We were playing baseball at the end of this dead-end street where there weren't any houses around—and they sent some kind of drunken cop to basically beat our ass. And as a kid, I always thought cops were good guys.

JOURNAL: *Was this your first confrontation with authority?*

SPAIN: Yeah, the first confrontation with official authority. When EC comics were banned I never thought that sort of thing could happen in America, so as a kid you take that stuff kind of hard . . . and I took it hard, and became a kind of bitter kid.

JOURNAL: *Can you give me a time frame here?*

SPAIN: Well, this was the '50s, actually paralleling the time of EC comics. It was a time of coming of age. *Mad* comics seemed to have that bitter edge to it. It seemed to be one of the few things you read that rang true.

JOURNAL: *Earlier you said you had interest in fascistic . . .*

SPAIN: When I was a teenager . . .

JOURNAL: *When did that change into a dislike for authoritarian . . .*

SPAIN: It was never quite clear because it was never really sophisticated. I mean all that stuff seemed to be identified with losers of the world which myself and other guys I grew up with saw ourselves as.

JOURNAL: *Have-nots . . .*
SPAIN: Yeah, right, have-nots, people who were clearly the bad people of society.

JOURNAL: *Was there any one thing that you remember as radicalizing you so that you sympathized in a political way with the have-nots?*
SPAIN: I remember seeing a mural in a book in art school. It showed what were obviously wealthy people eating little cakes looking quite pleased with themselves. In the background were Mexicans, fingering rifles and machetes looking very sullen and I instantly understood who I was and who they were and that vision has never left me.

I started to read more things, and also as I investigated guys like Hitler and Mussolini, it's real hard to see those guys as being role models, heroes . . .

JOURNAL: *I assume you didn't see them as role models.*
SPAIN: Well, I saw that kind of image, that kind of tough-guy look . . . well, basically like Rambo.

JOURNAL: *Rambo's the other side of the same coin . . .*
SPAIN: Rambo is a fascist. Rambo basically—it's just like applied to this country—but basically it's the idea that you have the right to pull off anything you can pull off.

JOURNAL: *So how would you describe your political views? Were they leftist in the '60s?*
SPAIN: Oh yeah, definitely leftist. As I developed a more sophisticated view of things, I started to become interested in philosophy. I started to read all these different philosophers and stuff, a good deal of which confused me and seemed unclear . . . Schopenhauer and Hegel . . . and you know, all those different guys . . . John Stuart Mill.

JOURNAL: *Did they help you in any way?*
SPAIN: It kind of helps you in that it stretches your mind and makes you wonder about things. I read Plato. Plato was real fascistic . . .

JOURNAL: *He's not democratic.*
SPAIN: No, right, but he also seems to eulogize this SS . . . these guys are . . . the philosopher-kings, and then they had warrior castes where these Gestapo guys guarded this super society. It

had a certain appeal, and it also had a kind of respectability. Who could say anything bad about Plato?

JOURNAL: *And you believed in what principles at this time?*
SPAIN: At a certain point, as a late teenager, I just was searching around for stuff . . . kind of curious and confused, and basically alienated and trying to figure out what was going on, trying to find some sort of focus, some sort of political focus, too, because I clearly saw that standing by yourself, the guy that's standing by himself usually gets jumped on by some more organized force. I started to become interested in Marxism, but from a libertarian perspective.

JOURNAL: *A libertarian Marxist? That's an oxymoron.*
SPAIN: Well, not really; Marx himself was greatly influenced by anarchism. As a matter of fact, Marxism today is more influenced by Engels in a certain respect, than by Marx. I mean, Engels was a more realistic guy whereas Marx had a more ideal conception of what things could be.

JOURNAL: *Now at what point did you choose to express your political feelings and why comics?*
SPAIN: The first things I did were in Buffalo. I worked with a guy—an old Commie who was expelled from the Communist Party in one of the purges in the late '50s, and me and him actually did early stuff on the Vietnam war. We put out a periodical called *The Spirit and the Sword* and it was dedicated to John Brown.

JOURNAL: *And this would have been in the early '60s?*
SPAIN: This was around '64. So already there was a whole lot of political ferment with the civil rights movement . . .
ROBERT CRUMB: *[from audience]* When did you become a card-carrying communist?

JOURNAL: *Are you now or have you ever . . . ?*
SPAIN: It would take a whole lot of discipline to be a card-carrying communist. It's hard enough being a cartoonist. Being a card-carrying cartoonist . . .

JOURNAL: *Let me backtrack and ask when you started drawing?*
SPAIN: I started drawing when I was a kid, in second grade . . . it was always echoed by comics.

JOURNAL: *And what kind of comics did you read as a kid?*
SPAIN: Captain Marvel, and then I got into EC comics. I must have been about eleven or twelve.

JOURNAL: *When the ECs folded did you continue reading comics?*
SPAIN: No, because of the Comics Code I just stopped reading comics. As kids we had this idea that—Kurtzman did that great thing about the underground comics—we had this idea that there would be underground comics, and we used to do these kind of underground comics . . . my friends and I would draw. We did them in high school.

JOURNAL: *You mentioned Buffalo?*
SPAIN: Yeah, Buffalo, New York. That's my hometown.

JOURNAL: *When did you leave Buffalo?*
SPAIN: I went to art school for a few years.

JOURNAL: *Which art school?*
SPAIN: [Silvermine] Guild School of Art in Connecticut. You might be familiar with it.

JOURNAL: *Now, at what point did you leave Connecticut and art school?*
SPAIN: Nineteen-sixty.

JOURNAL: *Did you go to California?*
SPAIN: No, I returned to Buffalo and was working at a factory, which was another political education. I mean, over there Marxism really rang true. Everybody in the plant knew exactly who the enemy was, and these are your average working guys, not your political guys, or not guys who were leftists. Everybody knew that they were trying to squeeze as much work as they could out of you and everybody knew that you were trying to give them as little as possible.

JOURNAL: *So you became part of the laboring class?*
SPAIN: Yeah, well, right, but I have always been part of the laboring class. I've always had to work to live. Still do.

JOURNAL: *Okay, now back to my original question: Why comics? Why did you choose to express your political views in comics?*
SPAIN: I'd always considered myself an enthusiastic comic book type of person. As a kid, the Comics Code was too much to stomach, so I just stopped reading comics.

JOURNAL: *You were actually sufficiently politically aware in the '50s to realize that the Comics Code emasculated comics?*
SPAIN: But it wasn't political . . . it was political in that, as a kid, you believed that America stood for freedom and you could print anything you wanted. These weren't fuck books or anything, these were like stories that . . .

JOURNAL: *Even that suggests a degree of political awareness.*
SPAIN: I guess that when you look back upon it it was political consciousness because you felt that you had a right to read these comics. I count my last experience as trying to find these comics as . . . EC had a thing called picto-fiction, which were basically trying to get out of the Comics Code because they were magazine stories . . . and I remember seeing one with this great Jack Kamen cover and this guy with a leather jacket. I saw it on a stack in a drugstore behind the counter, and I was waiting for the guys to put it out on the stands, and a week went by and it wasn't out, and so I asked the guys, "Do you have this specific comic?" and they said, "No, we don't carry those," and I said, "Well, how about that one behind the stands?" and this guy said, "Oh, you don't want to read that, you'll become a juvenile delinquent! You want to become a juvenile delinquent?" And I said, "You're fucking right!" [*laughter*] Being a juvenile delinquent like, you know, images of Marlon Brando and *The Wild One* . . . these guys that weren't these sniveling conformists.
CRUMB: [*from audience*] Did you ever want to be a boy scout?
SPAIN: As a matter of fact I was a boy scout.

JOURNAL: *Subverting from within . . . Well, now, speaking of* The Wild One, *did you belong to a bike gang?*
SPAIN: I belonged to a bike gang after I got out of art school.

JOURNAL: *Did that have any kind of political significance?*
SPAIN: The thing is, in the '50s you had all these youth gangs. When the '50s ended, things kind of got more conservative in this way. The guys that couldn't adjust, becoming bikers in the '60s. At a certain point you figure that that stuff's okay for teenagers . . . but here you are twenty years old . . . you don't do that stuff. I was one of those guys who did that stuff.

JOURNAL: *Slicked your hair back?*
SPAIN: I always did that. I used to use Dixie Peach Hair Pomade . . .

JOURNAL: *Oh my God.*
SPAIN: I mean, the thing was, you could comb your hair straight out, and it would kind of stand up there for a while.

JOURNAL: *You started to draw comics. Now, the reason you drew comics was essentially to express your political views.*
SPAIN: Well, I just had political views. I'd always had this thing and had a small core of friends who somehow believed these comics would come back and people would have dreams and walk into a drugstore and they'd find some EC comic they'd never seen before . . . I mean, I had these dreams, but I knew other guys who had these dreams. EC comics really touched people deeply, and me, too. With Marvel, at some point, the psychedelic pop came back, and you knew that underground comics were just down the line and had to happen.

JOURNAL: *Did you read Marvel in the '60s?*
SPAIN: Yeah, I did.

JOURNAL: *Did you like them?*
SPAIN: Yeah, I liked *Thor, Fantastic Four* . . . they had some kind of psychedelic quality about them. I haven't been into Marvel comics recently . . . I've heard that they don't have that psychedelic quality anymore.

JOURNAL: *Had you ever considered working for one of the established companies?*
SPAIN: I thought about it when I first started doing comics. I thought ultimately, I don't know how long this'll last, I'll probably end up having to work for Marvel or something. But the more I did it the more it seemed as though maybe we could do this stuff . . . it seemed like such a logical thing. I mean, here you have an art tradition that I was put in contact with going to art school—the idea of the unbridled artist, the artist who could do anything he wanted, and here you have this whole area open for exploitation, I mean, you had literature being apprised here, you had artwork being apprised, why aren't they apprised when they're put together? And especially the whole thing that comic books were so sneered upon. When I first was in art school I started drawing these . . . actually, I was into Conan the Barbarian before anybody had ever heard of Conan the Barbarian. I'd draw these ancient barbarian

things . . . kind of corny today, but at the time nobody else was doing them. But in art school they were kind of sneered at.

JOURNAL: *Did you see underground comics as kind of a resurrection of what EC stood for in the sense that they were subversive?*
SPAIN: Yeah, right. I mean, the thing about the stuff you read about in EC comics was that it was incredible . . . and somehow you just knew everything else you got in the media was bullshit, you just knew that even these people who were conformists weren't really that way, they weren't really these nice people. They were basically as rotten as everybody else, but they somehow put on this goody-goody facade.

That was the great thing about *Mad* comics. *Mad* comics just cut through that shit and they . . . Veronica and Starchy and all that stuff, man . . . hearing the voice of truth out of all the chaos of smarmy niceness . . . It's still . . . I don't know, what is politically sophisticated? I like to flatter myself thinking that I have the correct insight and everything . . . think of myself as a well-intentioned person and all. [*laughter*]

JOURNAL: *Deluding yourself . . .*
SPAIN: Yeah, right.

JOURNAL: *Well now, correct me if I'm wrong, but was* Trashman *the first underground you did?*
SPAIN: No, I did *Zodiac Time Warp. The East Village Other* started going and I got something going with Walter Bowart and he told me to do a comic. Actually, it was intended as a comic book.

JOURNAL: *Were you living in New York City?*
SPAIN: No, I was living in Buffalo. What happened was . . . I'd been working on it for six months and came to New York, and laid the comic on his desk, and said, "You still interested?"

JOURNAL: *So, you did some work for* The East Village Other *and then after that?*
SPAIN: Doing *Zodiac Mind Warp* I found myself in New York with about a hundred bucks in the middle of winter and I basically . . . *The East Village Other* was kind of the only thing I could do.

This was what I wanted to do. I really wanted to do comics and I just felt, especially doing this thing, I mean, I wasn't too happy with it. When I did *Zodiac Mind Warp* I didn't like it all the way through, and when I was finished after about five minutes I didn't like it. But I worked for six months and just had to see if I could sell it. Which got me working with *The East Village Other* and kind of doing amorphous strips which later on evolved into *Trashman*. By that time Robert [Crumb] came down and I was living with Kim Deitch . . . this was on the Lower East Side. A lot of great tales came out of that period.

JOURNAL: *Now at what point did* Trashman *come out?*
SPAIN: *Trashman* must have come in '68.

JOURNAL: *And that was your first really major . . .*
SPAIN: That was my first really identifiable character.

MEMBER OF THE AUDIENCE: *You were taking LSD?*
SPAIN: Right, right.
CRUMB: [*from audience*] It was something inspired by that, it was somewhat psychedelic.
SPAIN: Yeah, right, sure. I mean, all that stuff started to happen then. I lived in New York for about six months in '65. It was kind of pre-hippie, but all that stuff was beginning to happen. This was before *The East Village Other*. All sorts of strange stuff going on, all kinds of weird communes and Kerista, this free love commune . . . and everyone fucked and sucked . . .

JOURNAL: *The good old days.*
SPAIN: Yeah, right! Free love . . . plentiful drugs. Call me old-fashioned, but I miss those days.

KIM DEITCH

KIM DEITCH IS UNUSUAL AMONG UNDERGROUND CARTOONISTS FOR COMING OUT of a cartooning family. His father is the noted animator Gene Deitch, who worked at UPA, headed Terrytoons, and emigrated to Czechoslovakia, where he directed the Academy Award winning *Munro*. Kim's career has been no less colorful, if not quite as well-known. He was one of the most prolific underground cartoonists. His drawing style evokes the '20s and '30s, and his favorite subjects are the occult and charlatanry, which are never far apart. Like several underground cartoonists, he now can make a better living in fine art than comics, but he still manages to stay active in the field. He's been more active than ever in recent years, with a new book (*Hollywoodland*), a continuing series of short stories in *Weirdo*, and a forthcoming comic book series from Fantagraphics.

This interview was conducted by Monte Beauchamp.

JOURNAL: *So after high school, what happened? Did you head off to college?*

DEITCH: After high school, *everything* went blank. [*laughter*] Well, miraculously, I graduated from high school. Rather well, too. I kind of pulled myself together during the last two years. I was kind of a geek/weirdo/outcast the first two years of high school, but then I

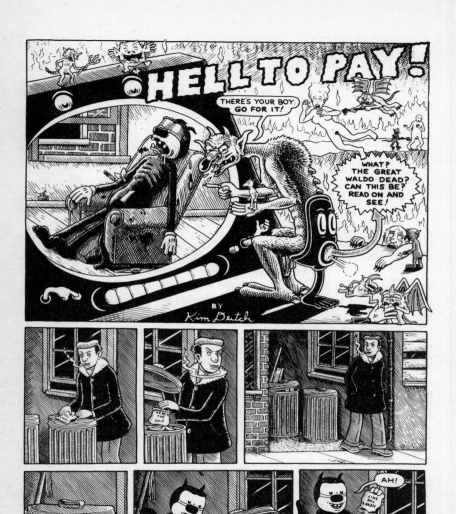

Waldo the Cat, from *RAW*

actually turned my individuality to my advantage. I remember during my senior year that CBS came to do a piece on outstanding kids in the high school, and because I wasn't like everyone else, I was one of the ones they picked. So I started getting the girls toward the end of the year. But getting back to your question, "What happened after high school?" Well, I really didn't want to go to college. I guess I was falling under the spell of the beatniks. I just wanted to get out and experience life. I was reading Thomas Wolfe novels, and I wanted to experience the juice of life. I wanted to do my *own* thing. The sum total of my ambitions upon graduating from high school was to join the army—because you could get around and see a little bit of the world—or just be a bum, just schlep around, travel, see the world. But everyone was supposed to go to college. And I had one big problem about going to college in that I couldn't pass elementary algebra! But one of the few colleges that didn't require that was Pratt Institute in Brooklyn, New York. So really, in an uninspired and rather lackadaisical fashion, I became a freshman at Pratt Institute. And I got by. But I was already smoking marijuana before I got out of high school; I would have started sooner if I could have gotten my hands on it. Really, I was more interested in things like good times with girls than anything else. The most interesting thing for me about college was suddenly being transplanted to Pratt and being able to live in a fascinating place like Brooklyn, which I did for the next two years. But I didn't really fit in at art school. I didn't really have any clearly defined ambitions. Plus, I wasn't especially impressed with the art that was coming out of Pratt. And the feeling was mutual—they weren't especially impressed with the art I was doing.

JOURNAL: *What type of art were you doing at the time?*
DEITCH: It had a tendency to be *somewhat* cartoony, but there was actually no point of view behind it. My efforts at Pratt were pretty halfhearted. I was getting by, but my work habits were poor. I was getting into drugs and laying the groundwork for a *big* drinking problem. I remember one evening in Brooklyn, I ended up getting drunk with a Norwegian sailor. He was telling me yarns about getting drunk and dancing on a bar in Hong Kong. And he also told me how easy it was to ship out on Scandinavian ships in Brooklyn. It sounded good to me. So, at the end of my sophomore year, I took a leave of absence and shipped out as a deck boy in the Norwegian

Merchant Marines. I did wind up in Hong Kong. But to tell the truth, I don't remember dancing on any bars.

JOURNAL: *[laughter] How long did this continue?*
DEITCH: Well, after six months of that, I got out—with even *less* ambition than I had before. I had some vague idea that I wanted to be a man of adventure. One of the first things I did toward achieving this goal was to enroll in karate classes. And it turned out that I was the worst in the class. I was getting hurt left and right. After two months, I quit in disgrace.

JOURNAL: *And then?*
DEITCH: Oh, I went through a battery of jobs. Like working as a stock boy at Macy's and working in a hardware warehouse.

JOURNAL: *How did you get started with* The East Village Other?
DEITCH: Well, I began planning to go to the lower east side to try my luck. So I saved 500 bucks, and at the end of 1966, I quit my job and headed for the big city. And, before I knew it, I was working at *EVO.* I brought in some samples of my stuff, and the editor liked them but said they were looking for something more psychedelic. So, I went back to my Tenth Street garret, smoked a bunch of marijuana, and created *Sunshine Girl*—an overstuffed flower child. And the editor really liked it, but he couldn't pay me for it. But what the hell did I care? I had 500 bucks.

JOURNAL: *I'm sure just seeing your strips in print back then was enough to get by on.*
DEITCH: No two ways about it. Yeah, it was a real turn-on. But many episodes of *Sunshine Girl* and many reefers later, I was running out of bucks.

JOURNAL: *And then what happened?*
DEITCH: Well, I was having various other problems, too. Like a growing drinking problem, losing my girl friend, robberies, and just generally coming unglued. To top it off, the comics got worse—if such a thing were possible—and finally stopped altogether. Soon I was in a murky, confused state, and I was living kind of dangerously.

JOURNAL: *How did you pull yourself out of this psychological cesspool you were sinking into?*
DEITCH: Willpower. I saw I was going down the drain and I didn't want to go down the drain. And one day I walked into the Integral

Yoga Institute run by somebody named Swami Sachidinanda. It was really quite amazing. After just one session, the desire for alcohol left me as easily as taking off an overcoat. I didn't have another drink for five months. I thrived on yoga. I responded amazingly to it. It made me happy, but it also didn't seem to do too much for my creative juices. But it shaped me up marvelously. I started working for the post office, and I actually went back to Pratt and started taking night courses there. I was very happy in some weird way. And it's had something of a lingering, permanent effect on me. This whole concept of karma has kind of stayed with me.

JOURNAL: *Did you ever try to get Spain to join? What did he think of all this?*

DEITCH: [*laughter*] That was before Spain was rooming with me. This was like, late '67. Actually one of the acute incidents that got me out of yoga was the time I got mugged. And I *swore* I would never let it happen again. So I started carrying a gun the day after I got mugged. And it just was not fitting with the "lovely" yoga experience.

JOURNAL: *Peace and love, and all that stuff . . .*
DEITCH: Yeah.

JOURNAL: *Did you meet any yoga chicks you had a crush on?*
DEITCH: Well, it wasn't doing me *any* good with the dames. One of the ironies of my life is that all of my really good times with the dames have been connected with the low-down lifestyle. I don't think I have ever picked up a girl in my life when I wasn't drinking. That's not quite true, but it's almost true.

JOURNAL: [*laughter*] *Yeah, it's that ol' liquid courage.*
DEITCH: It worked for me.

JOURNAL: *What kind of affect did yoga have on your cartooning?*
DEITCH: It had a *bad* effect on my cartooning. I was kind of in the middle of some insipid *Sunshine Girl* story, and I was keeping it going. But the strip was bad enough *before*. When I started to get all "lovey dovey" with yoga, then it really started getting rotten.

JOURNAL: [*laughter*] *Around this time, didn't you meet someone by the name of Joel Fabricant?*
DEITCH: Joel Fabricant. I'll never forget him. A great man. A great, great man.

JOURNAL: *In what sense?*

DEITCH: He saved my *career*. He saved Spain's career. I mean, he put the "peace and love" bullshit where it belonged, and put our careers on a paying basis. He wasn't paying us much, but we were getting a salary we could count on. And in his own crude way, we were getting good encouragement and support. He was a crude guy. He was no hippie. He didn't even read *EVO*, even though when I met him he was *EVO*'s new boss. He belonged to the Republican party. There was everything wrong with him, but there was something fundamentally honest about him. You knew where you stood with him. He was a *good* man. I liked him. I grew to love him. I wish I could see him now.

JOURNAL: *When did* EVO *start to run strips by R. Crumb?*

DEITCH: Right around this time. When I first saw his work for *EVO*, I was both entertained and yet devastated by the dynamic quality of these strips.

JOURNAL: *Devastated?*

DEITCH: Yeah.

JOURNAL: *Would you compare your work to Crumb's and then say, "Oh, shit . . ."?*

DEITCH: Yeah.

JOURNAL: *You felt your work was somewhat inferior?*

DEITCH: Yeah, to put it mildly. Yeah, greatly inferior. I mean, that stuff was, and still is great. I was so entertained by it. I couldn't be a sourpuss about it because I loved it. And ultimately, Crumb has been a *great* influence on my work and just about everyone else in the underground. He's kept us on our toes. He's made us all try harder. Hail Crumb! I have nothing whatsoever bad to say about Crumb.

JOURNAL: *So after you saw Crumb's work, and they put you on the payroll at* EVO, *did you continue with* Sunshine Girl?

DEITCH: Oh, I didn't want to do *anything* more with *Sunshine Girl*. Basically, the whole idea of it was originally to give them a psychedelic-type strip. I just started doing one-shot type strips.

JOURNAL: *Getting back to when you were getting robbed. Did you ever have to use your gun on anyone?*

DEITCH: Yeah, a couple of times. But I never had to shoot anybody. I did have to fend off a couple of *b-a-d* people. I never even fired that gun. I was told it had a tremendous kick to it.

JOURNAL: *So, were you rooming by yourself at the time?*
DEITCH: Well, I'd had a roommate by the name of Frank Schultz. But he listened to me and all of my merchant marine blather, and he went off and joined the merchant marines. [*laughter*] So I was briefly alone. But then Spain came over and he saw that I had plenty of room, and he said, "Hey, man, why don't you let me move in here?" [*laughter*] He was a big, burly guy and knew how to take care of himself. I was still kind of reeling from being mugged, so I was only too happy to have Spain move in. [*laughter*]

JOURNAL: *Did he pack a pistol, too?*
DEITCH: Well, whenever I was home and he went out, sometimes he'd carry the gun.

JOURNAL: *Did he ever use it?* [laughter]
DEITCH: [silence]

JOURNAL: *Or don't you want to comment on that?* [laughter]
DEITCH: [*laughter*] No, I don't think he ever used it. If he did, he didn't tell me about it. But Spain got robbed a few times, too.

JOURNAL: *Knife point? Gunpoint?*
DEITCH: I forget. But I remember once when Spain got mugged, it rated an article in *The East Village Other.* Everybody got mugged on the Lower East Side. Before I got mugged, I'd been on the Lower East Side for about a year and a half, and I was really surprised by it because earlier in my life I cultivated a way to strut around and really look *b-a-d.* See, people can't tell with me. They don't know whether I'm a cream puff or not. I'm sort of mysterious. I look sinister. Fortunately, it's helped me. I've got menacing eyeballs.

JOURNAL: *Didn't you meet Trina Robbins about this time?*
DEITCH: Yeah, I met Trina in 1968. About six months after my second era at *EVO.*

JOURNAL: *So what happened after you and Trina met?*
DEITCH: Well, it turned out that she had been following my recent stuff in *EVO,* and was full of compliments about it. Trina was twenty-nine at the time, six years older than me. She'd been around. I was somewhat in awe of her, but not so much that I was a shrinking

violet. Soon we were going together, and right from the start it was a pretty stormy relationship.

JOURNAL: *How did you two wind up in California?*
DEITCH: Well, it was our stormy relationship that led to my introduction to California. See, about three months after our meeting, Trina and I were living in a tiny apartment on Mott Street. There were lots of good times, bad times, and plenty of battles in between. And at one point, Trina told me she needed a breather from me and was going to go to San Francisco. So I made a *big* stink about her going and talked her into taking me with her. It was in the spring of 1969 that I saw San Francisco for the first time. And it had been the first time I'd been back to my beloved California since 1949.

JOURNAL: *How'd it feel being back?*
DEITCH: It felt great. It was such a high being there among those comic strip artists. I was staying at Crumb's place in Haight-Ashbury. Crumb was out in Detroit at the time drawing *Motor City Comics*, but his wife, Dana, offered to put me and Trina up.

JOURNAL: *Did you draw any comic strips when you were out there?*
DEITCH: Yeah. You see, I was so exhilarated to be out there that I started drawing comics at Dana's. I did a page for *Bogeyman*, a big page for *Yellow Dog*, and I started another page called "Hector Perez, the Boy Vivisectionist," which I ended up finishing when I got back to New York. It was a glorious trip, and when we left, about two weeks later, I swore I was coming back.

JOURNAL: *When you first arrived, were you immediately introduced to some of the cartoonists whose work you enjoyed?*
DEITCH: Yeah. I made it a point to visit Rick Griffin. And one place I wanted to go, that I heard about—I just *had* to go—was the San Francisco Comic Book Company. That was kind of a focal point where I met both Gary Arlington and Rory Hayes.

JOURNAL: *What was it like walking in there?*
DEITCH: It was *great*. It was incredible. Gary gave us the *big* hello.

JOURNAL: *His store was one-of-a-kind back then.*
DEITCH: Oh, yeah. There wasn't anything else like it. He had all of the new undergrounds, and I scarfed them all up. There were ECs pinned up on the wall. It was *incredible*.

JOURNAL: *Didn't a lot of the cartoonists hang out at his place? In a way, wasn't it like a comic book coffeehouse, where the artists would congregate?*
DEITCH: Yeah. The same day I met Gary and Rory, Willy Murphy wandered in and I ran into Roger Brand.

JOURNAL: *What happened when you landed back in New York?*
DEITCH: The first thing I did was to go over to the newsstand and buy the latest issue of *EVO.* I flashed through it to see what comics were in it, and was thunderstruck to see a page featuring my character, "Uncle Ed, the India Rubber Man." But it wasn't drawn by *me.* Well, it turned out that it was drawn by my brother Simon. So, I headed straight for Simon's place.

JOURNAL: *Were you mad about this?*
DEITCH: No, I wasn't mad. In fact, I was tickled to death. The first thing that Simon said when he opened the apartment door was, "Well, what do you think of it?" As it turned out, Simon had been drawing Uncle Ed pages at Joel Fabricant's instigation during my absence. In fact, Simon had a half-finished Uncle Ed strip going when I came over, and I finished penciling the second half of it for reasons I can no longer remember.

JOURNAL: *When did you split back to California?*
DEITCH: Well, I still had unfinished business in New York, so it wasn't for a while. Earlier that year, Joel Fabricant had started a tabloid comic magazine called *Gothic Blimp Works.* Vaughn Bode was the editor and I was his assistant. But after a few issues, Vaughn couldn't take the heat of the bizarre hippie life, and frantically backed out of the project. Well, Spain had split to California, and it fell upon me to edit the *Blimp.* So Joel gave me fifty dollars a week over and above my *EVO* salary to do it, and I did it.

JOURNAL: *What happened next?*
DEITCH: Well, around this time I was beginning to get a little unglued myself. I'd been drinking more, and even worse, taking lots of speed. After six more months in New York, Trina and I embarked for San Francisco. I was in somewhat of a wet-noodle-ish condition at the time of our departure, privately worried that I might have permanently messed up my ability to do comics anymore from taking speed.

JOURNAL: *Did it affect your motor skills?*

DEITCH: I was starting to walk around dragging my ass on the sidewalk. It was debilitating my body. It's *terrible* stuff. Nobody should mess with speed.

JOURNAL: *Was it just frying you out?*

DEITCH: Yeah, totally. In every way.

JOURNAL: *So you headed off to California and . . .*

DEITCH: Yeah, we rode across country with Gilbert Shelton and his girl friend, who were about to break up. Me and Trina were doing our usual bickering routine. So you can imagine what a jolly ride that was. But once again, San Francisco proved to be a tonic for me. Trina, with her usual brilliance, found us a swell place. It was an entire house that we split with another couple. Soon, I had *plenty* of comic work to do. I more or less swore off the speed, and kept the boozing to weekends. Oh yeah, by this time, Trina was pregnant. And it was *no* mistake. It was a baby that both of us wanted. My relationship with Trina was curious. It was stormy, but we had our good times, too. And I'd be the biggest lying asshole that ever lived if I tried to say that what went wrong between us was her fault. I was as much to blame as anyone for the failure of our life together.

JOURNAL: *When you first got involved in underground comics, did you view cartooning for the underground press merely as a transient, counterculture activity? Did you have any idea it was going to develop into a way of life for you?*

DEITCH: The whole thing just grew like Topsy. When I went to New York on the lower east side in 1967, I didn't really know I was even going to do comics. My plans were vague. I just knew I wanted to do *something* good in art. And one thing led to another.

JOURNAL: *You've done some work in the film industry. How'd that come about?*

DEITCH: In 1980, I was approached by Brian Yuzna, who wanted me to do a movie project for him.

JOURNAL: *How were you introduced to Brian?*

DEITCH: He was familiar with my work. He wrote a letter to the Cartoonists' Co-op Press asking how he could get in touch with me. Bill Griffith forwarded the letter to me, and I wrote a letter back to Brian. About three days later, he was on my doorstep.

JOURNAL: *So he contacted you about doing a story. How'd you feel about this?*

DEITCH: I felt great about this. I had been taking all of these classes in screenwriting and submitting all of these fledgling screenplays, and I was getting nowhere fast with it. And then, suddenly, to have someone out of the blue, who knew absolutely nothing about all of this flailing around that I had been doing, show up on my *very* doorstep, and offer me a thousand dollars for openers to start developing something, well, it was a very exhilarating feeling. Especially since I didn't know where the next month's rent was going to be coming from. So I started developing stories, but things just kind of fizzled out. But I never gave up on Brian. I kept submitting stuff for the next couple of years, until finally, in the summer of 1982, I ended up in Hollywood, working for Paul Bartel, doing a comic based on a movie he had just directed called *Eating Raoul*. I hired a staff of about four people, and we cranked the sucker out in about six weeks. It was just about the worst six weeks of my life because my relationship with Sally [Cruikshank] was going to the wall at the same time. By the time that comic was done, I was ready for the river. I'd been on the wagon for eight months, but as soon as *Eating Raoul* was done, I fell off with a resounding thud. But not for long. Then, out of the blue, Brian Yuzna contacted me while I was still in Hollywood, and said he had raised fifty-thousand dollars and wanted to use it to produce a ten minute, 35mm film of a comic strip of mine called "Born Again," which originally appeared in *Insect Fear* #2. My life was in a pretty bad state at that point, so I jumped at the opportunity to go to North Carolina and work on that. But when I got there, it was only the tip of the iceberg. What Brian really wanted to do was a whole anthology film. He even worked out other stories of mine he wanted to see. I spent about four months in New York working with Simon on it, and then about eight more months working in North Carolina on it. A lot of storyboards and art went down that year. I lived in Brian's office and slept on an old broken down couch. Took showers at a floating tank therapy joint next door. There was a lot of tension on the job and finally, the combination of the job getting sour, and feeling blue about Sally, all caught up with me. Once again, I fell off the wagon, which I had been on for five months this time, and drank for an *entire* week.

JOURNAL: *For a week solid?*
DEITCH: Yeah. I was rolling around in the gutter drinking beer. I wasn't really working. At the end of that week, though, I walked into a branch of Alcoholics Anonymous and joined up. I haven't had a drink since.

JOURNAL: *Have you been tempted to give in?*
DEITCH: There've been times.

JOURNAL: *But you've stuck to your guns.*
DEITCH: Yeah.

JOURNAL: *Did Brian ever meet with any major success?*
DEITCH: Brian met with *great* success. He produced *Re-Animator*, directed by Stuart Gordon, which was surprisingly a hit of a movie.

JOURNAL: *I was surprised to hear that you appeared in* Re-Animator.
DEITCH: Well, it was a very small part.

JOURNAL: *Fantagraphics Books is coming out with a book by you called* Hollywoodland. *How'd that project come about?*
DEITCH: Well, at the end of 1983, my movie work for Brian was over. He was getting set to go to Hollywood and try and sell the property we'd created. I didn't really feel like going back to Berkeley, so I drifted to Hollywood to keep an eye on things. Besides, I'd saved over six thousand dollars and decided to do a story project with a Hollywood theme. It's something that I'd been wanting to do for a while. In fact, I was in L.A. researching that idea in '82 when I met Paul Bartel, got involved in *Eating Raoul*, lost Sally, and ended up in North Carolina. This time I was back and in a position to live off my savings. I managed to sell my idea to the *L.A. Reader* as a weekly comic strip. Ordinarily, the fifty dollars a week they paid me could never have supported me, but my North Carolina money filled the breach. So, in 1984, I buried myself in the *Hollywoodland* project. Meanwhile, Brian got sidetracked in an exploitation horror film project, *Re-Animator*, which turned into a surprise hit.

JOURNAL: *What happened to the project you two had been working on?*
DEITCH: It sort of got lost in the shuffle, and I hung around L.A. for another year, but ultimately ended up coming to stay in Elm Banks, Virginia with the Bergdolls, where I have been working my

butt off doing paintings and comics. I don't know what the future holds in store for me, but at least for the next two years, I hope to devote as much of my time as possible to comics. As of right now, I plan to return to Berkeley in early 1988. I have enough money saved to back myself for at least one more intensive year of doing comics. I've been doing comics more on than off for twenty years, and I think I'm still getting better. I've done a lot of growing up in the last few years, and really do feel like I've got some unfinished business yet to go in this racket. I see doing this stuff almost like some kind of holy mission. God willing, there's still some more good shots in the old cannon yet.

JUSTIN GREEN

IF YOU ASKED SOMEONE FAMILIAR WITH THE MOVEMENT WHAT THE BEST SINGLE underground comic was, chances are it wouldn't be anything by Crumb or Shelton, but Justin Green's *Binky Brown Meets the Holy Virgin Mary*. Behind the facetious title is a harrowing tale of a guilt-drenched Catholic boyhood, as painful as it is funny. While other underground cartoonists tended to skate over deeper feelings and spiritual questions, Green faced them so openly that he's a bit uncomfortable with his earlier work. Unfortunately, the cost of raising a family and the low returns of cartooning have sharply curtailed his output. Still, he keeps his hand in, and what work he does is very much in demand. His family is not a total loss to cartooning either; his wife, Carol Tyler, has done some fine work for *Weirdo*.

This interview was conducted by Mark Burbey.

JUSTIN GREEN: Three hundred dollars worth of signs today, and they have to be done tomorrow and the rest of the week, and so tonight I have to do my patterns.

JOURNAL: *So, you're going to work while we talk?*

GREEN: No, I'm not going to work, but I'm always afraid of making engagements because of just this thing, and it makes me appear

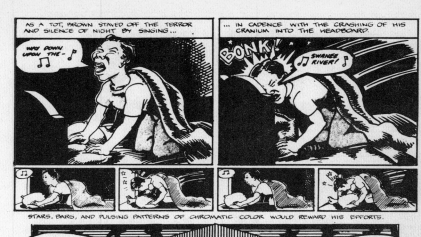

From *Binky Brown*

From *Binky Brown*

very flaky, but [this interview] has fallen through so many times that we have to get on with it.

But I want you to know this was all a very long time ago for me, this underground cartooning, and I still have plans of doing more cartoons, but my early work, to me, is like the trail of a snail. I am the work of art. My work is my shadow. I don't associate myself with it that much. I still feel empathy with some of the work that I've done, but I'm not that proud of it. I'd say I was "on" ten percent of the time, and a lot of it was just potboiling, just to make the rent.

JOURNAL: *Well, a lot of people don't seem to agree. They look at it differently. They see it as being some of the better stuff that was done, and that it stands apart from a lot of what was being done in underground comics.*

GREEN: I take that as a compliment. I don't consider myself to be that thoroughly immersed in the comic tradition. I had a very eclectic kind of orientation.

I learned how to read and write from *Fox & Crow Comics* when I was four or five years old, and then I went through the standard Scrooge, Donald Duck routine. Then I became kind of fixated on *Superboy*, as a budding neurotic. Then I totally disavowed comics, oh no, wait a minute, I had a brief fling with *Sgt. Rock*. It was kind of like the . . . it gave vent to my repressed macho fantasies, the need to become a man and thinking that I had to prove my manhood at some future time on the battlefield, that there was something to be learned from the camaraderie of men under stress. But mainly I wanted to look like *Sgt. Rock,* but it slowly dawned on me that I would never have these highly masculine characteristics. [*laughter*]

JOURNAL: *Was there a gap between when you read* Superboy *and* Sgt. Rock, *or was it around the same time, or what?*

GREEN: Yeah, it was, you know, steamy adolescence. But I always liked the way *Superboy* was drawn in the late '50s. There was something, the clarity about it, there was something about this world that, to me, expressed objective truth.

I just remembered; one of my great influences was *Treasure Chest* comics, which was a Catholic comic that was distributed free, although the nuns thought it was kind of a questionable venture.

JOURNAL: *Why?*

GREEN: Because, *the comic book*, the tainted medium, even though it espoused . . .

JOURNAL: *It was such a wholesome comic, though.*

GREEN: Yeah, but still, it was slightly risque to be getting this comic book. Nevertheless, Sister Cora Maria would give us our *Treasure Chests*, and I would really get off on it. In fact, I prayed that I would someday be a cartoonist. It was a toss-up between fireman, priest, or cartoonist.

And also, I really liked *Heckle & Jeckle* as a kid.

JOURNAL: *The cartoons or the comic book?*

GREEN: The comic book. But mostly, it's *Fox & Crow* and *Superboy*. And then I had this total disavowal of comics all through adolescence.

JOURNAL: *How did that happen?*

GREEN: I grew out of them, I guess. I started to like Salvador Dali, Edward Hopper, the socio-realists; I used to go down to the Art Institute of Chicago all the time, the great Impressionists . . .

JOURNAL: *What age was this?*

GREEN: From fourteen on, all through my teens. The world of art opened up to me, and comics seemed pretty thin fare indeed. It wasn't until I was in Rome, studying painting, as a senior painter, that I saw Robert Crumb's work in an underground comic, and it was an electrifying experience. I had seen his work in an underground paper in Philadelphia in 1966. In fact, I even met him, unknowingly: I was crashed out on speed on a pile of coats at a party and there was this scrawny guy drawing me, that I found most annoying. And it wasn't until I met him years later that I realized, and he confirmed, "Yes, I was in that circle of acid-heads in Philadelphia in 1966."

The underground paper was an issue of *Yarrowstalks*, and I submitted a drawing of some asinine thing; two pigs in a police car, and it said "pork" on the side instead of police.

But when I saw "Itzy & Bitzy" [a Crumb comic] in Rome, to me it was like a call to arms to take up the pen again. And also, being in another culture, I became acutely aware of my own roots. I couldn't relate to this Renaissance art, this varnish-encrusted, largely Christian or royalty inspired kind of patronage art. It seemed very distant. So I started out to think about the things that had formed my own aesthetic, which were, of course, television, movies, and comic books. I'd always been kind of ashamed of that and felt that I had to look to other cultures and other eras for inspiration, but something happened when I saw that Crumb piece.

So anyway, I saw the Crumb piece in Rome, I came back, my conscientious objector appeal was voted down, and I was in constant turmoil, and it looked like I was going to be drafted all the time. It seemed like comics were a very vital medium in the late '60s around the time of *Yellow Dog* and *Gothic Blimp Works*. It seemed that they were a real forum for this alternate culture. There was a great belief that this alternate culture was undermining the repressive powers that were causing all this suffering, which, of course, didn't turn out to be all that it was cracked up to be.

JOURNAL: *So what was your first published strip?*
GREEN: It was "When I First Knew There Was Something Fishy About the FBI." It was about a counterfeiter who published these flawless bills, and nobody could spot these twenties. They were just impeccable. But finally, through a series of chemical tests they found out that the ink he used would fade when a certain kind of acid hit it. But to all appearances the ink was the perfect color. So finally they bust the guy, and in the last five minutes of the show, it shows this guy being hauled away by his Commie cohorts and being pulverized, and he's saying [*assuming Russian accent*] "But comrade, those bills was perfect!" [*laughter*] Because the FBI wouldn't give this guy the satisfaction of telling him that he'd done a good job, they said, "Oh, a common clerk spotted these bills."

When I was a kid I'd seen this TV show, and it seemed like dirty pool so I linked the FBI with this foul play. It was just kind of an anecdotal cartoon, which I seem to find the easiest to script. It's much harder to do an ongoing slapstick piece than it is to reminisce and select details. Sort of tell a story about the past.

JOURNAL: *At one point in our last conversation, you were saying that with the world in such a state of turmoil, it seemed rather trivial to be sitting here talking about comics.*
GREEN: I think underground comics came out of a very volatile period in American history. It was a time of heavy polarization of ideas between generations, and we had youth on our side, with this tremendous righteousness and optimism. Things that had absolutely no artistic merit, had more of a political thrust. As the years go by, it's more difficult to rely solely on sloganeering and heavy-handed symbolism to make an artistic project valid. Very little, oh I can't say that, I won't say very little, but as the years pass, you look over the body of your own work or the work of your peers, not everything is gold. Everyone's career was uneven.

JOURNAL: *That was all during a time when the hippie movement was very big and it was lots easier to live on nothing.*
GREEN: That's right. The sheer economics of producing comics was such that you could live on three to four hundred dollars a month. You could get by on that amount of money, whereas today

that's entirely impossible. So there just isn't the available space to create work that there once was.

JOURNAL: *I don't assume that the artists thought so much about it as a "career," or as furthering their career, as they did about the work on the drawing board at that moment. I don't know if they really thought of it as, "Well, I'm an underground cartoonist and this is my career."*

GREEN: Well, there was a bit of ego involved, in the sense that there was a tremendous hope that one's vision would be appreciated and realized by thousands of readers, as we were speaking to a mass audience. I, myself, at the time, had letters that I more or less solicited from famous people who I sent my work to and returned letters of praise. As the years go by I see that those letters had their value. They made me, in my mother's eyes, a legitimate artist, not a pervert. They made *Binky Brown* somehow a bona fide work of art, instead of this tormented, perverted exposé of my own worst fears.

And also, I used one of the letters to get laid. I showed this woman that I cared nothing for fame, and I ripped up this letter from Fellini. I was laid twenty minutes later.

JOURNAL: *Was it worth it?*
GREEN: Yeah!

JOURNAL: *Who were some of the other letters from?*
GREEN: Well, let me explain: the letters were somewhat ambivalent in their praise. Kurt Vonnegut wrote this really, uh, this postcard that had a strange gratitude. "Thank you for doing this. Now I understand what it's like to have a Catholic boyhood. You are a beautiful revolutionary." Stuff like that. I called him up. I got his number because we had the same dealer on the East Coast.

JOURNAL: *The same dealer?*
GREEN: He was into weed for a while. And I said, "Hello, this is Justin Green." "Who?" "You remember, I sent you my comic." "Oh, yeah, yeah, yeah." "Gee, did you really remember? Did you really, all those things you said, did you really mean that?" And he said, "Well, yes, uh, I was mildly amused, but I could see that the whole production came from a permanently damaged brain." [*laughter*]

You get your fingers bruised a little if you go searching for a star. But that postcard helped me with my mother.

JOURNAL: *Did you show your parents* Binky Brown Meets the Holy Virgin Mary?

GREEN: Well, my father passed away in 1970, and I bet that I never could have done *Binky Brown* if he were alive. In fact, while I was working on *Binky*, I had dreams about my father, in the form of a dangling telephone. I was going down this long spiral staircase and there was like a dangling phone. He was always on the phone, he was an industrial realtor, and his voice on the phone said, "Such things have never been discussed in public." It was an indictment.

JOURNAL: *But you did the book anyway.*
GREEN: Yeah.

JOURNAL: *What did your mother think of it?*
GREEN: Well, she said she laughed and cried, but I learned later she had terrible health problems at the time. So, who knows what she felt. In the end, you can only do the work out of internal necessity. Anyone else's acceptance or rejection or praise is immaterial. The work has to stand up on its own merit.

JOURNAL: *Another topic we got into last time that never made it on tape was religion. Religion has played a very big role in much of your work, not too unlike the films of Luis Buñuel. You went to Catholic school for only three years, right? But it left a real dent in your psyche, nonetheless?*
GREEN: Afraid so.

JOURNAL: *That you still can't shake?*
GREEN: No, I can't. I think that the Christian cosmology touches on a very fundamental orientation to life that people from all cultures have, and that you can be an absolute monarchist and a Christian, you can be a Marxist and a Christian, you can still find solace in this person who supposedly lived 2000 years ago and who died on the cross for our sins.

JOURNAL: *But do you believe in God and the whole thing?*
GREEN: Do you mean am I a practicing Christian?

JOURNAL: *No, do you personally believe in God?*
GREEN: This is on tape? [*laughter*]

JOURNAL: *Would you go so far as to say you're an agnostic, or do you believe there is a God of some sort?*

GREEN: Well, today I was driving along and you know how it is when you're in a two-lane situation, and there's some obstacle in the traffic in front of you? In the first lane, there are the people behind the guy who get trapped there and try to get out, and then the people in the fast lane just drive by. The other people are kind of screwed, they can't get out, they have to wait. So I slowed down and I honked my horn so that one of these trapped individuals could get into the fast lane. First he thanked me, and I didn't acknowledge his thanks; it was all right. But he wanted to make sure that I was well-thanked. So he was driving ahead of me, waving his hand out of the window. Like there was this current of energy that we built, from my act to him and from his acknowledgment of my . . . [*laughter*] . . . I know this sounds trivial. I'm just trying to explain, you asked me if I believed in God. There's definitely a current of benevolence we generate toward each other as human beings. Maybe because of the horrific responsibilities of vengeance and cruelty that we are capable of giving vent to, we have to codify our aspirations for good in symbolic figures like Christ and his sacrifice. It's a myth, and yet orthodox Christians claim it's more than a myth, that it's an actuality, an historical fact. I guess I can't buy that, yet I can subscribe to the myth. The message therein is that we have to die to this world, to go beyond it. And yet, to me, it's so complicated with sexual repression that the message of organized religion is all but meaningless.

I believe in Man. I think we're still capable of extricating from this cliffhanger of nuclear holocaust that we've somehow backed into. I think that the whole global situation now is an external manifestation of the psyche of man that is polarized into opposites of good and evil. The whole human consciousness has evolved to the point where we have this very strong fear and very concrete sensibility of ourselves, that we are good and bad. We've done it on a global scale now. The Russians feel the same about us as we do about them, that we're good and they're evil. It's possible that we can take that leap now, that we can go beyond that, that we can seek a higher ground, somehow this arsenal that can kill every one of us, and incidentally all hamsters, 340 times over, you know, there's enough for death to the thirtieth power for all of us, every living being on earth, that somehow, human consciousness can make that leap that we can somehow squelch this. You have to believe that.

BILL GRIFFITH

BILL GRIFFITH COULD JUST AS EASILY GO IN THE NEXT SECTION AS THIS ONE; HE and art spiegelman are transitional figures between underground comics and the comics of today. Though both spiegelman and Griffith were active throughout the underground era (Griffith especially so), they didn't really find their mature styles until the mid-'70s. Perhaps for this reason, they were among the most energetic in finding new venues for underground comics. Together they edited *Arcade*, which was the most important underground anthology comic after *Zap* and *Bijou*. It was underground comics' last stand, a quarterly magazine designed to break into mainstream newsstands and bookstores and provide a steady outlet for the future. It was not to be; *Arcade* folded after seven issues. *Arcade* did allow Griffith to develop his bread-and-butter character, Zippy the Pedigreed Pinhead. Zippy is a walking random factor, a wrench in the works of any situation he walks into. His non-sequitur adventures have struck a popular chord; *Zippy* has moved from a weekly strip in alternative papers to a daily that appears in several major newspapers. It should be noted that when Griffith and spiegelman moved into the mainstream, they didn't adapt to it, they made the mainstream adapt to them.

This interview was conducted by Joe Sacco.

Griffith Observatory · "THINK EIGHTIES"

The *EIGHTIES* will be a decade of intense *CULTURAL UPHEAVAL*... for instance, the long-awaited *"UNDERWEAR-ON-THE-OUTSIDE"* fashion trend will be seen sometime before *1984* — — THANX TO J.L. OF CHICAGO, ILL.

© 1979 BILL GRIFFITH

The *"HIGH-TECH"* furniture craze will finally find it's way into *K-MART* stores —

OOOH!! HOW *DARLING*!! TWIN *GIANT FILE CABINET BEDS*!!

..WITH A *"VINYLETTE"* FINISH!!

MOM

DAD

NOSTALGIA for the late *SIXTIES* and *EARLY SEVENTIES* will sweep the country.. *"BE-IN DISCOS"* will feature *ACID ROCK, LIGHT SHOWS* and TIMOTHY LEARY *"YOU CAN BE ANYTHING THIS TIME AROUND"* TAPE LOOPS — —

I AM HAVING A *FAR-OUT* EXPERIENCE...

...YOU CAN BE *BUDDAH*!

REMEMBER *SONNY BONO'S "CAVEMAN VEST"*??

RUNNER-UP in the NUTLEY, N.J. JUNIOR HIGH SCIENCE FAIR will disprove all of EINSTEIN'S findings with his *"SQUARE UNIVERSE THEORY"* —

$M = CE_2$!!

A *PARA-MILITARY YOUTH MOVEMENT* will pull off a *BLOODLESS COUP* of the U.S. GOVT. in *1989*.. A CLONED, GAY *NELSON A. ROCKEFELLER* will take over as *DICTATOR* — —

JOURNAL: *I'd like to know how you view the momentum you and Zippy have gathered in the last year or so with the mainstream syndication and the upcoming movie project. Are you surprised at all?*

BILL GRIFFITH: Yeah. But by my own perceptions, I haven't changed what I do. So the explanation can only be that the outside world—to whatever degree it has—is seeking out what I do. That surprises me a great deal, because I don't see what I do as being mainstream. Frankly, I don't think it will ever get as mainstream as something like *The Far Side* or *Bloom County*, even though they're both strange in their own, mainstream way. I don't think I'll ever achieve that kind of acceptance, but it is amazing to me that something as bizarre as *Zippy* can be surfacing in daily newspapers in Omaha and places like that. Of course, it remains to be seen whether *Zippy* will confuse readers to such a degree that it's just going to be a brief flirtation. But the movie—that makes more sense to me. That's not very surprising to me because Zippy has always been a living, breathing character to me. And it makes complete sense to me that he should be translated into film. It's been something I've wanted to have happen for about eight years.

JOURNAL: *To what do you attribute your success? Has something paved your way? Why are people coming around now?*

GRIFFITH: I think most of the reasons are media-connected. Maybe Americans are catching up with Zippy's disconnected qualities, his fractured attention span, and his seemingly unrelated sentence structures. These things are hitting some kind of nerve in people, perhaps because of the incessant bombardment of information we're all subjected to every day. Zippy has a kind of healthy way of dealing with it that maybe people respond to. I don't know if they're responding consciously or whether it's an unconscious release mechanism that they get from reading *Zippy*. Perhaps that's combined with the acceptance of so-called absurdist humor that I deal in (which I don't think is absurd, but a lot of people say that). That acceptance was boosted by the post-hippie humor of the original *Saturday Night Live* show. Let's face it, people who wrote for *Saturday Night Live* wouldn't have been as zany had they not smoked marijuana for five years. So if you want to go back to what paved the way—things like that released people from linear thinking. Enough people, I hope, now accept humor that doesn't have a traditional structure. And that helps *Zippy* get more acceptance.

JOURNAL: *Now that* Zippy *is appearing in mainstream daily newspapers, what sort of response have you been getting? Is a new audience appreciating Zippy?*

GRIFFITH: Yeah, I get a lot of appreciative fan mail from people who just can't believe that *Zippy* is appearing in their daily paper.

JOURNAL: *Are these old fans?*

GRIFFITH: They don't always say. I would say a lot of them are new just because they seem kind of giddy about *Zippy*. It's obvious they're reading him for the first time. Other people are saying, "I've read it for years in undergrounds. It was always hard to find. Now it's in my daily paper, and that's great." On the other hand, a lot of people are writing to the papers that they're outraged. It's not pleasant to be told you're the scum of the earth by a trailer-park resident in Memphis, Tennessee, but I feel that shows I must be doing something right. After fifteen years of doing *Zippy* for an audience that was ready to accept him, I'm doing *Zippy* for an audience that is sometimes completely confused and then hates *Zippy*. They don't get it. That's kind of nice in a way. It sort of justifies—I wonder sometimes if I'm changing, if I'm getting less and less individualistic. And then I get these letters and they make me feel better, even though I put my chin out there and it gets bopped. But I get enough positive feedback to keep me going.

JOURNAL: *Do you get tired of explaining* Zippy, *especially now that there's been a lot of media attention?*

GRIFFITH: I was for a while, but then, like with any questions you get asked often enough, you begin to have an answer you know people will like. [*laughter*] You have little catch phrases. I get tired of it, but not to the point of not answering, because people have the right to ask such questions, especially if they've just been exposed to *Zippy*. I feel a paper in Shreveport, Louisiana, has every right to ask me who Zippy is. But the only way to understand Zippy is to read the strip for a period of months.

JOURNAL: *I agree. I think it's a cumulative effect.*

GRIFFITH: It's like brain damage. If you read enough, it will seep into your brain cells and make its changes without your being aware. All of a sudden you'll get up one morning and understand *Zippy* before you even read it.

JOURNAL: *What makes Zippy relevant today?*
GRIFFITH: It has a lot to do with these remote control devices for TVs. I think they've made a major impact on our society that's yet to be studied. We have the ability to sit in front of our information device, our stimulation device, and be able—not only able, but have this uncontrollable urge—to change the information we're receiving every five or ten seconds. Eighty-five percent of the country has these things now. I think the way Zippy's mind works is very similar to the way a remote control device works on TV. It makes its own logic. Whether you're consciously aware of it or not, people in our society are rearranging reality in a non-linear, bizarro-world way, like a reversal image of what's really out there. I think it's possible that people will surpass even Zippy's non-sequitur personality pretty soon and find Zippy rather tame.

JOURNAL: *How do you think this will manifest itself? In someone's personality?*
GRIFFITH: Well, the attention span is the first to go, and that's been going on for years. However, I think there's a possible beneficial result of it all. Life and reality—to bring in two huge subjects—are not linear. They don't have logic. We force logic on them by believing in appointments and goals and that events have reasons for happening that ought to be traced back very specifically. When you believe all that, you're kidding yourself to a large degree, although you have to subscribe to some amount of it in order to survive in this culture. But Zippy breaks that up and shows you that the logic is a construction. That's the basis of Zippy's humor. I think the more that people are made aware of that, the healthier, ultimately, they'll be, although they'll go through a kind of shock process before they get that point. As heavy as I'm sounding, I'm really talking about humor, because humor is a release of anxiety or tension that's been built up either inside you before the joke got to you or built up by the joke and then released by the joke.

JOURNAL: *Are you saying that in some ways Zippy is saner than the world around him?*
GRIFFITH: I don't necessarily like to use the word sane, because that implies that insane is not preferable. Zippy isn't sane.

He's nuts, but to be nuts is not necessarily an inappropriate response to the world. Of course, I'm being somewhat facetious, because I don't think people should go about their lives not accepting all the reality around us—because they would starve to death rather quickly. But a healthy awareness that what's around you is a construction is good. It lets you take things a little less seriously. I wish I could believe it as much myself as I tell other people to sometimes.

JOURNAL: *You haven't reached that ideal yourself?*
GRIFFITH: Not twenty-four hours a day. When I do, I'll probably retire and go live on a mountain somewhere.

JOURNAL: *You work really hard, don't you? You're putting out a daily strip.*
GRIFFITH: I work harder now than I ever have, even though I have always worked hard. It's the first time in my so-called career I feel like I have an actual job. The way the daily strip happened, I was contacted by the *San Francisco Examiner* and asked if I wanted to do a strip. They never said the word daily, so I thought they wanted my weekly strip. They said, "No, no, no! We're talking about a daily strip here." At first it was very hard because, like any cartoonist, I have good days and bad days. I sit down to work some days and I don't feel funny. Before I had the luxury of saying, "I'm not going to work today." Now I can't do that. At first I had a freak-out period, and then an adjustment period. And now it's easier to do the strip than it used to be. Tons easier.

JOURNAL: *Let's shift gears again and talk about what initially inspired* Zippy. *I've read that you saw the movie* Freaks—
GRIFFITH: I think that's what planted the idea of doing a pinhead character.

JOURNAL: *And you've actually met some pinheads?*
GRIFFITH: Yes. Back in the mists of the '70s. "Pinhead" is a sideshow term, of course. The real name is microcephalic. I met one in about '71 or '72 when I was just starting *Zippy*. That was sort of an accidental meeting, where I was visiting a friend of mine in Connecticut. He was a cab driver, and he picked up this guy every day to take him to work. When he picked me up at the train station, he'd already picked up this guy. I quickly realized he was microcephalic, which is fairly obvious from their small domes. A microce-

phalic is very short and has a very small head. Anyway, he sat in the back seat with me, and I looked at him, and he looked at me, and he said, "Are you still an alcoholic?" He was going from one thing to the next in rapid succession with a huge vocabulary, and I was so knocked out I couldn't even laugh. The humor was register-ing, but it was happening so quickly—the absurdity of everything he was saying, the strange interconnectedness of it all that didn't make any sense, was so intense that after it was over I was dizzy. And I wanted to see him again. I called up his house, but his father wouldn't let me talk to him. His father said I was making fun of him. It was really sad. I couldn't get through at all. I couldn't convince his father that I was interested in his son as a person, not as a specimen, but as an enlightened being. This did not compute with his father. But two or three years later I met a whole bunch of them, which was very frightening, in a very liberal institution here in the Bay Area.

JOURNAL: *Did you visit the institution for that express purpose?*
GRIFFITH: Yes, with the illusion I could interview them. I even brought a tape recorder. A friend of mine was a nurse in this place, and she told me I could go and that it was a very experimental place. She said that they don't separate the sexes. And I asked, "Why is that so liberal?" She said, "Well, microcephalics are very sexual." They just don't have that censoring thing. And they don't keep them apart. So they're always in the halls fucking. So she said I should be ready for that. But I wasn't prepared for the way they deal with outsiders, which is—they climb on you. They're very little and they're very talkative. You've seen *Freaks?*

JOURNAL: *Yes, I have.*
GRIFFITH: Do you remember that scene at the beginning where Tod Browning, the director, is in a little idyllic country setting, and all the circus freaks are dancing around him? The pinheads are clinging to him very affectionately, and he's stroking their heads and looks very fatherly. Well, that's what they did to me, except it wasn't as idyllic. They ran for me and jumped all over me, basically wrestled me to the ground, and my tape recorder immediately was smashed. Not that they were being aggressive or hostile. They were being affectionate: "Oh, a new human! Let's explore his every crevice!" And not only were they physical, but they were talking a mile a minute. And so I spent fifteen minutes in a com-

pletely altered conscious state in that place, without any ability to do something as logical as interview them or gain a perspective on their lives. I was just inundated by them. Actually, it was a big education for me.

JOURNAL: *Did it scare you off from doing* Zippy? *Did it make you think twice about it?*

GRIFFITH: It briefly dried me up. I had to digest it for a few weeks. Until then, except for that brief encounter with the other pinhead, I was sort of making up what a pinhead was. And what I did realize after a while was that I had to continue to make it up, because to deal with the way an actual pinhead is, even though it was an inspiration for me to see them, would be an assault on people. It would make an interesting strip as a one-pager once in a while, but it's just too fractured. It was an overwhelming experience.

JOURNAL: *Let's talk about your other projects*—Young Lust, Arcade, *and* Griffith Observatory.

GRIFFITH: I was lucky because I did *Young Lust* early in my struggling career, and it was a real big hit. The first issue of *Young Lust* came out in October 1970, and it's been through several dozen printings. I started getting a monthly check right away. And *Tales of Toad*, of course, was nothing near that. I thought of *Young Lust* as just a one-shot parody of girls' romance comics when I started it with Jay Kinney. When it became a big seller, we decided to do more and get other artists. Issue #2 was still fairly much a parody, but less so stylistically. And by #3, it became a social satire on male-female or sexual relationships. *Young Lust* showed me I could make a living at this racket.

JOURNAL: *When did* Young Lust *start to fade out of your life?*

GRIFFITH: In terms of my needs as an artist, it faded within a few years, although when we did *Young Lust* #4 in color, in '74, that was a big boost. So I guess it was after that, actually, when *Arcade* picked up.

JOURNAL: *That was a collaboration with art speigelman.*

GRIFFITH: Yeah. We saw a real need for underground comics to have some kind of life raft. We thought we'd provide, first, a place for underground cartoonists to do their work, because it was getting harder to get published, and, second, a place to jump out of the underground audience to a wider audience, which only minimally happened. Print Mint never had enough of a budget to push *Arcade* the way *Weirdo* is pushed by Last Gasp.

JOURNAL: Arcade *was a very strong magazine.*
GRIFFITH: Well, we were demanding what art demands of people he puts into *Raw*, that everybody do his best work. But the reaction in the marketplace was basically slight interest and then disinterest. *Arcade* didn't fit. It was a bastard form. It wasn't a comic book; it wasn't a magazine; it didn't have advertising; it didn't have coated stock—all the things you're supposed to have to break into the newsstand distribution world. We were asking to be put next to *National Lampoon* and the Warren publications, *Creepy* and *Eerie*, and we briefly got there, but not for long. One distributor that took us briefly didn't sell the numbers they wanted, so that was the end of that. And then *Comix Book* came along from Marvel, edited by Denis Kitchen, which tried—in a crass sort of way, I thought—to do what we were trying to do with more integrity. It got wide distribution because it was put through the Marvel system, but they didn't make it either. And distributors were looking at *Arcade* as an imitation of *Comix Book*, even though we'd already been around for over a year.

JOURNAL: *Were you very disappointed with what happened to* Arcade?
GRIFFITH: Yes. We took it pretty hard at the time. Looking back, I see it was all very logical that it happened that way. We were trying to buck a system that was so rigid and still is. We were trying to gain some middle ground between undergrounds and the mainstream distribution system, and it didn't exist. We thought we could make it exist, but not with one magazine you can't. It was artistically a success and financially a failure. But that's okay.

JOURNAL: *Did you worry at all that the underground comics scene had really finished? Did you feel that the audience had dried up, too? And that* Zippy *wouldn't—*
GRIFFITH: Yeah. It was a frightening time. I mean, *Arcade* started out of a need to reestablish an audience because a lot of the audience for early undergrounds had drifted away. When we didn't make it commercially, I retreated back to *Zippy*, which was probably the healthiest thing I could have done at the time. *Arcade* was a group effort. We were all trying to pull together, but Art, Diane, and

I were largely the ones that were pulling. It was a tremendous drain. In college the first week of freshman year was called hell week. This was like hell year. The amount of work we had to put into it never stopped. The fact that it wasn't commercially successful just kind of made me want to hole up in my studio for a while. But I had no choice. I do what I do. What else can I do but keep being a cartoonist? Out of a sort of compulsiveness, as well as feeling that there was no other thing I was suited to, I just kept doing it. I still had *Young Lust* and a few other ways of making money, so I wasn't totally broke. And luckily the Rip Off Syndicate came along a year after *Arcade* died, so I was able to have some steady place to put stuff, and I always had access to the publishers out here. My way of making ends meet with comics was always to produce a lot of work. Aside from *Young Lust*, if I couldn't do something that was going to be a big hit, at least I could do a lot of things so I could keep money coming in as well as keep myself going. So the idea of quitting or stopping never occurred to me. It seemed that all I had to do was retreat into my own work more after *Arcade*.

JOURNAL: *And it was about this time you launched* Griffith Observatory?

GRIFFITH: Well, I started doing that in '76 through the Rip Off Press syndicate, which is also where I started syndicating *Zippy*.

JOURNAL: *You were doing two syndicated pieces at once?*

GRIFFITH: Yeah, I was alternating *Zippy* with *Griffith Observatory*. That kept up for four years, and I collected the *Griffith Observatorys* and put them in a book. The Rip Off Syndicate died in 1980, and I asked for the list of papers taking *Zippy* so I could keep doing it.

JOURNAL: *And you dropped* Griffith Observatory *at that point?*

GRIFFITH: I dropped the *Observatory* because *Zippy* was the one they wanted. I've always intended to do the *Observatory* again someday, but so far, in its pure form, it hasn't happened. When people ask me what happened to that, I say, "It's still going on because I've incorporated it into *Zippy*." And I use the Griffy character quite a bit in *Zippy,* with his penchant for obsessive viewing and observation of everything around him.

JOURNAL: *When I started picking up undergrounds in the late '70s, the* Griffith Observatory *collection was my favorite because it sums up the mid-'70s so well.*

GRIFFITH: It was a great time to caricature things because everything was so exaggerated. Now everything is fairly conservative, but in the '70s everybody was flipping out. Everybody was walking around with a clown suit on, just asking to be lampooned and caricatured. It was a great mine for satirists.

JOURNAL: *In one of your* Observatory *panels, you predicted that nostalgia for the late '60s and early '70s would sweep the country, and I think that's starting to happen.*

GRIFFITH: Seventies nostalgia? I dread the moment, but it's going to happen. [*laughter*] I think Prince has already started it. He's wearing platform shoes.

JOURNAL: *[laughter] I think that's because he has to. Anyway, when did you start to feel that things were beginning to work out for you?*

GRIFFITH: I started sensing *Zippy* starting to build around '76 or '77. I realized I had a cult following, which was better than no following. An artist needs some encouragement. And little by little it just picked up, until *Zippy* took over both right and left brain. [*laughter*]

JOURNAL: *It must be gratifying after all this time, and the struggle, to feel that a large segment of people have come around.*

GRIFFITH: Sure. I still feel that there's a lot of struggle and hard work going on, but I'm luckier to have had it happen to me in this slow way, as opposed to overnight success. When overnight success happens, a person tends to burn out rather rapidly. Of course, a lot of overnight successes have ten years of work behind their overnight success. I think the slow haul, the way it's happened to me, has kept the work from pandering to an audience. To me the worst thing a cartoonist can do—or any artist—is to consider the audience while he's working. And if I ever sit down and think that, then there's no reason to do it. Even working for King Features—that thought is in the back of my head, because I know that all of a sudden I'm [appearing in] Omaha. But I can't, and it doesn't, have any effect on what I do. It just can't. I've been doing it too long the way I do it. I didn't start out saying, "Hmmm, what can I do to really appeal to the mainstream? I know! A character with polka dots and a tapered head and a five o'clock shadow! And make him say non sequiturs! Yeah, that's just what America wants!" That isn't how it happened. That isn't how it's going to develop. *Zippy* is my mission in life.

JOURNAL: *Will you continue to work with your* Zippy *character throughout your career?*

GRIFFITH: Right now that's how I think. I have had some people say I have done everything I can, that I'm repeating myself. I think that might have been true occasionally. When you're doing something long enough, that is a risk. But to me *Zippy* is so flexible that if I'm repeating myself, I would be repeating myself if I was doing some other character, too. It would be a reflection of my own state of mind. As long as I'm thinking and reacting and interpreting things around me, *Zippy* will be my vehicle for me to express that stuff. If you look at the strip, especially these days, the other characters have become more important, too. Zippy is a part of a universe. Any strip tends to develop a cast of characters. That's what I've done. So Claude Funston, and Shelf-Life, and Mr. Toad, and Griffy, and Vizeen, and Dingy, and all these other characters are all pieces of me. And they can express different points of view. Zippy's isn't the only point of view, although he does have many points of view. Yes, I see myself doing it for years. I see myself in the tradition of Chester Gould or somebody who continues a character for the rest of his life. I don't foresee it not being that way, although I suppose it could change. I could look back on this and see it as a twenty-year period that stopped. It's possible. But not in the foreseeable future.

JOURNAL: *Well, I wish you all the luck in the world.*

GRIFFITH: Well, as long as my hand doesn't fall off, I'll be okay.

PART IV:
THE
NEW COMICS

ONE OF THE ODD THINGS ABOUT UNDERGROUND COMICS IS THAT THEY HAD NO second generation. All of the cartoonists who would make a name in the underground were present almost from the start; the few new faces that did break into underground comics in the '70s seemed to lack the fire of the first generation. It would take until the '80s for younger alternative cartoonists to begin to match or surpass their underground predecessors. Indeed, in a very important sense, the underground cartoonists of the '60s are the established cartoonists of today: the ones with a significant body of work behind them. It might just have been a matter of waiting for the cartoonists who grew up with *Zap* the way the underground cartoonists had grown up with *Mad* to mature.

If the emergence of underground comics was an explosion, the emergence of today's alternative comics was a slow crawl. While the counterculture that sustained underground comics allowed them complete freedom, when it collapsed underground comics went with it. Today's alternative comics had to sink new roots and find a way to exist within the mainstream. The current era began with the first issues of *RAW* in 1980 and *Weirdo* in 1981. These two magazines developed a pool of new talent that would fill other magazines and slop over into more mainstream magazines like *National Lampoon* and *Heavy Metal*. In the meantime, the proliferation of weekly entertainment papers in major cities created a venue for cartoonists like Bill Griffith, Lynda Barry, and Matt Groening. These strips have even begun to slip into major daily newspapers. Some cartoonists went even farther underground, publishing (if that's the word) photocopied "mini-comics" and selling them through the mail. Publishers like

RAW Books and Graphics and Fantagraphics Books began giving cartoonists larger venues (solo magazines and anthologies) to present their work. Though they cater primarily to the costumed character market, comics shops have helped revitalize the surviving underground publishers.

The cartoonists of the '80s brought in a whole new set of influences. On the one hand, most have a more than passing affection for the junk culture of the '60s: cheesy television; monster magazines; the latter-day *Mad* of Al Jaffee, Mort Drucker, Sergio Aragones, and Don Martin; the grotesqueries of Ed "Big Daddy" Roth T-shirts and Topps bubble gum cards; and so on. It might surprise some that after Robert Crumb, the name that you'll hear most often as an influence is Charles M. Schulz. On the other hand, the best of them have a much deeper concern with character than their underground predecessors, who favored a broader kind of humor. Among the current group, even humor as frenzied as Peter Bagge's will have, beneath the wild exaggeration, recognizable human beings. Following the example set by Harvey Pekar, they are increasingly inclined to delve into autobiography and the facts of everyday life.

To say that comics have suddenly ceased to be "kid stuff" and turned into an "adult" medium is the shallowest sort of trendmongering. For half of this century newspaper comics were among America's brightest cultural achievements, producing talents like Winsor McCay, George Herriman, E.C. Segar, Al Capp, and Walt Kelly. The comic book was a bastard cousin, uncouth, ill-mannered, and ignored whenever possible. As newspaper comics descended more and more into triviality and dreary, mediocre artwork, cartoonists began to look to the comic book as a new home for the art of cartooning. Since the '60s a new sort of comic book has been growing, embracing all the capabilities of the medium. The talent has always been there. What is needed is an audience that can support comics in the style that newspaper readers once did. If the recent inroads of comics into bookstores and mainstream publications can provide this audience, the comics' greatest days may yet be ahead of them.

ART SPIEGELMAN AND FRANÇOISE MOULY

AFTER THE OFTEN HELLISH EXPERIENCE OF PUTTING OUT *ARCADE*, THE LAST thing art speigelman wanted to do was another magazine. By his own account, it took some convincing from Françoise Mouly before he agreed to co-edit and co-publish *RAW*, which arguably has become the most influential comics magazine of the decade. Mouly was a French emigré with a wide range of interests in the arts, as well as an interest in printing and publishing (her popular *Streets of SoHo and Tribeca Map and Guide* kept *RAW* solvent for years). She rekindled his enthusiasm and introduced him to the excellent comics coming out of Europe.

RAW represented a clean break even from underground comics; with a few notable exceptions, *RAW* avoided the established underground cartoonists. Instead it favored a mixture of European cartoonists and a new generation of American cartoonists who would become the core of the comics revival, including Drew Friedman, Gary Panter, Mark Beyer, and Charles Burns. It eschewed the word "comics" in favor of "graphix." In large part this was calculated to sidestep the stigma comics have acquired among adult readers, but it also signified the magazine's intent to blur the distinction between comics and fine art. The tone of clever irony was set by the magazine's various subtitles, such as "The Graphix Magazine That Lost Its Faith in Nihilism" or "The Graphix Magazine of Abstract Depressionism." Starting out as a nonprofit venture, it surprised everyone involved by becoming an instant success, going from a press run of 5,000 in 1980 to 20,000 in 1986. The success of *RAW* allowed spiegelman and Mouly to publish a series of solo books by Panter, Burns, Sue Coe, and others.

Anonymously, spiegelman is probably one of the most ubiquitous cartoonists in the country; as a consultant for Topps Bubble Gum, he masterminded the wildly successful "Wacky Packages" and "Garbage Pail Kids" bubble gum card series. His underground cartooning career began with well-done but superficial forays into sex, violence, and scatology. He found his true voice in 1972 with the original three-page version of *Maus*. In telling his father's experience of the holocaust in funny-animal terms, it heightened the irony of a child growing up hearing tales of the concentration camps rather than fairy tales at bedtime. Though his subsequent work was for the most part not so openly autobiographical, starting with *Maus* spiegelman dealt more and more with serious themes. His shorter pieces shatter and examine the comics form in much the same way Jean-Luc Godard and Alan Resnais do with cinema. An extended version of *Maus* had been at the back of his mind since the '70s, and in 1981 he made it a regular feature in *RAW*. When Pantheon published the first six chapters in book form in 1986, it was immediately hailed as an important contribution to holocaust literature.

This interview was conducted in 1981 by Joey Cavalieri, Gary Groth, and Kim Thompson.

JOURNAL: *Where did* Maus *come from?*

ART SPIEGELMAN: The 1972 three-page *Maus*? Well, that was an interesting strip for me. It's a good place to start because to me it's the point where my work starts. Up to that point, I feel like I'd been floundering. I didn't know that I was floundering when I was floundering, but all of a sudden, I found my own voice, my own needs, things that I wanted to do in comics.

There were several sources for *Maus*. The very specific birth was that somebody was putting together a comic book called *Funny Aminals* [sic] and I was invited to do a story for that book, whose only guideline was that it involve anthropomorhic characters. I was just puttering around trying to figure out what I'd do. At one point I was going to do this kind of EC story with animals, which I think has been done by a lot of cartoonists now. I was tinkering with that, and it wasn't satisfying. I didn't see why I should waste all my

FOR ME IT WAS HARD HERE, BUT FOR MY FRIEND MANDEL-BAUM IT WAS MORE HARD.

IN SOSNOWIEC, EVERYONE KNEW MANDELBAUM. HE WAS OLDER AS ME... NICE...A VERY RICH MAN...

...BUT NOW, IN AUSCHWITZ, MANDELBAUM WAS A MESS.

HIS PANTS WERE BIG LIKE FOR 2 PEOPLE, AND HE HAD NOT EVEN A PIECE OF STRING TO MAKE A BELT. HE HAD ALL DAY TO HOLD THEM WITH ONE HAND...

ONE SHOE, HIS FOOT WAS TOO BIG TO GO IN. THIS ALSO HE HAD TO HOLD SO HE COULD FIND MAYBE WITH WHOM TO EXCHANGE IT.

ONE SHOE WAS BIG LIKE A BOAT, BUT THIS, AT LEAST HE COULD WEAR.

IT WAS WINTER, AND EVERYWHERE HE HAD TO GO AROUND WITH ONE FOOT ONTO THE SNOW.

CAN I USE YOUR SPOON, VLADEK?

OF COURSE, BUT WHERE'S YOURS?

I DROPPED IT, AND BY THE TIME I BENT DOWN, SOME-ONE STOLE IT.

FOR A SPOON YOU COULD GET A HALF DAY'S BREAD.

I SPILLED MOST OF MY SOUP, TOO. WHEN I ASKED FOR MORE, THEY BEAT ME!

I HOLD ONTO MY BOWL AND MY SHOE FALLS DOWN. I PICK UP THE SHOE AND MY PANTS FALL DOWN....

BUT WHAT CAN I DO? I ONLY HAVE TWO HANDS!

MY GOD. PLEASE GOD... HELP ME FIND A PIECE OF STRING AND A SHOE THAT FITS!

BUT HERE GOD DIDN'T COME. WE WERE ALL ON OUR OWN.

From *Maus*, Chapter 7

From *Maus*, Chapter 7

energy doing it. Anyway, I decided I didn't want to do the funny animal comic anymore, and wrote back saying, "No," that I just didn't have any idea that was worth bothering with. Then I got a really nice letter back from a cartoonist crony with some amphetamine in it, saying, "Take this and do the comic with us!" I didn't really want to do it, but it was just this letter of encouragement saying I really should do it, and we don't want to do the book without you: please do it.

So, I was still fishing for my ideas, and I was looking at some films that were being shown at a film course up there that included a lot of early animated cartoons. I was really struck by the cat and mouse cartoons. I saw that the mice in those cartoons were very similar to the negroes in the other cartoons that were being shown in the same days, and realized that this cat and mouse thing was just a metaphor for some kind of oppression. I wanted to do a comic strip in which the mice were blacks and the cats were the whites, using funny-animal style, and so I started trying to research things about black history. And then just short-circuited there, realizing that I was never going to be able to give this any authenticity, because I just didn't know the material, and I'd just be some kind of white liberal simp. On the other hand, there was an involvement with oppression that was much closer to my own life: my father's and mother's experiences in concentration camps, and my own awareness of myself as a Jew. That was the next step in creating that comic strip. I wasn't in contact with my father anymore, but remembered a lot of stories from my younger days at home. That's the genesis of that particular strip, I guess.

JOURNAL: *Did you get any reaction to it at all?*
SPIEGELMAN: Not much.

JOURNAL: *Really?*
SPIEGELMAN: I got reaction from other cartoonists, who thought it was very good, and also seemed to feel that I'd stepped onto some other place as a cartoonist. I didn't receive too many letters. I did have some interesting reactions that I can remember. I got back in touch with my father when I was about two-thirds through this thing. My father was struck by the fact that a building on page two looked exactly like a building that he had been in. It was just surprising to him that I'd got everything right; where things were in relation to each other, where the train was in relation to the house.

JOURNAL: *Was there anyone who was offended . . . ?*
SPIEGELMAN: Well, let me get there. My father played cards with other friends of his every few nights. And all of his circle of friends were concentration camp survivors. Now, none of them, my father included, have any orientation toward comics whatsoever. If you're growing up in Poland in the early part of the century, you're just not exposed to that. It's not part of your life. So while they were playing cards, I showed them the strip, and they all read it. They all know each other's stories, what happened to each particular one of them, and they didn't notice that it was cats and mice. They just noticed that it was my father's story, and that triggered conversations about each other's stories. "I remember when you were here I was blah-blah-blah, and this was happening." And nobody at any point in the evening said anything about cats and mice, which I thought was very interesting. I was happy about that.

The next day, I went to Alan LeMond, my friend at *Dude, Gent* and *Nugget*. It happened to be a Wednesday, which was called "look day," when gag cartoonists would come in from Long Island with their pile of gags to sell to the magazines. I was just hanging out with him and these cartoonists were coming in. And this guy named Don Orehek and another gag cartoonist from Long Island—balding, cigars, loud clothes—came in to tell Alan LeMond a dirty joke to grease him up and sell him their little tit cartoons. I was there so Alan said, "Oh, Don Orehek, art spiegelman, this is another cartoonist." He says, "Oh yeah? What 'zines ya draw for?" And I said, "I guess I draw what's called 'underground comics.'" He said, "Oh yeah, what's that?" And Alan said, "Well, here's a piece of his work right here." And then he showed *Maus* to these two cartoonists, and they read it. They had this very taut expression on their faces, and they weren't sure how to react, and there was real silence after they finished reading the script. Then, one of them turns to the other and says, "Good mouse, man." And the other one says, "Not bad on cats, either." And that was the response that I got from them on *Maus*. Between the two days, I got this complete response to my work.

This was the correct way to approach this material. The reason was, if one draws this kind of stuff with people, it comes out wrong. And the way it comes out wrong is, first of all, I've never lived through anything like that—knock on whatever is around to knock on—and it would be a counterfeit to try to pretend that the drawings are representations of something that's actually happening. I don't know exactly what a German looked like who was in a specific small town doing a specific thing. My notions are born of a few scores of photographs and a couple of movies. I'm bound to do something inauthentic.

Also, I'm afraid that if I did it with people, it would be very corny. It would come out as some kind of odd plea for sympathy or "Remember the Six Million," and that wasn't my point exactly, either. To use these ciphers, the cats and mice, is actually a way to allow you past the cipher at the people who are experiencing it. So it's really a much more direct way of dealing with the material. One thing that happened in the three-page version that's different than what I'm doing now, is that in the three-page version I consciously chose not to mention the word "Jew" or the word "Nazi" at any point in the strip. And, in a three-page comic strip, it was possible to maintain that kind of delicate balance where everybody would know what I was talking about and yet not have to say . . .

JOURNAL: *Well, there's a code word. It's "Die Katzen."*
SPIEGELMAN: Well, "Die Katzen" is German for "cats," and "Maus" is German for "mouse," but it's still not stated. And it led to this very kind of natural joke, "Mauschwitz," which, I've heard later, some people seem to have read as the punch line of the strip. To me it was an organic thing that just grew out of using the German word for "mouse," and wasn't to be avoided. And yet, would help, in a sense, to keep that distance, to keep that alienation element in play.

Now, doing the longer version, it's impossible not to talk about Jews and Nazis, because I want to talk in detail about what happened. One can't keep changing it to metaphor. It would come out like some clumsy version of *Animal Farm* or something. It wouldn't ring true. I would have been better off, then, creating my own completely fictional version of Nazi Germany and what happened, and making something that worked a lot tidier. And, since I'm not interested in doing that, if I want to keep to the real story of what happened, I have to drop that element of the artifice so that what dichotomy exists is in the fact that the cats and mice are drawn as cats and mice but referred to as Nazis and Jews.

There are places in the story where the rupture becomes very strong, and it's hard to accept. There's a point where my father talks about "being killed like animals." Well, you're made very aware of the devices at that point. I think that sort of works with me rather than against me, and something I'm happy to have happen in the course of the book.

JOURNAL: *What made you want to do an enlarged version of Maus?*

SPIEGELMAN: That's complicated. There are many . . . like, nothing's ever simple. When one asks for causes, one cause probably has something to do with the Boer wars. But one reason is, the story is far from told in three pages. All that was was just one tiny anecdote. So, one impulse for doing it is just that there's information there that I really wanted to deal with. Being a Jew, not necessarily a practicing one but coming from that particular cultural heritage, there are things that have happened to me in my life that make me very aware of the fact that I'm a Jew. I suppose that growing up with parents who survived concentration camps is important in whatever else is operating in my life. So I wanted to deal with that more directly. I reapproached my father, and spent a long time taping conversations with him.

JOURNAL: *Was that hard?*

SPIEGELMAN: Getting him to talk about it? He was willing to talk about it. He never understood or doesn't understand what I'm doing or why. He'd rather I did more work for *Playboy* and the *Times*, because it's safer. I could make more money. More secure. He's understandably oriented toward security.

Another cause is, when I was a kid I remember my mother wishing she could write about her experiences and not being able to. Not feeling able to. I remember vaguely her saying, ". . . and then someday maybe you'll write about this stuff." And that was an impulse, an input. It was a concern that my mother had that my father doesn't have. He has no desire to bear witness.

Another impulse to do the book was the fact that, I'm in a particular situation now with my comics, which is, more and more I've found myself involved with things of more and more esoteric interest. Being involved in plasticity of a page and how one's eye moves across a page is interesting as subject matter to only a few people. And, like I said, I was being polemical when I said I'm not interested in communication. That since it is one of my interests, I wanted to deal with subject matter that could matter. I've often been involved in *stretching* what narrative is, seeing how far one could go and still have something that can be called a narrative. And yet, what people seem to want is *story*. They just want to be hypnotized more and more.

If I'm left in a position where what the comics people want to see are stories, then, I'm going to deal with a story that people have to think about. The problem is, that most stories aren't worth telling. Most stories that you come across are just one more chase adventure, or one more boy and girl meet each other. As a result, if I was going to do a story, it had to be a story that was born of some kind of necessity, and the only story that I know at the moment that really has that kind of necessity, that should be told, is this one.

Also, I was tired of working on very, very small pieces of work. Because, whether I was doing a one-page strip or a seven-page strip, I find myself working on it for four or five months, and the amount of paper consumed by the strip wasn't relevant to how long it was taking me to do. I was putting all that energy out; I really wanted to start on something that would take a sustained effort, something that would take me further. Also, I feel it's possible to do a long book. That's one thing, and it's serious, and since I feel capable of doing it, I have the obligation to try.

JOURNAL: *You experimented with several styles of drawing before settling on the one you eventually used. Why did you choose the one you did?*
SPIEGELMAN: There was a temptation after doing the breakdowns for *Maus* to stick with them as the finished art, because everything else I tried seemed to be a step down from it. It had the immediacy and the simplicity of a diary and the quality of sharing information rather than pontificating it. The problem with it for me was first of all, it just wasn't comfortable. A lot of times the drawing just looked too bad to me, just embarrassing. It shouldn't have disturbed me, but that was a factor. The other, more important factor, was that there were things that weren't clear, and clarity is what I wanted.

What I did—the final solution [*laughter*], which is the right phrase for *Maus*—was to continue the way I'd worked out these breakdowns and just carry the process several stages further.

I've always tried to find a proper voice or a proper style for each piece of work, so that a strip like *Little Signs of Passion* looks very different from *Prisoner on The Hell Planet*. I made other forays, including trying to draw something loose, but drawn much larger and then reduced into being a neat, tight picture. The problem was that I found myself putting too much irrelevant pictorial information in.

One solution I thought was interesting involved using this Eastern European children's books wood engraving style that I'd seen in some books of illustrations. But I found myself thoroughly dissatisfied with these woodcut illustrations after a day or so. My problems with the drawing are, I would hope, obvious. First of all, it banalizes the information by giving too much information and giving too much wrong information. It becomes like a political cartoon, like on the page you're printing. The cat, as seen by a mouse, is big, brutal, almost twice the size of the mouse creatures, who are all drawn as these pathetic furry little creatures. It tells you how to feel, it tells you how to think, in a way that I would rather not push.

JOURNAL: *There's also the danger of it falling into cliché, it seems.*
SPIEGELMAN: Heavily into cliché. Well, political cartoons are like that.
FRANÇOISE MOULY: It's also very dogmatic. It puts the artist in this situation of superiority, kind of like this castle fortified by his drawings, and he can't be attacked for any reason.
SPIEGELMAN: It makes me more impregnable.
MOULY: When he's doing a story on this subject matter, nobody's going to criticize and say, "Yeah, they should have killed all the Jews!" The subject already has a certain sacred element to it, and the scratchboard drawing reinforces this.

JOURNAL: *With the mice and cats caricatured that way, there's a value judgment in the visuals that's a very shallow moral judgment.*
SPIEGELMAN: Yeah. That's a problem using mice and cats, and I'm very aware of it. That's why I'm very happy when the metaphor breaks as it does in some parts of the story, which you'll see eventually.

JOURNAL: *It also seems to me that using the mice accommodates the more obvious gestures you put them through, whereas if you used a more representational illustration of people the gestures would be too blunt and too obvious.*
SPIEGELMAN: Yeah. This lets the story take place in your head better. And that's more important. That's why in a sense comics are

perfect for this and it would have a hard time being adapted in any other medium, even animated cartoons or something, because it has that totemic quality that allows you in.

Unfortunately, even if everything else were going fine with it, these woodcut illustrations don't work as well for comics. I have the same objection to Hal Foster: As illustrations they're fine, but what they're doing there is illustrating the text rather than moving the story through word and picture, and each picture on that half page I did in scratchboard is too fully realized as an illustration to flow comfortably from picture to picture. Your eye gets trapped too long in the picture.

JOURNAL: *And it gets captured by the wrong things.*

SPIEGELMAN: Yeah. It just doesn't move along the way it's supposed to, and I obviously couldn't go for that.

I had this unhappy experience of showing a slide of the scratchboard *Maus* to my students, who all thought, "Hey! That's really good! You should do it that way!" This was near the end of the semester, after talking to them for sixteen weeks. And their opinion was, "Well, that's a really nice drawing. That's nice to look at."

JOURNAL: *This is sad.*

MOULY: Yeah, but they are art students. All they can think about is . . .

SPIEGELMAN: The way it looks, the surface.

JOURNAL: *At that point in their development, maybe they've become obsessed with technique.*

SPIEGELMAN: Yeah, well, when you're trying to learn how to do it, all you want to do is to be able to do it as refined as possible. In any case, my reason for not doing *Maus* that way has nothing to do with the time factor, which is what some of the students were trying to pin me to: "Ah, you don't want to do it that way 'cause it'll take you longer to draw." When you're in it for eight years, you might as well be in for fifteen, you know.

Using *Maus* in *RAW* led to some interesting aesthetic questions, about *RAW* and about *Maus*. I think we've solved them satisfactorily.

One interesting thing about *RAW* is that it's a large-size magazine, and therefore, almost as a result of the format, stresses the graphic element of comic strips, because its pages are very large and there's not 200 of them, but about 36. So it asks that every page be very graphically compelling. That tends to emphasize one element, the graphics, over the storytelling—hopefully not at the expense of the storytelling.

This led to a dilemma for *Maus*, which I conceived of primarily as a comic wherein the pictures were in service of the story. I wanted very much to keep the pictures subservient to the idea. In fact, it's drawn quite small—the original for each page is about five by seven or something like that.

I didn't quite know how to make use of *Maus* in *RAW*. On the other hand, if I didn't combine these two projects, my head would go rolling off down the sidewalk, bounce into a sewer somewhere and never come back, because it was just spreading myself way, way too thin.

First thought was, well, we'll blow up the pages. Now, that makes a very strong graphic statement, to take a relatively simple drawing, and blow it up so the hairs at the edge of the line are all showing. I kind of liked the way that looked. But I think it's all wrong for *Maus*. Also, it would be seventeen pages of the magazine.

The final solution was a separate small-sized booklet, like "Two-Fisted Painters" in the first issue. I found that it involved very little reduction. The pages remained very clear. Although it looks very dense, it has some of the qualities that I really wanted to catch in *Maus*. It makes it look like a manuscript. Seeing these small pages of kind of doodle drawings, almost—they're rough, quick drawings—mounted together makes it seem like we found somebody's diary, and are publishing facsimiles of it. And that's kind of nice.

I'm not sure how *Maus* fits in with the material that's been in *RAW* so far. It's something else. And yet, as we quoted in the introduction to the magazine, the introductory editorial, there was this line from Juan Gris, "The question of what will emerge is left open. One functions in an attitude of expectancy. You are lost the instant you know what the result will be." Although *Maus* doesn't feel like the kind of material I would've predicted would be in *RAW*, there's no reason why it can't be.

MOULY: You should mention the other reasons why you want to see *Maus* published in *RAW*—having some kind of discipline.

SPIEGELMAN: Yeah, the requirement of having to produce it, rather than just let it be a project that could easily take the rest of my life if I allow it to. The fact that every time an issue of *RAW* is ready to come out I've got to have another chapter ready. That's good. I think if the deadline were *too* tight, it would become really excruciating.

JOURNAL: *Why was RAW #1 "The Graphix Magazine of Post-poned Suicides"? A postponed suicide is just a stall till suicide, isn't it? That doesn't sound very hopeful at all . . .*

SPIEGELMAN: Let me answer that with a quote from Nietzsche: "The thought of suicide is a great consolation: with the help of it one has got through many a bad night." To think about suicide isn't necessarily to commit suicide. It's to acknowledge the possibility and to acknowledge the precariousness of being alive and to affirm it. Every moment that you don't commit suicide is an affirmation. It's deciding to live some more. The reason I think it's actually an optimistic notion is the fact that . . . well, that quote that's in the inside front cover by Cioran, "A book is a postponed suicide," to me implies an act of faith has been committed. Which is, to create a work of art, a book, a painting, a poem, a magazine, a comic strip, whatever, and that the work is in itself a justification for remaining alive. In that sense, at least, I felt it was provisionally optimistic.

One thing that bears mentioning is that neither Françoise nor I were aware when we were collecting material for the magazine that it was all going to be so downbeat. We were just looking for strong comics. And we found that looking for strong comics ended up meaning finding comics that were personal in some sense, and were filled with anxiety, since most of the artists, for one reason or another, tended to be filled with anxiety and were able to express it. As a result, it creates an interesting tension in the work, because what one usually associates with comics is anything but existential despair. Maybe *RAW #1* is really *Despair Comics #2*.

In any case it was a posteriori—after the fact—that we discovered that all of this work had a common denominator. We had come up with this catchy subtitle without realizing that the material inside tended to rally around these themes, urban madness and suicide.

MOULY: And again, it was not to make a statement about suicide—not to either advocate it or provide a solution or pretend we had one, in any way. Simply, when we looked at the work, we had a strong response to pieces that had this element in it.

SPIEGELMAN: In a sense, suicide is like a case of terminal alien-ation. And alienation in its less terminal stages seems like the only appropriate response to me to the society I'm living in. Did you register for the draft?

JOURNAL: *No, I'm a tad too old for it, thank you very much. So there are more hopeful ways of dealing with this alienation than suicide?*

MOULY: We think so.

SPIEGELMAN: Producing the magazine is one of them. That's what I mean by an affirmation. The existence of the magazine is an affirmation. The magazine was not produced cynically to make money. The magazine is produced . . .

MOULY: . . . with a certain belief in what we do . . .

SPIEGELMAN: With a certain belief in what we're doing. With a commitment to the medium. With a commitment to the art and to the works within. All of which we see as—to one degree or another—affirmations.

JOURNAL: *With a commitment to change the way comics are perceived?*

MOULY: Maybe, maybe not. It's not—

SPIEGELMAN: I would've said "Yes" to that. If you want to expand on it . . .

MOULY: Well, it seems to me that comics provide a certain function: entertainment. Comics are a pleasurable thing to read—in some ways easier or more enjoyable to read than a piece of text. And this is never going to be changed. There's no reason to change it. It's one way comics are perceived, one way they perform. It would be pointless for us to try to say, "We don't want this to happen anymore—this is forbidden." It would also be very presumptuous, and unrealistic. We're not trying to change that.

We're trying to widen the perception of comics, in that its only specific is that it combines words and pictures. But it doesn't have to be one page and it doesn't have to be twenty pages. Or 250 pages. It doesn't have to be well-drawn or badly drawn. It doesn't have to be a humor strip or an adventure strip. It doesn't even necessarily have to have words in it. These are not the things that define comics. What defines comics is more an element of time, of placing things in a certain order on a page which indicate a certain temporal relationship, or a spatial relationship. In his strip, Kaz plays with both time and space.

SPIEGELMAN: Which is not to say there isn't room for entertainment in *RAW*. I think there are some strips that qualify . . .

MOULY: Yeah. [Jacques Tardi's] "Manhattan" is very entertaining.

SPIEGELMAN: In a sense it is. Hey, entertainment doesn't mean happy endings. And certainly Gerry Capelle's "Canal Street" is an entertaining bit of business. I think essentially "Two-Fisted Painters" is an entertainment. It's just that we'd like to entertain a more literate audience than comics usually reaches for.

MOULY: But this point is very important to me: We're not trying to get people who are now reading Marvel to stop reading Marvel and start reading *RAW*. We're just trying to get people who might have similar interests to ours, who right now do not look at comics because of whatever negative connotations it has, to start looking at it and hopefully finding something of interest to them in it.

Part of the way to do this was to use a totally different format than comics have been printed in up to now. To combine comics, text, and graphics without any emphasis on any one. The main denominator of all the pieces is that they should be paid attention to. The artists have worked on them and have tried to express ideas and visual concepts in them, and it's up to the reader to pick it out. It's not to spend five minutes with it in the bathroom.

JOURNAL: *So that's why it's "the graphix magazine" as opposed to "the comix magazine"?*

MOULY: Yes. We were afraid that if we had put "the comix magazine," that would have kept away everybody that did not read comics.

SPIEGELMAN: To whom comics has bad connotations.

MOULY: So we tried to fool those people.

SPIEGELMAN: In a sense, the packaging of *RAW* is a deceit. This is essentially comics. There are texts in it, there are graphics in it; they're all integrated in the magazine.

MOULY: By putting it out of its usual context, we tried to get people to pick it up without the a priori ideas they might have about comics. And maybe after they read it, they would figure out, "Oh, this is comics! I should have known!"

SPIEGELMAN: And what's wrong with that? But the big size does perform a very specific set of functions for us. For one thing, there are at this point a handful of large-size magazines. *Wet* Magazine.

Skyline, which is an architectural magazine, *Picture*, a photo magazine, *Fetish*, which is I don't know what kind of magazine.

MOULY: A consumer magazine.

SPIEGELMAN: A consumer magazine? A bunch of these advertising magazines. All of which come under the banner of new wave or whatever, and are sort of put in their own section on the newsstands that carry them, and tend to be carried in large newsstands, urban newsstands, "hip" newsstands . . .

MOULY: This was to overcome the distribution problems that Art had when he did *Arcade*. Even if some newsstand wanted to take *Arcade* it didn't know where to put it. At best, they'd put it with *National Lampoon*. There was no slot for it. By doing *RAW* large-size, it gives it an automatic slot. It goes with the other large-size magazines.

The other reason—which is harder to explain—is that, by having a very luxurious format it somehow gives the feeling when you pick up the magazine of a very elaborate display of the piece of work. I think that you look at work differently if it's printed on newsprint in eight-and-a-half by eleven, or if it's printed on very good paper in a larger format. Your attitude toward it has changed. For one thing, this is not a magazine you will throw away after you have read it.

SPIEGELMAN: Not at four dollars a shot.

MOULY: So it creates this almost automatic respect for the work.

SPIEGELMAN: Which isn't to say that it's an excuse to print empty work and get the respect that way, just by fooling people with the format. It's a way to make people accept our attitude toward comics by presenting it in a format that deserves that respect.

MOULY: For those reasons we did *RAW* this size, we did the insert inside, we did this elaborate work of tipping-in the color picture onto the black-and-white cover of the first issue. And we've had people thinking—quite a few, actually—that the tip-ins on the cover came from a mistake. That we made a mistake on the black-and-white, or it was supposed to be printed in color and we couldn't afford it, and therefore, we tried to cover up our mistake by gluing this other piece of paper on top.

JOURNAL: *Had they peeled it away?*

MOULY: Yeah.

SPIEGELMAN: We're one step ahead of them. There's another image underneath. But this thing with the large size: It's a mistake to leave it at this on the record, because it does allow for the pictures to be seen. One doesn't have to squint and find one's way through tiny little boxes. There's something very pleasant to me about reading things in this format. It also just happens that pragmatically, it's useful to us to find a new audience.

JOURNAL: *What struck me about the magazine as soon as I saw it was, that it wasn't so much a magazine as a printing orgy.*

SPIEGELMAN: Well, we both like objects.

MOULY: We could have rationalizations for why we did that, but the main reasons, I guess, is the fact that we do like it. We enjoy doing this.

SPIEGELMAN: It's nice to get a well-made book. Independent of what's in it, even. It's just a wonderful thing.

MOULY: That's something that we want to keep.

SPIEGELMAN: That's important to us.

MOULY: There's something about comics being a printed medium which is really fascinating. We're in touch with a certain number of artists in New York, who are trying to work the "gallery circuit." And are stuck in that. For us, that seems to be almost a certain dead end. In working for galleries, in being elitist, in doing an original work of art that can't be accurately reproduced. And that group of well-meaning doctors and lawyers on Fifty-seventh Street going to see it in a gallery. Somehow it is so perverted. Artists have tried everything for the past fifty years or more to come out of that ghetto. They have not succeeded.

A number of things have been tried out—doing multiple works of art, and so on—and none of them has really gotten the artist out of the vicious circle, the elitist market of art.

On the other hand, there's commercial art for magazines, advertisements, and mass media. That's also a problem for most people who are in that field, because they have to compromise themselves, they have to sell out to appeal to the commercial values of the editors, publishers, and so on. Not because the editors are old, nasty people, but because the things that sell the most are the most bland. There's a certain logic to that. If you want to appeal to a very large audience, you have to have no specificity to your work. It has to be acceptable to everybody. And you lose a lot of the edge that could have been in the work.

Though we are doing a printed magazine, we're not doing a

mass media magazine. We are trying to fall somewhere in between. A unique object, yet not a unique object. There's 5,000 of them. It's available to most people that want it. At this point, to us, that's a pretty satisfactory solution. We feel more fortunate than our commercial artist friends or fine artist friends, each in their ghetto.

SPIEGELMAN: I'm afraid that our comments make it sound very pretentious, and yet, there's something that I like about the fact that comics are such a gritty medium. That they're so ignored. There's something to be said for that. And I don't think we're necessarily losing that grittiness in *RAW*. Some pieces in *RAW* express that element in comics more than others. I think that in my own work, in "Two-Fisted Painters," for example, there's a lot of respect for what's gone down before, for the kind of comics that have been coming out—an attempt to play with all those things. We're not necessarily rejecting them.

JOURNAL: *What are your criteria for selecting artists for* RAW? *What is it about their work you find interesting?*

SPIEGELMAN: I would just say, "They're good."

MOULY: This is not a direct answer to your question, but we have a different relationship in a sense with the artists in Europe and the artists in America. Part of the reason is that the guys in Europe have been working for a while. It's easier for us to look at their work because it's finished work and if we're interested in it, all we have to do is contact them, see if they like the magazine, want to be printed in the magazine. We know exactly what we're getting.

In America, it's much harder for us in a sense to solicit work because since there hasn't been any magazine like *RAW* and there hasn't been that approach to very good quality comics being printed, it's very hard to get in touch with people who have already done work. Most of the people we know are people who have the potential and the interest in doing great work and see the magazine, get interested in doing something for it, and we end up with a situation like, "Go ahead" or "Wait awhile" and then seeing something.

SPIEGELMAN: But in terms of what we look for, I have this specific liability of not being able to read any language other than English, so primarily I look for good graphics, and then find out later if the content even remotely comes close to being worth printing. And it's actually one of the biggest problems, because usually being able to read it is a disappointment. The main difference, I think, between the European comics that I've been seeing and the American comics that I liked and was involved with in whatever decade that was, is that the European stuff is much more heavily graphics-oriented than the American stuff—I think that if I was from another country looking at the American stuff, very little of it would stand out, because they're not splashy graphics. Most of the drawing in its own way is very utilitarian.

JOURNAL: *You're talking about what kind of American comics?*
SPIEGELMAN: Underground comics, things like that. Even somebody like Robert Crumb, whose drawing is exemplary of its kind, it's still usually in the service of the story, and therefore I think if you couldn't read it and were just looking at it a lot might pass by. So it's possible that we're missing a lot of interesting cartoonists in Italy or Spain. Less so in France, where Françoise at least is able to rapidly monitor if somebody's got something to say.
MOULY: It's not that likely, because those people work within a certain culture and certain magazines that promote them, and most of the magazines are oriented toward the visual. The clearest example is that they do print a lot of people who can draw but have absolutely no idea what a comic strip is, having nothing to say, no story to tell. And there is a higher proportion in terms of the adult comics magazines of people drawing for somebody else who writes. There's not much of a conflict here.
SPIEGELMAN: The one thing that is interesting to me is that *RAW* plays right into this—I don't know if the word is "dilemma"—plays right into the situation of being attracted to these European graphics, and *RAW*'s size brings with it some concomitant factors, like when a thing doesn't look that hot but reads well, very often I'm attracted to it in American comics. The drawing is often secondary. But because the paper is so fuckin' valuable, it costs us so much to buy each one of those sheets, and because it gets printed so large, it's very hard to go with something that reads well but looks terrible—terrible in relation to the way it reads. And this isn't by way of making a definitive statement, it's just something that's an interesting problem, that *RAW* because of its format tropes toward well-designed graphics.

PETER BAGGE

In 1981 Robert Crumb did it again. In the late '70s Crumb's comics (which mostly appeared in Stewart Brand's *CoEvolution Quarterly* and the *Village Voice*) took the form of a bitter jeremiad against all aspects of contemporary American culture. Though they were often quite astute, well, let's just say that Jeremiah was probably not the most popular man in Israel, either. Crumb had come to feel more and more like a misfit, and in a typical act of defiance he launched *Weirdo,* a celebration of misfits. First reactions were negative; reviews of *Weirdo* #1 read more like obituaries. As time went on Crumb, much to his surprise, began discovering kindred spirits. *Weirdo* soon became the second part of a tandem that revitalized comics; where *RAW* emphasized graphic excellence and cool intelligence, *Weirdo* embraced primitivism and impassioned self-expression. As it came out more frequently than *RAW*, it gave new cartoonists more of a chance to develop. While Crumb was no less dismayed about modern America, the bitterness had evaporated from his work, and having given up drugs some years earlier, he showed a new mastery of the medium.

One of the most important of Crumb's newfound kindred spirits was Peter Bagge, who would eventually become the editor of *Weirdo*. Bagge's own comics are hysterical in both senses of the word; it's as if he thinks the only adequate response to the passivity and bland insanity of suburban living is a sustained scream. During his tenure at *Weirdo*, Bagge accelerated the trend toward new talent. In 1986 he resigned to devote more time to his own magazine, *Neat Stuff.* (*Weirdo* is presently edited by Aline Kominsky-Crumb.)

This interview was conducted by Michael Macrone.

Junior, from *Neat Stuff*

The Bradleys, from *Neat Stuff*

JOURNAL: *Something that surprised me—because I didn't realize it until I made a list of artists that you had used and that Robert Crumb had used—is that you've used almost exactly as many different artists in your first four issues of* Weirdo *as Crumb had used in nine. In* Weirdo #1 *Crumb is the only artist, aside from Bruce Duncan and Stanislav Szukalski. Something that Crumb did a lot of was "found weirdness": the SubGenius Foundation pamphlets, Eugene Teal . . .*

BAGGE: Well, that was the main idea of the whole magazine. I think he was convinced that the whole underground comics movement was dead, and that anything he would find that would be interesting was super-duper oddball stuff that some guy did because it was in his system and for no other reason. Crumb had no idea that there were people like me and J.R. Williams and Kaz and Drew Friedman. Then as time went on he started using more and more comics by new, dedicated artists. But I imagine he originally thought that nothing was going to happen anymore, because he hates mainstream comics. There's nothing that he likes, except for his early influences like *Pogo*. If you asked him who his favorite cartoonists are, I imagine he'd name all the old underground guys, like Kim Deitch. He's still a big fan of his underground peers.

JOURNAL: *Obviously, as an editor, you're trying to shape a package around some coherent concept. I know Crumb used to get lots of letters complaining that there was no editorial control. His attitude was, "If you don't like it, go start your own magazine." I think the magazine was meant to reflect a state of alienation that Crumb was coming to terms with in his own life, the death of the '60s and their supposed idealism, the death of the undergrounds, mid-life crises, having a kid. For me, those ideas didn't really cohere until the third issue.*

BAGGE: I think that *Weirdo* #1 gives the best idea of what the magazine was supposed to be about originally, but it gradually changed because Crumb became aware that there were a lot of new people who wanted to make a career or subcareer out of cartooning in the underground fashion. He just hadn't known they were out there, but they were, and in fact, one of them is now the editor of *Weirdo.* I think I tend to be more sympathetic to people who are or were in the situation I am or was in. I mean, I have all sorts of wacky things back at my house, and for all I know, the average reader would get a much bigger kick out of something like that than out of interesting artwork by some new guy, but I think it's better to run something by someone who's alive, who would benefit by having his work run in *Weirdo,* or who might, just from seeing it in print, get better.

JOURNAL: *It seems to me that, especially in Crumb's issues,* Weirdo *reflected and employed a very urban sensibility, with gritty, bleak urban backdrops and a city rat's sense of alienation.*

BAGGE: I guess when Robert lived in cities, which was in the '60s, most major cities were falling apart. And I guess he always lived in the poorest parts. He must have thought he was seeing all of western civilization crumbling. And of course, he's a real pessimistic guy. I suppose that's one of the reasons why he's living up in the boonies—to get away from it all.

The ironic thing is that Crumb, as pessimistic as he is, seems to truly believe that *Weirdo* will last forever. He thinks it's just this thing that has to be. He's made it pretty obvious to me that if I suddenly quit, he would pick it up again, or find someone else to pick it up the way I did. He's really dedicated to the magazine, and though he doesn't brag about it or admit it, he really did start the whole underground genre. If *Weirdo* was gone, it would disappear; I'm sure he'd hate to see this whole genre he created just suddenly disappear off the face of the earth. He loves it; when *Zap* came out, that was exactly what he wanted to do, it was the perfect format for him. If *Weirdo* was gone, that format would be gone, too. One thing that Crumb seems to believe is that, technically, anything in the format of an underground comic book on up to slicker thing is big time. He looks at the self-published, Xeroxed mini-comics thing as homemade, handmade, small-time cheapo stuff. He still feels underground comics is big time; he's still real proud and real excited to see his work published in that format.

JOURNAL: *What do you feel is* Weirdo's *place in the field? You've said that it's the last "regularly published" underground comic, or magazine. What sorts of submissions do you receive?*

BAGGE: Submissions come pretty much from everywhere. Maybe it's just because I've been doing it—I've just done my fifth issue—people are starting to pick up on what I'm trying to do. One thing that makes me feel bad sometimes is when someone makes a real, honest-to-God "statement," even if it's real liberal, or knee-jerk, or real sensitive. Sometimes I'll get a submission that'll be a clear-cut antinuke or antipoverty or antiReaganomics thing . . . and it'll be real obvious . . . and I sort of feel like I should run something like that. A complaint that a lot of people have about *Weirdo* is that it's too insensitive, that it's too "punk wise-ass." A lot feel that what underground comics were about was being part of a cause—which, generally, isn't true. They just came out at the same time as everybody was doing all kinds of protesting. But right from the start, undergrounds spoofed on all the bleeding hearts and do-gooders. Underground comics were always real wise-ass. I remember reading that the guy who started *Bijou Funnies* . . .

JOURNAL: *Jay Lynch and Skip Williamson . . .*

BAGGE: . . . I think they put together the first *Bijou* when they were having those riots outside the Democratic Convention [in Chicago, 1968]. And even though I don't think there was anything in there dealing specifically with that . . . hippies were all so serious then . . . I guess when you're getting your head bashed in, you take things seriously . . . but they said they had a real hard time getting the hippies to accept the comic. Their first impression was that the hippies had absolutely no sense of humor. Frank Zappa said the same thing. You know, when you hear *Absolutely Free,* or *We're Only In It For the Money* or just look at the way the band looked you would think that this was a real hippie thing. But it was antihippie, Zappa said that he hated that flower power generation because they hated his stuff—they didn't see or appreciate the satire. As soon as he picks on them, they think he's a bastard, no matter who else he picks on.

Anyhow, sometimes I'll get something really sincere, like Carol Moiseiwitsch made a poster which was actually a comic strip, about a family that got disintegrated in a nuclear blast. Crumb thought it was very powerful, and it was really well done, but I thought it was too obvious. I mean, even people in government who say we have to build up our nuclear arsenal call it a necessary evil. Everybody calls it an evil, nobody's gonna say, "Wuh, nukes are the greatest thing!" [*laughs*] But if somebody could do a strip that could actually convince someone who's in favor of nuclear power to oppose it, I would run that. I don't want to just keep all these antinuke people happy by telling them stuff they already know. Another thing that people can't believe is that a lot of *Weirdo*'s contributors and readers do have super-conservative, Reaganite ideas. Anybody who has liberal feelings seems to automatically assume that everybody who reads *Weirdo* is a liberal.

JOURNAL: *There seems to have always been a lot of autobiographical or semiautobiographical stuff in* Weirdo, *Carol Lay's "Midwestern Wedding," most of Dori Seda's stories, Crumb and Aline Kominsky's things, your "The Reject" and "In My Room," not to mention "The Bradleys." I suppose reality is "weirder" than fiction.*

BAGGE: Yeah, that's true. That's something that took me a long time to realize when I first started doing comics. The comics that I did that were the funniest were always based on things from real life. And every time that I sent in a strip that I thought would really impress Crumb, it was something that was really fanciful, that got away from real life, and he always complained about it for that very reason. He made a big deal out of that, being autobiographical—not necessarily writing about something that exactly happened to you, opening yourself up the way he and his wife do—but just drawing from real life. That's what writers always say; any writer you talk to will say that that's what makes the best stories. I don't think it's that cartoonists don't think about that, it's just that what really sells in cartoons, generally, is the exact opposite. I get the feeling that most comics fans find real life so grim that they're really looking for escape. Just the fact that they've got those crazy costume contests [at comics conventions] . . . probably the rest of the year people that win that contest don't even leave the house.

JOURNAL: *An inability or refusal to cope . . . or an inability to realize that you're just not that different from everybody else.*

BAGGE: That's why I think the general comics fan might not only be turned off by the weirder, wide variety of artwork in *Weirdo,* but also by the fact that it does touch so much on real life.

JOURNAL: *"In My Room" reminds me of what Harvey Pekar is doing . . .*

BAGGE: Which is indebted to what Crumb is doing. One thing that nobody ever points out is that Pekar is really influenced by Crumb. I think everything about what Pekar does is an extension of Crumb. And I like him, I think what he does is very good. I know a lot of people who think Pekar is a better writer than Crumb. I don't think he's better; he's different, but he's not better. But I think he's been really inspired by the way Crumb writes. Crumb did low-key stories even before he was working with Harvey, although he was inspired by Harvey, too.

JOURNAL: *Who else has influenced you?*

BAGGE: People have always compared me to Basil Wolverton and Ed "Big Daddy" Roth, but I never collected their stuff. In fact, when I was younger, I thought I didn't like Wolverton, that I was repulsed by his stuff. But I could still stare at it for hours [makes gestures of disgust and fascination] . . . and I guess it really sunk in. But my biggest influence is probably Charles M. Schulz; I liked him the most when I was a kid. I wanted to be the next Charles M. Schulz. And *Mad* magazine; I liked a lot of the guys in *Mad* magazine: Al Jaffe and Don Martin. And then when I saw Crumb . . . Crumb was the only thing that existed for about a year of my life. And Harvey Kurtzman . . . I like the way Kurtzman draws his own work, I prefer it a million times . . . I like Will Elder a lot, but when Kurtzman draws his own stuff it's fantastic . . . which I guess he hasn't done in about twenty-five years, on a regular basis.

JOURNAL: *What do you see in the future for* Weirdo?

BAGGE: I have a funny feeling that *Weirdo* is going to take off sooner or later—even if it only goes up fifty percent in sales. But maybe it'll go up to 100,000, who knows? As long as we can hold out, that's the thing, it could be a long time before there's a sizable chunk of people out there who are willing to get into *Weirdo*. I think right now it's getting worse, that there are fewer and fewer potential *Weirdo* readers. Then again, there are probably a lot of people out there who would like *Weirdo* if they could only get to see it. It's probably going to have to bottom out somewhere along the line before it gets better.

JOURNAL: *You never know. It may have bottomed out already. I'm more hopeful about kids now—I think they're by and large a lot more interesting than they were five or six years ago.*

BAGGE: Well, you never know how they're going to think, or if your thoughts are in line with whatever present-day teenagers are going to think when they come of age.

JOURNAL: *But, of course, it's impossible to second-guess. As you say, the response you get on anything is always split.*

BAGGE: So you have to follow your own instincts. One thing I know for a fact, although I don't always stick by it, is that every single time I haven't followed my strongest instincts, I've wound up regretting it. But I guess *Weirdo* will keep going; if I quit—and it has a lot to do with this *Neat Stuff* thing, too—I guess Crumb would start doing it.

JOURNAL: *Maybe you should get Kaz [a cartoonist who has had work in both* RAW *and* Weirdo*] to edit the magazine.*

BAGGE: I've thought of that, but he might turn it into *RAW, Jr.* He's one person I know that could do it, but my main thing is that I think *Weirdo* should be a flip-flop from *RAW*, attitude-wise, and I think his natural inclinations are way too close to *RAW*'s. Otherwise, he'd be the first person I'd think of. I'm a pretty stable person, and I find it really tough to deal with all these crazies that you work with. I'm not going to put *Weirdo* in the hands of somebody who's even more sensitive or shakier. I'm surprised Crumb put up with it as long as he did.

HARVEY PEKAR

FOR THE PAST ELEVEN YEARS HARVEY PEKAR HAS WAGED A ONE-MAN CAM-
paign to advance the comics form. While he was impressed by underground comics, he thought they had far more potential as literature than
they had yet shown. In 1976 he set out to prove it with *American
Splendor*, a comic he wrote, published, and distributed himself. By his
own estimate he's lost thousands of dollars on the deal, from a file clerk's
salary, no less. The passionate commitment that such a quixotic enterprise
requires comes through clearly in his stories. They portray the minute
details of everyday life that even serious fiction ignores; those moments
that don't lead to any conclusion but still stick in the memory. They are
animated by Pekar's abrasive personality, made up of equal parts gut-
wisdom, crankiness, and an intense involvement with every aspect of life.
His commitment finally began to pay off in 1986, when Doubleday/
Dolphin published a collection of his stories. This notoriety led to a brief
career as a professional guest on NBC's *Late Night with David Letterman*, a
career that promptly ended when he tried to expose the malfeasances of
General Electric, the network's parent company, on the air (he didn't succeed,
but the host's frantic attempts to silence him revealed far more about the
company than Pekar could have). He is often cited by cartoonists as an
inspiration for following an independent path.

This interview was conducted by Gary Groth.

The Last Supper

STORY BY HARVEY PEKAR
ART BY R. CRUMB
©1983 by Harvey Pekar

JOURNAL: *I want to talk about you and your work and I'd like to talk about your interests, particularly with regard to literature, but let's start talking about your work in* American Splendor. *Based on the assumption that a lot of our readers might not be familiar with your work, could you describe your place in comics today—how you fit in, or don't fit in, as the case may be!*

HARVEY PEKAR: *American Splendor* is a rather typical comic book in form; that is, I use illustrated panels with balloons, but it's atypical in content. Most comic books feature fantasy of one kind or another, superhuman characters, science fiction, or talking animals. My writing is autobiographical, as realistic as I can make it. I focus on writing stories about everyday life, not thrillers dealing with aliens invading earth. Also, for the most part the illustration in my books is more realistic than in other comics. I generally don't care much for artwork in which characters are idealized.

JOURNAL: *Well, I think that attitude is a distinguishing characteristic of your work. Why do you write autobiographically?*

PEKAR: Well, I may have a bigger ego than most people—that's for others to decide—but the main reason I write autobiographically is because I find it hard enough to understand why I myself do things, let alone why others do them. I want my writing to be as accurate and plausible as possible. I find that when others write fiction, they project their own ideas, impressions, sensations, and experiences on their fictional characters. Sometimes, of course, with magnificent results. For my purposes, though, I figured that I'd cut out the middle man, the fictional people, and write about me, the person I know best. Not that everything in my book is completely true, but an awful lot of it is. I·will change peoples' names or occupations sometimes, or maybe compress events that took place over a period of time into a few days.

JOURNAL: *The people who populate your book also, I assume, populate your life.*

PEKAR: Except Ozzie Nelson. [*laughter*]

JOURNAL: *Right. Except viscerally, through the television. But how much freedom do you give yourself in reconstructing incidents, situations, and so forth?*

PEKAR: Well, I start by trying literally to stick to the way things are because that works best for me. The more accurate the details of my stories are, the more people can believe in them, identify with the people in them. However, if for some reason it makes more sense to depart from the literal truth, sometimes I will. As I mentioned, I'll sometimes compress the time in which incidents have taken place—I remember once I changed the sex of a character. I've changed the ethnic identity of people on a couple of occasions.

JOURNAL: *But I assume your primary focus is to tell the truth, or to convey some aspect of the truth as you see it.*

PEKAR: Yeah, I want to write literature that pushes people into their lives rather than helping people escape from them. Most comic books are vehicles for escapism, which I think is unfortunate. I think that the so-called average person often exhibits a great deal of heroism in getting through an ordinary day, and yet the reading public takes this heroism for granted. They'd rather read about Superman than themselves.

Also, I think we see and hear stuff during the course of our ordinary days that is a lot funnier than what's happening on situation comedies. I incorporate some of this everyday humor into my work. Truth is funnier than fiction.

JOURNAL: *Do you need a specific amount of time to lapse between when something happens to you that you feel would make an interesting story, and the actual writing of it? Or do you write it immediately . . . or are there any set rules?*

PEKAR: Often I do it immediately, especially if I'm writing a story in which dialect is important. I'll take notes right away and try to write the dialect as accurately as possible, because a word here and a word there can make a lot of difference. There are things at work that happen and I'll write a story about them within a half-hour. Shorter things, anyway—vignettes.

I'm usually not in a position to write the longer stories right away, but I'll try to take notes and set up an outline while the facts are still fresh in my mind. I mentioned that the more believable my work is, the more people can relate to it. If you give them a generalized account with generic details it often has less impact.

JOURNAL: *Well, insofar as* American Splendor *is far more believable than most comics, how do you account for the comparatively small sales?*

PEKAR: Well, there are a lot of reasons *American Splendor* doesn't sell well, some having to do with virtually no advertising, poor media coverage, and pretty spotty distribution. But it's true that there are some people who aren't going to take a lot of comfort from what I write. It depresses them to read about themselves; when you shove their faces into their lives it bums them out. They don't want to deal with it, they say, "Hey man, I have to live through this stuff. When I go home I want to watch something on the tube with romance and excitement and stuff like that. I don't wanna be reading about the kind of life I have to live." And it bothers some of them, it seems strange to them sometimes.

JOURNAL: *Do you think that's a valid point of view or do you think it's the product of aberrant cultural conditioning?*

PEKAR: Generally, I think it's best for people to face their lives and their societies, to think about them, to deal with unpleasant facts rather than trying to make believe they don't exist. But it's hard for many to do that. When they get through with their daily work, some probably don't want to be reminded of it, it may seem like a busman's holiday for them to read *American Splendor*, which focuses on their everyday struggle. I'll tell you this, though—I've had surprising results when people I've worked with have seen the book. A lot have liked it, and maybe if I had better distribution and publicity it would sell better.

Of course, some comic book fans don't know what to make of *American Splendor*. They think a normal comic book should be about super beings who can fly, that a comic dealing with everyday people doing everyday things is weird. Ordinary is weird to them. Wow, that's really ironic.

JOURNAL: *Why did you choose the comic form to write in? Your greatest passion, it seems to me, is the novel.*

PEKAR: Comic book storytelling is particularly attractive to me for a few reasons. For one thing you can tell a story very concisely in comic books. A lot of the background details is in the illustration, which makes it easier to say what you want to say directly and economically. When I got into comic book writing, I was a street corner comedian. I actually had certain bits I used to repeat and it was easy to translate them to comics form. Using panels you can time stories the way a good oral storyteller would, sometimes using panels without dialogue for punctuation.

JOURNAL: *Right. So you can concentrate on dialogue.*
PEKAR: That's right. But to continue about comics: they've got both literary and visual aspects. I thought it was a great medium that had hardly been used, that there were so many things you could do, in addition to what I was doing. You could use it primarily as a visual medium, employing any number of graphic styles. There were experiments in the '60s that were not pursued, not vigorously pursued anyway. Guys like Victor Moscoso and Rick Griffin were doing abstract and surrealistic work, but not typical comic book abstraction and surrealism. It was like these guys were coming out of a "fine arts" bag. All sorts of possibilities that people had started to deal with in the '60s were let go.

JOURNAL: *Were you very familiar with comics prior to this?*
PEKAR: From the age of about six to twelve I collected and read them. Then my interest fell off to zero. In 1960, I married a woman whose little brother was reading a lot of comics and I started to read them again out of curiosity. At that time I got laid off work and started buying them again. They were only twelve cents. But I got bored with the Marvel and DC stuff real quick.

In 1962, I met Robert Crumb and his roommate Marty Pahls, who was a talented writer and cartoonist. They were living in Cleveland, about a block away from me. They interested me in comics again, but in good stuff like Jack Cole and Will Eisner and Walt Kelly and Segar, of course. I was familiar with their work, but I hadn't looked at it in some time. Unlike most of the '40s', super-hero stuff, it stood up quite well, it wasn't just of period interest.

Crumb was working on his *Yum Yum Book* then, and I was very impressed with it. I thought, "Man, this is tremendous."

JOURNAL: *How had you known Crumb?*
PEKAR: I was introduced to both Crumb and Pahls by a mutual record-collecting friend. This was just after Crumb had come to Cleveland from Philadelphia, just before he got his job at American Greeting. We all collected records in those days.

JOURNAL: *And your shared interest was jazz?*
PEKAR: Yeah, right. Originally when Crumb, Pahls, and I used to get together, we'd talk about records. The comic book stuff was in the background. I built myself up a new collection of comics, a small representative one, and later in the '60s, I got into under-

ground comics. I visited Crumb in San Francisco in 1968, he visited me in Cleveland in '70-'72. At this time I was thinking about doing realistic stories in comic book form. I also started thinking about something that has become increasingly important to me over the years, although I don't have the control over it that I have on my writing, namely realistic illustration, illustration that is not cartoony, but in which the characters are not idealized either, like they are in Marvel and DC comics.

JOURNAL: *To say the least about Crumb's work.*
PEKAR: Well, I was thinking about the realistic stuff that Gerry Shamray has done for me, or in the latest issue, Val Mayerik.

JOURNAL: *Do you make a distinction, when you refer to artwork as being realistic, between someone like Shamray, who I think draws from a lot of photo reference—*
PEKAR: Traces photos, as a matter of fact.

JOURNAL: *Okay, and someone like Crumb, whose work conforms more to a cartooning idiom, but who conveys a tremendous amount of realism? There's a difference there. At least there's a difference on the surface.*
PEKAR: Good point. Crumb exaggerates and distorts people's proportions, but he's tremendously observant—he notices how people walk and gesture and dress. When he exaggerates, he draws attention to peoples' unique, distinctive characteristics. In that sense, his cartoony style is as realistic as anyone's. But most cartoony illustrators lack Crumb's powers of observation. They merely employ techniques of drawing they've derived from other artists. They're not as insightful as Crumb and for that reason I prefer not to work with them.

JOURNAL: *Maybe "truthful" would be a better word.*
PEKAR: The stuff I've given him to do, he's always figured out a way to do it right.

JOURNAL: *Let me ask you how you work. Do you write a full script and give it to the artist?*
PEKAR: I write the stories in panel form using stick figures with balloons, and I indicate in the panels or on a separate sheet of paper what I'd like in the backgrounds, what I'd like the characters to look like, and so forth. Then I talk to the illustrator and we

have a meeting of the minds about what the drawing is going to be like and then we go from there.

JOURNAL: *Do you feel in any way that your vision is somewhat attenuated or diminished by having to work with artists that obviously can't feel what you feel when you write a story?*

PEKAR: Sure, to some extent, but in general I feel they've gotten the message across. People have told me they liked many stories where the illustration wasn't particularly good, so I guess the stuff is getting over. I know that the artwork has improved, in general, steadily since the first few books, but still some of those first stories and the early books remain among people's favorites, particularly the third book.

JOURNAL: *Yeah, that's right, a very good issue. Well, let me ask you this, since your stories and work in general are so autobiographical in nature, you really do lay yourself quite naked in the work. How naked are you in those stories? In other words, how honest can you be about yourself?*

PEKAR: There are a few things in my life I can hardly bear to think about, and I don't write about them. The things I do write about are things that I believe I'm doing with about as much honesty as possible. If I'm embarrassed about something, if it's too painful to write about, I just don't attempt to.

JOURNAL: *There seems to be a real danger, for someone like yourself, who uses himself as the protagonist, whereas other authors create characters through which they speak or see the world. And your problem seems to be that since you don't have that kind of mask, and since you're using yourself as the protagonist, there's the danger of your trying to color events or sort of seeing things happen, through your own eyes, and I'm wondering, have you found that a danger?*

PEKAR: Sure. It's a danger for me, and also for the many other writers who write autobiographical fiction and merely change the name of the protagonist from theirs to a fictitious one. But I err on the side of making myself look bad. I must be conveying some of my faults because when I read reviews of my work, people are always talking about me being cheap, gloomy, inconsiderate, and having a bad temper. It would be crazy for me to whitewash myself. In that case nobody would want to look at my stuff; they couldn't relate to it. If anything, I tend to exaggerate my flaws, I think.

JOURNAL: *How do you handle the problem of depicting other people? Since you obviously don't know what they were thinking when they're engaged in conversation or some other situation with you, you sort of have to recreate their own thought process and their behavior and mannerisms and so forth. How do you tackle that problem and remain as truthful as possible?*

PEKAR: Well, first I think all storytellers, whether they write about real people or not, have to give them plausible reasons for acting as they do. In a sense I have an advantage over some writers since my characters really exist and I have an opportunity to think about what motivates them. I don't have to worry about why generic, really fictitious people do things.

Anyway, I try to report what people say accurately and even if I really dislike them I try to see things from their point of view. For instance, in my story "Free Ride" I'm talking about a guy who was in some ways, I thought, a real drag. But I was getting on his nerves and there was a reason for it: He was doing me favors and I wasn't doing anything for him. He was helping out not only me but other guys who came to him at work and bugged him, not because he had a kindly disposition but because he felt obligated to.

He knew he was being taken advantage of, though, and he didn't like it. I tried to put this information into the story to give people a balanced view of what was going on. I mean maybe I think this guy's a jerk, but maybe he thinks I'm a jerk and maybe the readers will, too. Even if I come off as a shit, at least people will have an accurate opinion of what happened.

JOURNAL: *Well, you could put a few super-heroes and barbarians in it . . . What do you see ahead for yourself and for comics?*

PEKAR: Well, I just see myself plugging away at this with the same commercial results for years. As for the aesthetic future— that's a good question. My latest book, the ninth, was the subtlest, most low-keyed one I'd published. One of the reasons for this was because I'd written so much in the past about nasty conflicts between men and women and the pain of alienation, that I decided to leave those topics alone this time. So in the ninth book I dealt with some pretty subtle things. I've already talked about a few stories in that book, "Free Ride," "One of Life's Pleasures," and "Hypothetical Quandary." There was also a story in there called "Semi-Bummer Weekend," in which I describe the tensions that develop between me and an out-of-town friend when things start to go wrong during his visit to Cleveland. Another story ends with Joyce jumping on me because I'm reluctant to identify myself as a writer, rather than a file clerk, to a stranger. She thinks I'm being too humble, selling myself short, and doesn't want to stand for it. In the future I'm going to probably do stories about my attempt to control my temper, my impatience, and my compulsions. I've got a story I'm using in issue ten about how I first freak out and then try to get a hold of myself when I lose my glasses. These are the kinds of problems we deal with all the time but which are seldom written about. From a structural standpoint—I introduced an unusual guy named Toby in my last book. In the next one, issue ten, I'm going to have more about him, show you more about what he's like and why.

As far as the future of comics is concerned, who knows? Prospects for the near future don't look good. Even in the anti-intellectual 1950s there were important developments in comics—*Mad* and other EC books, Charles Schulz, Walt Kelly, Jules Feiffer. In the mid-'60s to the mid-'70s, there were underground comics. Since then—I dunno, man. Comics can be a wonderful medium, but not many serious, gifted people consider working in them because there're so many comics that are commercial garbage. It never occurs to them that anything good can be done in comic books.

JOURNAL: *Well, for someone who works in the medium, Harvey, you seem particularly uninterested in it. In other words, you don't keep up with it; you're not terribly involved.*

PEKAR: That's because the vast majority of comic books are not interesting to me. Look, there's medium and then there's genre. Would you say to someone, "You write these realistic novels about everyday life, so why don't you read more trashy Harlequin novels and hard-boiled detective novels?" I don't want to read junky novels or comics. A huge majority of comic books are comparable to schlock, formula commercial novels or TV shows. I'm not going to waste my time reading or watching or listening to cliché-ridden stuff, no matter what form it takes, what medium it's in.

JOURNAL: *What you're saying is that comics have almost been reduced to a single genre.*

PEKAR: Well, what I can see—the super-hero stuff. I don't care about that stuff. I'm sure that here and there are good comics I'm not aware of. But I mentioned that I'd taken a look at what passes for alternative comics. These days—I don't want to mention names, but I don't see where they differ much from Marvel and DC stuff.

JOURNAL: *You sure you don't want to mention names?*
PEKAR: I'm sure. There's no point in it.

JOURNAL: *Libel suits aren't so bad.*
PEKAR: Nah, I don't even care about it from that standpoint. It's just the idea that I don't want to sound like a schmuck, like I'm envious, because I'm not. These super-hero guys aren't taking away my bread. If Marvel and DC books didn't exist, most comic book fans wouldn't read my stuff. The genre is more important than the medium to them. If they didn't have their super-heroes they'd go see a horror movie. So that Marvel and DC don't hurt me, don't take business from me.

JOURNAL: *Right.*
PEKAR: I should mention that there is a certain kind of comic collector who'll buy my books, even though he might not like them; the kid that has to have everything. That's the kind of record collector I was. I'm sure there are comic book collectors out there who are into Marvel stuff but still buy my books. Good for these compulsive guys! For all I know, they're a majority of my buyers. But the people who *write* to me to tell me they like my book are not mainstream comic book readers. I don't think I've got a potentially much larger audience among the collecting junkies.

JOURNAL: *To change the subject, did you get any response from the* Village Voice *over your tirade against the* Voice?
PEKAR: No.

JOURNAL: *Not a bit, huh?*
PEKAR: No, because, those people don't give a shit. That's the point. They don't care if I'm happy or I'm mad. They don't care. They don't take any notice of you.

JOURNAL: *Did you find any irony in their doing a story on you almost immediately after that issue came out?*
PEKAR: I knew the story was coming out. The guy who wrote it called me months before to tell me he was doing it.

JOURNAL: *What do you think of his comparison of you to the Russian writers?*
PEKAR: Well, that's one stream of writing my work is related to. Dostoevsky and Chekhov are tremendous writers. Gogol is very fine—underrated. But my style is drawn from a lot of other sources, too, as I mentioned earlier. I think I learned from comedians like Bob and Ray, and Lenny Bruce, for example.

JOURNAL: *Well, I think that influence comes across in your work, especially when you address the reader in a kind of monologue.*
PEKAR: Yeah, and the timing thing, too, the pauses, the panels without dialogue that I write into the story.

JOURNAL: *The silences.*
PEKAR: Yeah, right. The silent panels.

JOURNAL: *Yeah, I think you use those quite effectively.*
PEKAR: Yeah, thanks. [*pause*] Let's end the interview right here—a Harvey Pekar ending.

GARY PANTER

GARY PANTER EXEMPLIFIES THE MERGING OF COMICS AND FINE ART. AS MATT Groening has written, Panter "applied his fine art training to the comic strip, and the result was an explosive series of graphic experiments that are imitated in small doses all over the world today." Panter grew up in a succession of Great Plains states, finally ending up in Sulphur Springs, Texas. Exposed to a strict fundamentalist climate in Sulphur Springs, he reacted by drawing "fighting dinosaurs, monsters, Roman soldiers, musclemen, amusement parks, spies, robots, spaceships, and Rat Finks" all the way through public school. Disturbed by the weird and often morbid subject matter of his drawings, his father arranged employment for him in a funeral home, "to give me an idea of the reality behind the things I portrayed. I cleaned up the vile fluids that result from the preparation of the dead for their burials, helped dress corpses in their suits-with-no-necks, and worked as an ambulance attendant getting accident victims in hospitals."

In 1969, the Jefferson Street Church of Christ sent him to Belfast, Northern Ireland, on a missionary crusade ("It was a strange thing to try and sell a new religion to the people of a city at war over religion.") Returning to the U.S. later that year, he studied painting at East Texas State College and, in 1971, won a scholarship to the Yale/Norfolk Summer School of Music and Art, where he studied under noted illustrator Don Ivan Punchatz. During the early '70s, he completed his education at East Texas State—"My senior painting project was a puppet show entitled *Godzilla Gets a Hot TV*"—briefly worked at a color-separation company, and helped form a musical group called Apeweek ("We pretended that we could perform rock music but did puppet shows instead.").

From *Jimbo*

JIMBO ERECTUS. Their feeding habits have been the subject of much speculation in the past, but it is now Reliably known that they are mainly Preddaceous.

From *Jimbo*

After moving to Los Angeles in 1976, his career began to take a more definite shape. He began drawing *Jimbo* for *Slash* (a punk rock magazine) and exhibiting his paintings in various galleries, did album covers for Frank Zappa, and saw his first book, *Okupant X,* published by Diana's Monthly Press. Since then, his work has appeared in such diverse publications as *Coolest Retard, Hoo Be Boo, Fool's Mate, New West, New York, RAW, Time, Rolling Stone, Weirdo, Wet, Women's Wear Daily, Mother Jones,* and *Illustrations.* His comics and paintings have appeared in numerous galleries and shows around the world, including the Whitney Museum's Contemproary Art show.

This interview was conducted by Dale Luciano, who also provided material for this introduction.

JOURNAL: *Maybe we could begin with a question about the origin of* Jimbo. *How did he come into being?*

GARY PANTER: Okay, well, let's see . . . I guess it was about 1973. I was just starting to try and draw some longer comic strips while I was in college. And I just drew him outright. That was one character who just sort of popped up, except that he had a pompadour and was a lot more baby-faced back then. But he first popped up as a parent in a story called—uh, what was it?—"Bow Tie Madness." He was the parent of some kids who get kidnapped by a kiddie-show host. That's a story that I've not really finished yet. *Jimbo* just sort of popped up.

JOURNAL: *Where did the name come from?*

PANTER: Jimbo . . . When I was growing up in Sulphur Springs, Texas, there was a kid in my neighborhood named "Jimbo" Thompson. He was a funny little kid—he was always getting picked on but he always managed to joke his way out of a tough situation, so I think I just liked his nickname, "Jimbo." His real name was Jimmy, but everyone called him "Jimbo." As to who the character *is*, he would represent to me an Everyman or a certain kind of Western man. My brother, my friend Jay Condom, and myself are probably the main source material for the character.

JOURNAL: *Looking over all the* Jimbo *stories—except for the* Jimbo *book itself, where there's clearly some consistency of character among the stories—I sometimes lose track of him as a consistent character. Is there supposed to be a consistency about him in all these various manifestations of Jimbo?*

PANTER: Umm, yeah . . . I think there's something consistent there, but he's got moods. Sometimes he's totally stupid and can't think at all. At other times, he's really thoughtful. He's really more of a soap box for me in those moments . . .

JOURNAL: *When he's being thoughtful?*

PANTER: Yeah. Then again, sometimes he's just acting and doesn't say anything. That's just his nature, how he is, what he does . . .

JOURNAL: *What inspires you to do a story like the one that opens up the* Jimbo *book, in which Jimbo mutilates himself while trying to perform normal, everyday morning functions?*

PANTER: At the time, I was writing for a really hard-core punk magazine . . .

JOURNAL: *Most of these originally appeared in* Slash?

PANTER: Yeah, originally, starting in about 1978 or something like that. Yeah, early 1978. And so it was intended for that audience. I was an older guy, I wasn't a young punk kid—I'd been more of a punk in the early '70s—and I guess the point I was making in that story is that Jimbo never starts a fight or anything, but still faces disaster. He just lives in a calamitous world. There was a lot of talk at the time about violence and style . . . so I just had Jimbo not start any fights. He's just trying to get by, and the world's violent enough. That's what I was trying to say.

JOURNAL: *Uh, I see . . . I notice—*

PANTER: It's all about the funny things that happen to you which you can't seem to get away from, like stepping on a piece of glass.

JOURNAL: *[laughs, a little confused] Well, sure, a piece of glass. A calamitous world . . .*

PANTER: Or when you see someone else fall for it and become a victim, or you hope they don't . . .

JOURNAL: *Man's loss of control over himself, yes? He slips on a banana peel and, in Bergson's terms, becomes an automaton . . .*

[Pause]
PANTER: Okay . . . yeah, that's part of it . . .

JOURNAL: *In the* Jimbo *book, there's a long story about the search for the missing girl that's kidnapped by cockroaches . . .*
PANTER: Right.

JOURNAL: *Then, uh . . . I'm not sure if this is all one continuous story, or if this is a separate story, but all of a sudden Jimbo is dismantling a thermonuclear device . . .*
PANTER: Right.

JOURNAL: *[still confused] I guess this was for* Slash *magazine? I notice in the latest issue of* RAW, *you've got the aftermath of the nuclear explosion . . .*
PANTER: That's a continuation of the last twelve pages in the *RAW* one-shot *Jimbo.* It's a continuation of that story. I started that story in *Slash* and worked on it over a period of years. I hadn't carried it through the conclusion that you see in *RAW #6.* That was where I was headed, though. Also, there are other loose ends, like Judy's disappearance, which feeds into a story I haven't done yet.

JOURNAL: *In this* RAW #6 *story, you depict the aftermath of the nuclear blast. [thumbing through the pages] This seems to achieve a level of graphic horror that is different from much of your work.*
PANTER: Yeah. I get real depressed and worried from time to time about that stuff. Doing a comic's a good outlet for those fears. Turn it into propaganda . . . maybe, unfortunately, that's what it turns into, just some wild opinion. And in the story I'm telling, it's about one tiny terrorist bomb going off in a city somewhere, not even a big war . . .

JOURNAL: *[quoting from story] "Forty miles around . . ."*
PANTER: Yeah. It's just about the fact that it's possible, it could happen, just like a car wreck's possible. If you live with the possibility that this may happen, you go on with your life and don't think about it that much, but occasionally people do think about it. I think publication's an ideal place to say something about that. I don't think it's been established well enough graphically what the horrors are. To do the story, I went and read as much and saw as many photos as I could of what happened in World War II—Hiroshima, Nagasaki—and it's pretty mind-blowing.

I'm going to do two more stories for *RAW*. They're going to get more literal and more horrible as they progress. It's pretty depressing to do those stories. I mean, if—

JOURNAL: *It looks like you're releasing a nightmare on paper.*
PANTER: Yeah, that's true. Sometimes it's fun when you get marks to go together right, or if I feel like this might provoke some sympathetic reaction. That makes me feel okay, but in general it's not much fun to draw stories like that. There's a morbid side to me that's always liked horror movies and drippy, gooey, awful stuff— you know, all that horrible stuff from the comics in the '50s. I find that stuff really neat.

JOURNAL: *[laughs]*
PANTER: It's just slop, but reality is something different. I think it just reflects anxiety about what can happen in everyday life. The "Jimbo" stories represent extremes of experience and you can come away from this stuff relieved and thinking, "Aren't you happy your life's not that exciting?" I mean, aren't you happy life's not as exciting as having some psycho guy chase you around with a hatchet? That's the Henry Webb end of things. That was just a black humor story, anxiety about there really being some psycho people out there who would hurt you if they could get to you.

JOURNAL: *[confused] Uh, you're referring to—oh, I follow you, you're referring to* The Asshole?
PANTER: Yeah, *The Asshole*, whose name is Henry Webb. That's what I usually call him, Henry Webb. That story was just totally anxiety-produced.

JOURNAL: *Tell me more about working in this childlike style.*
PANTER: Well, it's just following traditions. I don't think of my stuff as looking like children's drawing, really. In some ways, I'm just working to fill in a gap. If I see everyone doing slick, air-brush, beautiful, really "finessed" drawings, then I try to do something that's not being done as much. That's where my work comes from. But now, lots of people are drawing ratty.

JOURNAL: *[laughs] Drawing ratty? That's what you call it?*
PANTER: Yeah, ratty. That's pretty much what I call it. Ratty drawing.

JOURNAL: *But you like ratty drawing, correct?*

PANTER: Oh yeah, it comes right out of the human being. Ratty drawing is natural, like the marks people make on crates when they write the numbers on them to ship them off, or like bathroom graffiti when it's just scrawled onto the walls. The line has some kind of content. It's got the emotion of the person doing it. It's a testament that the person exists and that they made the marks.

JOURNAL: *So someone who has little or no training expresses something in a very primitive way that you would find moving or powerful, but if they gained technical skill, they might lose that natural quality . . .*

PANTER: Yeah. Well . . . I dunno. When you start trying to draw good, it's weird how people start not liking what they draw. *Most* people don't like what they draw, no matter how good or bad they draw. But sometimes I find pieces of paper on the street and people have done drawings on them. They're totally *un*self-conscious drawings because they're phone doodles, something that's going to be thrown into the trash, or maybe I find a little kid's drawing. It just seems to me that the way those marks go together is closer to the way, say, twigs would fall on a sidewalk. [*pause*] If you're walking down a sidewalk and you see all these squares of cement in a row, well . . . where the twigs and stuff fall on the squares, that's a composition made by nature on a square. That's what artists are trying to do all the time. They're trying to compose things in a rectangle. I study that. I think a lot of people study that. Unself-conscious drawing has that same kind of look to it, that naturalness of the marks. There are a lot of people whose marks I like a lot *after* they develop technical proficiency. I like George Herriman's marks—his shadows behind the characters, or the way he scratched through the drawing. Those are really the kind of marks I like. I'm really into marks.

JOURNAL: *You use the word "marks," where I hear most cartoonists or artists talk about "lines." What's the difference?*

PANTER: [*long pause during which he considers the question*] I think lines are the kinds of things an artist uses to construct an illusion. A line is a tool for making or defining an illusion. A mark is more of a thing that exists for and by itself. It's more abstract as a building block. I think the idea of "marks" is somehow closer to the natural. Marks get away from the sophisticated reality of an illusion of depth toward the reality of something that's closer to the natural order of things. Yeah, marks have the look of nature.

JOURNAL: *You're very concerned with the art work's self-consciousness, the degree to which it draws attention to its own qualities . . . Doesn't your work do that? Doesn't a lot of ratty drawing draw a lot of attention to itself?*

PANTER: Well, you see, it's a double bind. Work done with a lot of finesse draws a lot of attention to itself. You see a seamless, totally convincing illusion, but if you look at it closely, you just go, "Wow! How can someone draw like that?" On the other hand, you can also look at a piece of ratty drawing and in some way understand it as *more* self-conscious and drawing attention to itself, as you suggest, because of its crumminess. It's important to realize that this movement is inspired by the kind of art done by people who are totally *un*self-conscious. They just *draw*. That kind of *direct* drawing has a charm to it that, I guess, people like me are after.

JOURNAL: *Who do you feel your peers or colleagues are? Who are the people whose work you feel comfortable with, whom you feel are doing something like what you're doing?*

PANTER: There are a lot of people doing it that I didn't know about, that I eventually found out about. People like Savage Pencil and Ian Pollock in England—Pollock has an illustration in the latest *Rolling Stone*—Mariscal in Spain, Bruno Richard and Pascal Doury in Paris, Henrik Drescher, Sue Coe and Mark Beyer in New York, Rick Nictzman in Chicago. And there's a bunch of newer, younger guys that I feel really close to, like Mark Marek and Ron Hauge, both of whom do stuff for the *National Lampoon*. I could make a long list. I like to sit down and make long lists of influences sometimes . . .

JOURNAL: *Would some of these people be published in* Hoo-Be-Boo?

PANTER: Yeah, there are a lot of the younger guys in *Hoo-Be-Boo*. Will Amato, Jim Cotner, Rick Potts, Ehringer . . .

JOURNAL: *You feel a kinship with these guys.*

PANTER: Yeah, I really like looking at them. There's also a guy up in Oregon named Jim Williams whose work I like, and these guys in Memphis—"Box X" and XNO—who publish books as XEX Publishing. There's a guy in Iowa, Doug Holverson, who does good science fiction comics. It's just a process of mutual influence and what comes of these people having been exposed to similar kinds of things, making a vocabulary out of it, and starting to converse with it. It has a lot of very traditional roots, like . . . I dunno, I could name a hundred artists, like Klee, Arp, and Joan Miro . . . [*rummaging around, searching for something*] Uhh . . . Oh, here! Here's a Xerox list I have that I was looking at earlier! [*begins consulting list*] Forrest J. Ackerman is a really good influence on the youth of today . . . He started making those monster magazines.

JOURNAL: *Yes,* Famous Monsters of Filmland, *I'm familiar with them.*

PANTER: Ed "Big Daddy" Roth is another. These are the roots of my kind of stuff. The folk artist-type of guys. I guess you'd call them. Henry Darger was this guy in Chicago who wrote this really long novel they found after he died. It's really great.

JOURNAL: *Do you remember the name of it?*

PANTER: Uhh . . . something about the Vivien Girls. There's a catalog put out by the Phyllis Kind Gallery in New York. I think it's called *Realms of the Unreal* . . . that's the name of the catalog, maybe that's the name of the novel as well—I can't recall . . . Anyway, Darger had these tribes of girls who were menaced by all these armies. All the girls were traced out of the Sears Catalogue and collaged back into bigger compositions and water-colored. It's just crazy work. And totally catastrophic: train wrecks and wars and tornados! Also, all the little girls have penises. [*referring again to his list*] Here's a guy. Claude Bell, who built the dinosaurs out in the desert. All those kinda guys who build dinosaurs all over the place. Do you mind if I read this list?

JOURNAL: *No, I guess not. Go ahead.*

PANTER: Posada, the Mexican revolutionary artist. Tadanori Yokoo, a big commercial artist and illustrator in Japan. He's a painter now. Oyvind Fahlstrom, the Swedish pop artist who did *Charles Knight,* based on George Herriman's work, the dinosaur painter. Tex Avery. Claus Oldenburg. Salvador Dali. Cal Schenkel, the guy who did the Frank Zappa album covers. Fritz Lang, who directed *Metropolis*. Picasso. George Herriman. Segar. Kirby. Fellini. Sergio Leone . . .

JOURNAL: *Now, wait a minute, what's this list again? What list is this?*

PANTER: This is a list of guys who are really inspirational . . . to me and other guys, too. Like Mark Marek . . .

JOURNAL: *Yes, I just got some copies of* New Wave Comics *in the mail. Published by Manhattan Design . . . really nice production on the book!*

PANTER: Mark's from Texas also, and he's doing a strip about Hercules. He's really into Hercules. When I was a kid, there were *Hercules* movies, with a guy named Steve Reeves, which were really inspirational to me, and evidently they were really inspirational to him . . . [*returning to the list*] Uhh . . . Chester Gould. Al Capp. Jack Webb. Mouse, the weirdo painter.

JOURNAL: *What did you say, the weirdo painter?*

PANTER: Mouse? He became a psychedelic poster designer but he was a great weirdo artist who drew weird creatures with bug eyes and giant mouths with sharp teeth and their tongues hanging out . . .

JOURNAL: *Oh, he drew weirdos, you mean . . .*

PANTER: Oh, yeah, right. Not to be confused with Crumb's *Weirdo.*

JOURNAL: *How do you spell his name?*

PANTER: M-O-U-S-E . . .

JOURNAL: *[laughs] I had to ask, right?*

PANTER: [*continuing with his list*] Phil Dick, the science fiction writer. H. C. Westerman. Bob Zoell. Basil Wolverton. R. Crumb. Frank Zappa. Captain Beefheart. And the Chicago stuff like Jim Nutt and Carl Wirsum. That's just one day's list.

JOURNAL: *Do you have problems with the term "punk" being applied to your work?*

PANTER: Uhh . . . not so much. I don't like the term "New Wave." I never did. It always seemed like a term somebody came up with for getting all this stuff ready for a catalog.

JOURNAL: *[laughs]*

PANTER: "Punk." Well, I never felt like a guy who'd be a punk. As far as being screwed-up, I always felt my drawings tried to embrace all the smudges and mistakes. That's analogous to punk.

JOURNAL: *I notice, though, in conversation, you don't use the term "punk" to refer to your own work. . . .*

PANTER: No.

JOURNAL: *I saw The Pizz walking around the San Diego Convention in somber, dark clothing and dark glasses, looking very punk, but you were sitting there in a T-shirt, pretty anonymously. You looked—*

PANTER: Normal?

JOURNAL: *Normal.*

PANTER: I'm just a little older. About looking punk and feeling punk, well, I was a lot weirder looking when I was twenty-one than I am at thirty-three. I've never successfully been into fashion. Being into punk seems to imply a commitment to really standing out in some way, and I'm always under so much pressure to just try and look normal. You know, just being around people and having to consider what other people think. I guess if I were by myself, I'd be *really* weird, but since I'm around people all the time, I'm real modulated. Gotta be normal.

JOURNAL: *But a lot of your work has appeared in punk periodicals?*

PANTER: Yeah, well, I like punk! I love seeing kids standing around, looking really screwed-up, with their hair sticking straight out. I think they're doing a really good thing for the country, just shaking things up. It shocks a lot of people awake to see anything different, especially in their own town. It's a process. It spreads from one country to another, to a neighborhood, then to everybody's neighborhood. Once it's not creepy anymore, they'll invent something else that's equally offensive.

JOURNAL: *Are you occupied ten, twelve, fourteen hours a day doing art?*

PANTER: Yeah. I'm just determined to do what I want to do. To draw as weird as I want to draw.

JOURNAL: *You're developing a name, and there's certainly a style associated with your name . . .*

PANTER: Well, by being contrary, I stand out like a sore thumb. Most people are just trying to be accommodating, trying to do their jobs. I spend most of my time trying to figure out what my job *is*. I'm really pretty harried by the whole money thing. It would be nice if more people would buy my paintings, but . . . maybe they will sometime.

JOURNAL: *I notice there's an ad in* RAW *for your stuff through a New York Gallery . . .*

PANTER: Yeah, there's a gallery in New Orleans, a gallery in Massachusetts, a gallery here in L.A., and a gallery in New York, so I'm starting to be in galleries and shows, mostly from the cartoons. I'm in that comics show, "Strip Language: Contemporary Art as Comics and Caricatures," at the Gimpel Fils Gallery in London, along with a bunch of English artists.

JOURNAL: *You were in that show up in Toronto, too, "Kromalaffing," at the Chromazone/Chromatique Gallery in Toronto. Sybil Goldstein sent me a copy of the catalog.*

PANTER: Yeah! And the comics show at the Whitney in New York last year. People are slowly finding out that I paint, too. Most people who know my work have only seen the cartoons.

JOURNAL: *The work in* RAW #6 *seems much more painterly than some of the other work . . .*

PANTER: I've finally got my sketchbooks—I just draw in these sketchbooks all day long. I just draw out of my head or copy from photos. Then I make paintings from those, so the cartoons and the paintings are starting to overlap with one another. *Jimbo's* the closest I've come to combining all the stuff.

MATT GROENING

ARRIVING IN LOS ANGELES ABOUT TEN YEARS AGO, THE OREGON-BORN MATT Groening put his initial reaction to the City of Angels (i.e., revulsion) on paper. The inveterate doodler titled his satirical cartoons *Life in Hell* and photocopied them for his friends and relatives, selling some at local record stores as well. In 1978 the strip was picked up by the punkish *Wet* magazine, and in 1980 the newly formed *L.A. Reader* took over the feature, acquiring in the bargain Groening's services as a staffer. Eventually his personal projects began to absorb most of his time; Groening set up his own syndicate, and *Life in Hell* moved on to the *Reader*'s main competitor, the *L.A. Weekly*. It currently appears in sixty newspapers and weekly magazines.

Life in Hell is an often hilarious compendium of Groening's opinions and insights, starring a trio of neurotic and alienated rabbits, two fez-wearing gay midgets, and various hangers-on. Despite the occasional barb about his somewhat basic art style (he himself refers to it as "uh . . . functional," and helps maintain its integrity by often drawing it from scratch on the morning of his deadline), no one dispute's Groening's cutting and precise command of the language. It should come as no surprise that he considers cartooning an accidental sideline and, while loyal to the strip, he plans to expand his work into other fields in the future.

This interview was conducted by Kim Thompson.

HELL FOR BEGINNERS

A BRIEF INTRODUCTION TO THIS CARTOON FOR NEOPHYTES AND A REMEDIAL COURSE FOR THOSE WHO HAVEN'T BEEN PAYING ATTENTION

JOURNAL: *Do you have any particular affection for rabbits, as animals?*

MATT GROENING: No, not particularly. The reason I draw rabbits . . . I used to draw all sorts of animals back in high school. I drew a comic strip called "Tales of the Enchanted Forest," somewhat inspired by *Pogo* by Walt Kelly, but my bears didn't really look like bears, they looked sort of like big mice, and my mice looked like dogs, and people couldn't really tell what the dogs were . . . well, anyway, I had one rabbit character and they said, "Ah! A rabbit!" So that's why I stuck with rabbits; they're the easiest.

LIES MY OLDER BROTHER AND SISTER TOLD ME

© 1986 MATT GROENING

FROM *SCHOOL IS HELL* BY MATT GROENING, COURTESY PANTHEON BOOKS, NEW YORK.

JOURNAL: *How did you come up with the idea of depicting Bongo, the child rabbit, with just one ear?*

GROENING: Well, I had been drawing Binky the rabbit with two ears for several years and I wanted to give him an illegitimate son who would be the most alienated child in the world. I drew a number of prototypes for the son and I couldn't make the son look different enough from Binky so that people could tell them apart. Finally I hit on the idea of giving him one ear and it made me laugh out loud; I dared myself to use that character, and it's proven popular, although my mother thinks it's obscene.

JOURNAL: *Were you alienated as a kid—or just on the same level that any kid is alienated?*

GROENING: I don't think I was all that much different from other kids, but yeah, I had a strong sense of alienation and a good memory and a penchant for self-pity and bitterness [*laughs*] that had to do with the fact that I was unable to sit there quietly while the teacher was droning on and on, and I passed the time by squirming and drawing. When the teacher confiscated my cartoons, I was incapable of still keeping still so I drew on the desk. And then I would get caught for drawing on the desk and the teacher would draw this circle in chalk on the blackboard and make me stick my nose on it. There was nothing I could do. There was no chalk within reach for me to draw; that's how I learned to blow bubbles off the end of my tongue. You can't put me in reach of anything. I taught myself, by having to stand in the corner near the window for some time, how to tie a hangman's noose, which got me in further trouble. If you tie a hangman's noose with a venetian blind cord, I tell you, it's a one-way ticket to the principal's office. [*laughs*] [*In fact, the interviewee spent most of the interview toying with the venetian blind cord, although he never went to the extent of tying it into a hangman's noose.*]

JOURNAL: *I think that as kids, we all say to ourselves, "I'm going to remember this, and when I'm a grown-up I won't treat little kids this way"; it seems like everyone's forgotten but you.*

GROENING: People have put it in the back of their minds. But yeah, it evokes a lot of memories. I was an extreme case, a smart kid and a smart-ass kid, so my big mouth got me in trouble quite a bit. And I had a couple of really rotten teachers who went out of their way to make the lives of kids miserable rather than just boring the way most teachers do. Because of that, when finally in the fifth grade I had a teacher that I felt was *so* horrible, I decided to keep a diary, because I suspected I was right even though the authorities told me I was completely wrong. So I kept the diary that year and yes, upon rereading it, I think I was right. I think there was no point in making me write a thousand-word essay on the life cycle of the liver fluke for whispering in the library. Anyway, the diary has also been good basic material. I ran an edited version of it in my strip for a number of weeks a couple of years ago, and that will be my next book: *School Is Hell.*

JOURNAL: *I guessed as much.*

GROENING: Yeah. *School is Hell* is going to be my major opus on that subject, although not my only one.

JOURNAL: *There are very few cartoonists who legitimately write from a kid's point of view.* Peanuts *is brilliant, but it's not about kids—*

GROENING: Well, most traditional comic strips had so many taboos that they had to deal with—and also were a lot friendlier. [*laughs*] If those strips hadn't been done I probably would be writing in that kind of style myself. But because they have been done, I try to offer an alternative. There's a darker side of childhood that I try to make people remember. People forget how frightened kids are of adults and teenagers and big dogs and failure and other kids and all the rest, and I like to write about that. Despite my problems with teachers and principals, though, I had a pretty idyllic childhood in many ways. I grew up in Portland, Oregon, in a neighborhood that was in the middle of a park bordering on an arboretum which had very exotic trees. My family lived a half a mile from the old Portland Zoo, which closed down when I was five years old; they just shut it down and locked the gate and so when I was a very young kid we used to play war games in the abandoned zoo, which was great. Most kids pretend to be in caves, but we got to run through the hillside and in the grizzly bear grotto, hide inside small grizzly caves, pretend the bones found were real human bones, and actually swim in the bear pool, although that's probably almost as bad as swimming in these canals with the sea slugs.

When I was in the fourth grade, my friends and I became obsessed with monsters. We bought the magazine *Famous Monsters of Filmland* and saw on the back an ad for back issues, of which there were about forty at the time. We made a club called the Creature Club. Its motto was "I'm Peculiar," a take-off on a cigarette slogan of the time, which was "I'm Particular." I don't remember what cigarette brand that was. Anyway, the dues of the club were as much money as you could get [*laughs*] . . .

JOURNAL: *A communist at an early age.*

GROENING: Right. The club treasury was stored in the bottom drawer of a kitchen of an abandoned house we called The Haunted House because it had a toilet that flushed without stopping. And so we saved up thirty dollars and we took a vote on whether to buy a print of *The Creature From the Black Lagoon* in 8 mm or all these back issues of *Famous Monsters of Filmland.* We decided that the magazines would be better and we sent off for them; when they arrived they arrived in the mail one by one over a two-month period. They became a major part of our little afternoon rituals; laughing at these monster magazines or laughing at the *Playboys* that we had also accumulated. That's what our two pieces of reading material were: *Famous Monsters* and *Playboy* . . . until some big kids broke into the Haunted House when we weren't there and stole the *Famous Monsters* and *Playboys* and threatened to blackmail us by telling the principal that we had *Playboys* in our possession.

JOURNAL: *Was that the end of the club?*
GROENING: That was the end of that club. Also, by that time I had read, in *Time* or *Newsweek*, an interview with Forrest J. Ackerman that I had come across at random; they asked him about *Famous Monsters of Filmland* and he said, "Well, this magazine is made for little boys who are too old to play cowboys but are too young for girls." And right then the bubble was burst . . . all of a sudden, the limitations, the boundaries of that monster magazine were quite clear to me and I was no longer impressed with that kind of thing. In fact, that's my big problem with a lot of trash culture: I can see the boundaries in the audience for which it is intended and I feel like I'm not going to be surprised. For instance in so-called adventurous comics—you just know they're not going to go that far, that there are going to be boundaries, somewhere between PG and R, and I get bored with that.

JOURNAL: *That doesn't hold true for the undergrounds, though. I know you're a big fan of Crumb's.*
GROENING: Oh, definitely. Yeah, Crumb is great. A few years after the monster magazines, the whole hippie movement started and I first discovered that in *Ramparts* magazine. My father is a filmmaker who also runs his own advertising agency and as a result my family received just about every general-interest magazine in the country for free. So while I was growing up I read everything from *Ebony* to *Esquire*, and I read *Punch* and *New Yorker* from the time I was a kid. I was influenced by those cartoons from way back as well as the cartoon collections that were in my parents' library, which were the only things that interested me before I could read—these cartoons of people like Ronald Searle and a

guy named Rowland Emmett. They drew very complex cartoons for *Punch*.

My whole school career was a downhill slide from first grade on [*laughs*] through high school, as far as my attitudes toward school. I was a fierce believer in radical and progressive ideas about education, so I would carry around copies of *Teaching as a Subversive Activity*, hoping that a nifty girl would pop out of the crowd [*laughs*] and say "Yeah, I agree completely." Anyway, that didn't happen until I got to college, and went to a progressive school. I went to the Evergreen State College, in Olympia, Washington, which is a state-run school with no grades, no classes in the traditional sense, no football team, no fraternities, and once you graduate, no jobs . . . but that's true of a lot of colleges. But anyway, it was a blast being there, because the distinctions between education and socializing were a little blurred. A class—they didn't call them classes, they called them seminars or some other buzzword—they were fun. And if you didn't like being there, the way most kids don't like being in school, there was no reason to be there, because you didn't have to; as a result, there were some very motivated kids and I met a lot of extremely talented people.

I worked on the campus newspaper, called the *Copper Point Journal*, and that was where I met Lynda Barry, the cartoonist; another cartoonist who cartooned at the same time is Charles Burns, who has since gone on to cartoon for *RAW* and *Heavy Metal* and is extremely popular in Europe; Steve Willis, who is very prolific and popular in the mini-comics movement. We were all working on the same school newspaper at the same time. None of us, except perhaps Charles, had any plans for continuing professionally, and it was by fluke that both Lynda and I continued after we graduated from school. She moved to Seattle, and I moved to Los Angeles, and independently of each other we both cartooned for small newspapers in our respective cities and gradually built up from there.

JOURNAL: *You two are sort of the twin heads of the alternative cartooning world: It's always "Matt-Groening-and-Lynda-Barry."*
GROENING: Well, we decided a long time ago that we were going to do stuff together and not let our careers get in the way of our friendship, and we thought it was fun to mix our styles—not that rabbits and whatever those things that Lynda draws are [*laughs*]

are exactly compatible. Also, the same things made us laugh. Meeting Lynda in college was a real breakthrough for me, because it was a real treat to find someone who thought very much like I did. She was very influential.

Lynda and I both sort of developed a market that didn't exist much before we became cartoonists. Underground papers were dead and in their stead had risen in large cities around the country the so-called alternative newspapers, most of which are free entertainment guides with a smattering of coverage of local politics and things like that. Those papers were ready to give up a little space to new cartoonists, and we just happened to be coming along at the right time. So we were lucky. If we had tried to publish our own stuff and go through the comic book stores I think we would have been ignored completely. What we needed to do was to get in front of an audience that still considers cartoons kid's stuff and sneak up on them in the classifieds sections, which is just fine with me. I think most cartoons are strong when they are considered peripheral to whatever the main publication is. I think it's going to be a tough haul to make Americans go into a comic book store and walk out with a comic book under their arm. It's not quite as bad as pornography these days . . .

JOURNAL: *Tell me about your newspaper syndicate, Acme.*

GROENING: There's very little money in the alternative newsweekly situation—or at least so the editors tell me. But if you get enough of 'em you can pay the rent. So last year, with Lynda Barry and my fiancée Deborah Caplan, to whom I will no doubt be married by the time you read this interview, I formed Acme Features Syndicate. Acme syndicates Lynda Barry, me, and a Portland cartoonist named John Callahan. This has been a great thrill for us; I don't know how many newspapers Lynda's in, but I'm in sixty. I got picked up by the *San Francisco Examiner*, and by my hometown daily paper the *Oregonian*, and I'm amazed to this day that a daily newspaper will have the nerve to give me that kind of space with that title.

When I began *Life in Hell* in 1977 as a little Xeroxed comic book, my girl friend at the time said, "Why do you bother, there's no reason to do this, you're just wasting your time." But I felt compelled because of my lousy life in Los Angeles to do this little Xeroxed book, and it definitely was not done with commercial considerations in mind. [*laughs*] If I had to do it over, I probably wouldn't call it *Life in Hell*, and I think from time to time about changing the title. It doesn't seem to bother people anymore, although you can never tell what's going to stick in someone's craw. I get letters . . .

JOURNAL: *I assume there have been some tentative nibbles from syndicates.*

GROENING: I've been approached by daily comic syndicates off and on for the last few years. I love cartooning, I like to read good cartoons, but it's not the only thing there is in my life, and I certainly can't see me sweating over a drawing board every day [*laughs*] for the rest of my life writing something that is pasteurized enough to pass muster in the daily newspaper format. Newspapers don't give cartoonists enough space anymore, for one thing. But the real reason is that a daily strip would just eat up my time. I like working in different media, and I most strongly love to write. What I hope is that this weekly comic strip will prove lucrative enough that I can take it and finance some of the less commercial projects I have in mind. I tell you, having to draw one comic strip a week gives me plenty of time [*laughs*] at the moment to do other things.

JOURNAL: *Gee, and here I thought you spent all day every day doing a panel or two . . .*

GROENING: Well, I'm always working. For a long time, I felt guilty about random reading, but now I've convinced myself that it's research so I do quite a bit of reading and I fill up notebooks with ideas. For me, the hard part in the strip, believe it or not, is the drawing, although my drawing is as simple as you can get. I mean, I don't even fill in the black areas. It's still not quick enough for me. The ideas are there; I would much rather be writing than drawing. And as a matter of fact, that's what I appreciate more in comic strips that I do like: the writing. I love Robert Crumb's art, but I think he's really good as a writer. I like Lynda Barry as a writer. Gary Panter, another virtuoso artist, is also a terrific writer; his prose is fractured the way his images are, but he knows exactly what he's doing.

JOURNAL: *You were talking about writing projects.*

GROENING: Yes. This is another thing I'd really like to mention. One of the things I'm most excited about right now is a project which I call my Schoolkids' Notebooks project. A few years ago I used to write a weekly music column called "Sound Mix" for the *Los Angeles Reader*, and ostensibly it was supposed to be about music, but I got tired of writing about bands that everybody had already read about, and started to write about bands that had names I found amusing, like Grandpa Becomes a Fungus and Severed Head In A Bag. And it got to the point where I started making up names of bands. [*laughs*] Then I started reviewing my night out, and I didn't always make it to the night club, and sometimes didn't even bother *trying* to make it to the night club, and I was reviewing and writing about all sorts of wild stuff.

One of the things I wrote about was a walk that I took one night by a high school toward the end of the school year. I found a book report on the lawn, along with all sorts of bits of paper that were strewn all over the place by rambunctious teenagers happy to be free for the summer, and the book report was about the book *Cujo* by Stephen King. But the kid called it *Cojo*, and he obviously had not read the book, he had just seen the movie, and it was such a funny report that I started picking up other pieces of paper. I walked around the corner and there was a dumpster full of notebooks. I got a cardboard box and collected the notebooks and carted them home and ran the best stuff in my column for the next four weeks until my editor told me to knock it off if I knew what was good for me.

Anyway, I had so much more material than I could print in the column just from this little bit of stuff I picked up. The following year, this last June, long after my column at the *Reader* had ended and I had been fired by that newspaper, I went back to Los Angeles high schools and did the same thing on a much grander scale. (Actually, there's nothing grand about fishing around in dumpsters. I told all my friends that I had this project, that I was going to gather kids' notebooks. They said, "Oh, be sure to call me, I'll come help you out," but when the time actually came to go through this trash, everyone seemed to be busy.) So I was by myself in my little station wagon and I filled it up many times. I went to every high school I could find in Los Angeles and a number in the San Fernando Valley and I filled up my garage full of notebooks and I have been going through them.

I've gone through about half the material, and I have enough for a large book of kids' writings and the stuff is hilarious, scary, depressing, and astonishing, sometimes all at the same time. I've got everything from vocabulary lists where every word is used incorrectly in a sentence to love letters, notes passed in class, secret diaries, written threats to other students, lots of book reports that are obviously based on a movie watching experience. And some of the stuff's just wonderful. If I can publish it, the project will reach fruition, but right now I'm doing it for myself. I figure that with a few changed names and a few changed details I'll be able to get this out. But it is wild.

Somebody said, "Oh, this is sort of the '80s version of Art Linkletter's *Kids Write the Darnedest Things*" and it is, but if you were going to give it an equivalent title, it would be *Kids Write the Most Motherfuckinest Shit You've Ever Seen* [*laughs*] because what kids are writing about these days you or I either didn't know or wouldn't have admitted knowing when we were in high school. There's an incredible amount of profanity, confessions of drug abuse, lots of sexual dalliances, and then the more traditional high school stuff we're all familiar with.

But the stuff is just amazing, and the teacher's comments are equally funny. One of my favorite ones is the kid who had to write an essay on "The Person I'd Most Like to Meet in History" and the kid wrote "The person I would like to meet in History is this girl. She sits in row C . . ." and he goes on and on about this girl. The teacher's comment at the bottom is "This person should have died before you were born." Now if the kid doesn't get the point of the essay title, the kid's *not* going to get the comment either. [*laughs*]

Another girl, who through other papers I realized was sixteen years old, unmarried, living at home with a new baby and being knocked about by her parents, wrote in an essay, "Sometimes teachers don't understand that maybe students like me have problems that make it difficult to do our best school work, such as perhaps maybe we have a baby, no boyfriend, and we have a dad who knocks us around, and maybe we don't have any money, and . . ." etc. The teacher's comment is, "Too many run-on sentences. D minus." True, there were a lot of run-on sentences, but I don't think that was perhaps the most perceptive response to the essay.

One of the great things is that a number of high schools required the kids to keep journals for the entire year, usually with specific topics for the day, so you get a look at a kid's life. It's amazing stuff. That's another part of my interest in school satisfied. I'm fascinated by the idea of the words of people who are without a forum and generally remain unheard. These kids definitely have not memorized their *Elements of Style* by Strunk and White, but although they fail by arbitrary standards of correct English usage in this country, they are sometimes eloquent in their limited way.

I'm sorry not to be more energetic. I just got back from a book tour.

JOURNAL: *That's right. You and art spiegelman share a publisher.*
GROENING: Right, Pantheon Books. As a matter of fact, art spiegelman introduced my cartoons to people at Pantheon and they thought they were interesting, so I'm indebted to him. We share the same birthday, by the way—not the same year, though. Art was in town, so we compared notes on how we were being treated by the publishing company. We're both being treated fine. I've been all over the country now, signing books and doing obscure little radio shows. It's been real fun to get a whirlwind tour of the United States, looking at it from the windows of airplanes and taxis and from windows of bookstores, which is basically how I'm seeing the sights.

But I think that my books *Love Is Hell* and *Work Is Hell* have been pretty successful for Pantheon, as has art spiegelman's book *Maus.* I hope they'll open the door for other weird cartoon books. I think that's a step in the right direction toward getting more of the kind of cartoonists I want to see into print. Comic book stores are still unfortunately off limits to a lot of adult Americans who would not hesitate to pick up a book if it's endorsed by being on the counter of a book store.

JOURNAL: *You said earlier that if you'd gone through the direct-sales/comics shop market, you'd probably have failed. What kind of relationship do you have with that market at this point? I know you frequent the San Diego Comics convention . . .*
GROENING: That's because I just like to look at old comics and this gives me an excuse.

JOURNAL: *Do a lot of kids walk up to you and say "What do you draw?" and then get awfully confused when you show them?*
GROENING: Yeah. I did a book-signing at Golden Apple Comics up on Melrose last year for their grand opening, and I was seated between the Hernandez Brothers, Jaime and Gilbert. These kids came up with their little blank notebooks full of super-hero drawings and assumed I was the third Hernandez brother. I would draw Bongo in their books [*laughs*] and they would stare at me with this look of disbelief and disgust that I had ruined their books. A lot of them thought it was some sort of really cruel joke. [*laughs*]

But *someday* they'll realize that I'm not a cartoonist. I'm a doodle-god.

BILL WATTERSON

IF THE STATE OF MOST COMIC BOOKS IS BAD, THE STATE OF MOST NEWSPAPER strips is hardly any better. The great strip cartoonists of the '60s and early '70s, like Charles Schulz and Johnny Hart, are well past their prime. The funny pages are filled with dead-headed, one-joke strips with incompetent artwork. There are only a handful of cartoonists maintaining what used to be a national treasure, the most recent being Bill Watterson. Faced with the limitation of postage-stamp sized panels, he took the expedient of drawing postage-stamp sized people. *Calvin and Hobbes* is shaping up to be one of the great little kid strips. Calvin is neither a midget Groucho Marx nor an innocent font of wee folks wisdom; he's just naturally funny, the way a real child can be. Hobbes, his imaginary playmate, oddly enough represents realism and gives him tantalizing hints of the world he's growing up into. The artwork is a constant delight.

This interview was conducted by Andrew Christie.

JOURNAL: *Let's start with the basics: when, where, why, and how?*
BILL WATTERSON: Well, I don't know how far back you want to go; I've been interested in cartooning all my life. I read the comics as a kid, and I did cartoons for high school publications—the newspaper and yearbook and so on. In college, I got interested in

Comic strips should be treated as a serious art form, argues Watterson.

political cartooning and did political cartoons every week for four years at Kenyon College in Gambier, Ohio, and majored in political science there.

JOURNAL: *All in Ohio?*
WATTERSON: Yes. I grew up in Chagrin Falls, Ohio.

JOURNAL: *What kind of time frame are we talking about?*
WATTERSON: I was born in 1958; we moved to Chagrin when I was six, so from the first grade on, really. My whole childhood was in Chagrin Falls. Right after I graduated from Kenyon, I was offered a job at the *Cincinnati Post* as their editorial cartoonist in a trial six-month arrangement. The agreement was that they could fire me or I could quit with no questions asked if things didn't work out during the first few months. Sure enough, things didn't work out, and they fired me, no questions asked.

JOURNAL: *What was the problem?*
WATTERSON: To this day, I'm not completely sure. My guess is that the editor wanted his own Jeff MacNelly [a Pulitzer winner at twenty-four], and I didn't live up to his expectations. My Cincinnati days were pretty Kafkaesque. I had lived there all of two weeks, and the editor insisted that most of my work be about local, as opposed to national, issues. Cincinnati has a weird, three-party, city manager-government, and by the time I figured it out, I was standing in the unemployment lines. I didn't hit the ground running. Cincinnati at that time was also beginning to realize it had major cartooning talent in Jim Borgman, at the city's other paper, and I didn't benefit from the comparison.

JOURNAL: *I'm not familiar . . .*
WATTERSON: He's syndicated through King Features, and had been for a couple years by the time I arrived in Cincinnati. This is an odd story. Borgman graduated from Kenyon College the year before I went there, and it was his example that inspired me to pursue political cartooning. He had drawn cartoons at Kenyon, and landed his job at the *Cincinnati Enquirer* right after graduation. His footsteps seemed like good ones to follow, so I cultivated an interest in politics, and Borgman helped me a lot in learning how to construct an editorial cartoon. Neither of us dreamed I'd end up in the same town on the opposite paper. I don't know to what extent the comparison played a role in my editor's not liking my work, but I was very intimidated by working on a major city paper and I didn't feel free to experiment, really, or to travel down my own path. I very early caught on that the editor had something specific in mind that he was looking for, and I tried to accommodate him in order to get published. His idea was that he was going to publish only my very best work so that I wouldn't embarrass the newspaper while I learned the ropes. As sound as that idea may be from the management standpoint, it was disastrous for me because I was only getting a couple cartoons a week printed. I would turn out rough idea after rough idea, and he would veto eighty percent of them. As a result, I lost all my self-confidence, and his intervention was really unhealthy, I think, as far as letting me experiment, and make mistakes, and become a stronger cartoonist for it. Obviously, if he wanted a more experienced cartoonist, he shouldn't have hired a kid just out of college. I pretty much prostituted myself for six months but I couldn't please him, so he sent me packing.

JOURNAL: *Well, it was mercifully brief, then.*

WATTERSON: Yeah, in a way it was; and actually, I think the experience—now, in hindsight—was probably a good thing. It forced me to consider how interested I was in political cartooning. After I was fired, I applied to other papers but political cartooning, like all cartooning, is a very tough field to break into. Newspapers are very reluctant to hire their own cartoonists when they can get Oliphant or MacNelly through syndication for a twentieth of the price.

So I wasn't having any luck getting accepted anyway, and it forced me to reexamine what it is I really wanted to do. In my experience in political cartooning, I was never one of those people who reads the headlines and foams at the mouth with a rabid opinion that I've just got to get down on paper. I'm interested in the issues but . . . I don't know . . . I guess I just don't have the killer instinct that I think makes a great political cartoonist. I'd always enjoyed the comics more, and felt that as long as I was unemployed it would be a good chance to pursue that and see what response I could get from a syndicate, as I didn't have anything to lose at that point. So I drew up a comic strip—this was in 1980—and sent it off and got rejected. I continued that for five years with different comic strip examples 'til finally *Calvin and Hobbes* came together. But it's been a long road.

JOURNAL: *Were you submitting different strips to different syndicates, or did you go after one syndicate?*

WATTERSON: I didn't know a lot then—and don't know a lot now—as to what the best way to do this is, but my procedure was I would draw up the submission—a month's worth of strips, made to look as professional as I could, and send copies to the five major syndicates, and then just sit around and wait for their rejection letters. I would then try to see if I could second-guess them or imagine what they were looking for that I could put in my next submission and gradually get a more marketable comic strip. In hindsight, as I say, I'm not convinced that that's the best way to go about it. Trying to please the syndicates was pretty much the same as what I had ended up doing at the *Cincinnati Post*, and I don't think that's the way to draw your best material. You should stick to what you're interested in and what you feel comfortable with, what you enjoy, what you find funny—that's the humor that will be the strongest, and that will transmit itself. Rather than trying to find out what the latest trend is, you should draw what is personally interesting.

JOURNAL: *So after five years you just quit doing what you'd been doing and did what you wanted to do?*

WATTERSON: It was a slow process, and actually what happened is another odd coincidence. One of the strips I'd sent had Calvin and Hobbes as minor characters. Calvin was the little brother of the strip's main character, and Hobbes was like he is now, a stuffed tiger that came to life in Calvin's imagination. One of the syndicates suggested that these two characters were the strongest and why didn't I develop a strip around them? I had thought they were the funniest characters myself, but I was unsure as to whether they could hold their own strip. I was afraid that maybe the key to their wackiness was the contrast between them and the more normal characters in the rest of the strip. I wasn't sure Calvin and Hobbes would be able to maintain that intensity on their own. But I tried it, and almost immediately it clicked in my mind; it became much easier to write material. Their personalities expanded easily, and that takes a good seventy-five percent of the work out of it. If you have the personalities down, you understand them and identify with them; you can stick them in any situation and have a pretty good idea of how they're going to respond. Then it's just a matter of sanding and polishing up the jokes. But if you've got more ambiguous characters or stock stereotypes, the plastic comes through and they don't work as well. These two characters clicked for me almost immediately, and I feel very comfortable working with them.

That syndicate, oddly enough, declined my strip, so I started sending it around. Universal expressed an interest in it and wanted to see more work, so I drew another month's worth of art, sent that to them, and they decided to take it.

JOURNAL: *That's rather ironic: The syndicate that suggested you bring out those two characters rejected the strip?*

WATTERSON: Yeah.

JOURNAL: *Who was this?*

WATTERSON: Well, if you want to rub their noses in it, it was United Features. I was sort of mystified when they rejected the strip. They had given me a development contract, which meant I was to work exclusively with them and rather than completing everything on my own and turning it in to them and having it rejected or accepted, I was working much more directly with the syndicate, turning in smaller batches much more frequently, and getting comments on them. The idea was that they would help me develop the strip and then, assuming that they liked it, it would flow into a normal contract for syndication. I'm not sure exactly what happened; I gather that the sales staff didn't have much enthusiasm for it, I don't know—but apparently they couldn't convince enough people there in high places.

JOURNAL: *Is there a Calvin?*
WATTERSON: A real one? No.

JOURNAL: *Is he in some way autobiographical?*
WATTERSON: Not really. Hobbes might be a little closer to me in terms of personality, with Calvin being more energetic, brash, always looking for life on the edge. He lives entirely in the present, and whatever he can do to make that moment more exciting he'll just let fly . . . and I'm really not like that at all.

JOURNAL: *You manage a lot of complex shifts between fantasy and reality; between Hobbes as a stuffed tiger and a real-life playmate. He's frequently involved in what is apparently the real world, doing real things together with Calvin that he couldn't possibly be doing. Do you think that kind of thing out in advance or does it just come to you when the gag calls for it?*
WATTERSON: Could you name something specifically? I'm not sure I follow.

JOURNAL: *Well, when they're driving down the mountain in their wagon and flying all over the place. You think, after reading the first few strips, that you've got the idea; that this is a stuffed tiger and when he and Calvin are alone he becomes real—to Calvin—but then, obviously, when they're doing things like that in the real world, he has to be more than fantasy.*
WATTERSON: Yeah, it's a strange metamorphosis. I hate to subject it to too much analysis, but one thing I have fun with is the rarity of things being shown from an adult's perspective. When Hobbes is a stuffed toy in one panel and alive in the next, I'm juxtaposing the "grown-up" version of reality with Calvin's version, and inviting the reader to decide which is truer. Most of the time, the strip is drawn simply from Calvin's perspective, and Hobbes is as real as anyone. So when Calvin is careening down the hillside, I don't feel compelled to insert reminders that Hobbes is a stuffed toy. I try to get the reader completely swept up into Calvin's world by ignoring

adult perspective. Hobbes, therefore, isn't just a cute gimmick. I'm not making the strip revolve around his transformation. The viewpoint of the strip fluctuates, and this allows Hobbes to be a "real" character.

JOURNAL: *It has a lunatic internal consistency.*
WATTERSON: Yeah, I guess that's the best way of putting it.

JOURNAL: *Are you familiar with* Krazy Kat?
WATTERSON: Yes! I love it; I wish I thought that that kind of work were possible today.

JOURNAL: *Well, it sounds like it is. George Herriman didn't need to justify his reality, either.*
WATTERSON: Yeah, I agree on that point. I mean, the completeness of the art, the bizarre dialect, the constantly changing backgrounds . . . In the first place, I don't know who would put enough energy into their work anymore to do something like that; secondly, and probably more importantly, comic strips are being printed at such a ridiculous size that elimination of dialogue and linework is almost a necessity and you just can't get that kind of depth. I think of *Pogo*, another strip that had tremendous dialogue and fantastic backgrounds . . . Those strips were just complete worlds that the reader would be sucked into. For a few moments a day we could live in the Okeefenokee swamps or in Coconino County; the whole thing was entirely there. The dialogue was part of it, the backgrounds were part of it, the characters were offbeat . . . and you need a little space and time to develop that sort of thing. I know for a fact that nobody's doing it now and I don't know that anybody will do it. Garry Trudeau is the only cartoonist with the clout to get his strip published large enough to accommodate extended dialogue. It's a shame.

JOURNAL: *Well, let's talk about your peers for a bit.*
WATTERSON: You're gonna get me in trouble.

JOURNAL: *No, no; you can say anything you want.*
WATTERSON: Yeah, that's what's going to get me into trouble.

JOURNAL: *What about Gary Larson?*
WATTERSON: I really like the lunacy of *The Far Side*. It's a one-panel strip so it's a slightly different animal than a four-panel strip like mine. I don't really compare one-panel strips to four-panel

strips because there are different opportunities with each. Larson's working with one picture and a handful of words, and given that, I think he's one of the most inventive guys in comics. The four-panel strip has more potential for storyline and character involvement than just a single panel. But I do enjoy his stuff a lot.

JOURNAL: *What about Jim Davis?*
WATTERSON: Uh . . . *Garfield* is . . . [*long pause*] . . . consistent.

JOURNAL: *Ooo-kay . . .*
WATTERSON: *U.S. Acres* I think is an abomination.

JOURNAL: *Never seen it.*
WATTERSON: Lucky you. Jim Davis has his factory in Indiana cranking out this strip about a pig on a farm. I find it an insult to the intelligence, though it's very successful.

JOURNAL: *Most insults to the intelligence are. Well, how about the old school, are they holding up their end at all? Johnny Hart, Charles Schulz . . . ?*
WATTERSON: That's an interesting question. I have a tremendous amount of respect for *Peanuts*. Every now and then I hear that *Peanuts* isn't as funny as it was or it's gotten old or something like that. I think what's really happened is that Schulz, in *Peanuts*, changed the entire face of comics strips, and everybody has now caught up to him. I don't think he's five years ahead of everybody else like he used to be, so that's taken some of the edge off it. I think it's still a wonderful strip just in terms of solid construction, character development, the fantasy element . . . Things that we now take for granted—reading the thoughts of an animal for example—there's not a cartoonist who's done anything since 1960 who doesn't owe Schulz a tremendous debt.

Johnny Hart; I admire the simplicity, the way he's gotten that strip down to the bare essentials; there's nothing at all extraneous in the drawing, and the humor is very spartan. It doesn't grab me, though, because I look for real involvement with characters, and the characters in *B.C.* are pretty much interchangeable; they're props for the humor. I think his style of humor is mostly in the words, not in the characters. I look to strips like *Peanuts*, where you're really involved with the characters, you feel that you know them. I guess that's why I don't enjoy *B.C.* quite as much. It's better than many, though.

JOURNAL: *Do you see yourself doing this forever?*
WATTERSON: I'd like to, yeah, if the market will bear it.

JOURNAL: Calvin and Hobbes, *exclusively?*
WATTERSON: Yeah, I'm really enjoying the work. I feel that the characters have a lot of potential. I'd like to have the opportunity to draw this strip for years and see where it goes. It's sort of a scary thing now to imagine; these cartoonists who've been drawing a strip for twenty years. I can't imagine coming up with that much material. If I just take it day by day, though, it's a lot of fun, and I do think I have a long way to go before I've exhausted the possibilities.

JOURNAL: *Do you think you'll ever need a ghost?*
WATTERSON: No, that's against what I believe about comic strips. In fact, I'd go even further and say I don't think a strip should ever be continued after the death or retirement of a cartoonist.

JOURNAL: *Well, you know, a lot of the very good ones used assistants.*
WATTERSON: Yeah, *Pogo* did. Schulz has a good comment on that: "It's like Arnold Palmer having someone to hit his chip shots." I spent five years trying to get this stupid job, and now that I have it, I'm not going to hire it out to somebody else. The whole pleasure for me is having the opportunity to do a comic strip for a living, and now that I've finally got that I'm not going to give it away. It also gives me complete creative control. Any time somebody else has their hand in the ink it's changing the product, and I enjoy the responsibility for this product. I'm willing to take the blame if the strip goes down the drain, and I want the credit if it succeeds. So long as it has my name on it, I want it to be mine. I don't know, if you don't have that kind of investment in it ... I guess that's the difference between looking at it as an art and looking at it as a job. I'm not interested in setting up an assembly line to produce this thing more efficiently. There are certainly people who could letter the strip better than I do; I don't enjoy lettering very much, but that's the way I write and that belongs in the strip because the strip is a reflection of me. If cartoonists would look at this more as an art than as a part-time job or a get-rich-quick scheme, I think comics overall would be better. I think there's a tremendous potential to be tapped.

WOMEN IN COMICS: A PANEL

THE COMICS INDUSTRY HAS ALWAYS BEEN A BIT LIKE TUBBY'S BOY'S CLUB IN the old *Little Lulu* comics: except under extraordinary circumstances, no girls allowed. For the most part women have gravitated more toward magazine cartooning and newspaper strips. It's most likely due to a combination of the locker room atmosphere of most comics studios, the male-oriented fantasies comic books trade in, and simple discrimination. The following discussion, recorded at a National Cartoonists Society convention, features Shary Flenniken, a regular contributor for the last ten years to *National Lampoon*; Nicole Hollander, creator of the syndicated strip *Sylvia*; M.G. Lord, political cartoonist for *Newsday*; Wendy Pini, whose fantasy comic *Elfquest* helped create the independent comics movement; Trina Robbins, noted underground (and now mainstream) cartoonist and co-author with Cat Yronwode of *Women and the Comics*; Avis Rosenberg, curator of the traveling feminist cartoon exhibit *Pork Roast*; and Mary Wilshire, who has drawn for *Heavy Metal* and Marvel comics. It is aimed not so much at making up for the absence of women in this book as explaining it.

What do you all have to say about alternative publishing? What are the alternatives?
TRINA ROBBINS: Alternative publishing is exactly that—the alternative. I don't think I could exist without alternate publishing. I don't draw super-heroes; there goes a lot of money immediately. I don't want to do dope, sex and violence like they do in the underground anymore. All that's left is the alternative. The alternative has

been going on in Europe for a long time: good comics for grown-ups. That's just starting to happen here. It's the wave of the future; I think it's where the exciting work is going to be done. I hope that the few guys who are starting to do alternative publishing don't get run over by taxis, because I don't know what I would do without the alternative.

NICOLE HOLLANDER: I recently had what seemed like a forever experience with syndication, a way that is not good for most of us. It forces our work to fall into a certain kind of blank category. The only way we can handle it is to syndicate ourselves. Where are we going to do it? We can't do it in the major newspapers, so there has got to be the small press, a good avenue for all of us.

WENDY PINI: The first and most obvious advantage to alternative publishing is that you are under no censorship but your own. Alternative publishing, particularly if you are a self-publisher as my husband Richard and I are, enables you to say your own thoughts. If you have a point to make, you don't have anyone telling you that subject is taboo. You may have a chance to make that point in your own way. I don't believe a market would have existed for my personal art style unless my husband and I created a market for it. It's been a tremendous learning experience, and we're grateful it's been as well-received as it has, but I think that's just an example that this country is now ready for new kinds of ideas and styles. It's ready for women to be singing their songs now like never before.

MARY WILSHIRE: I would definitely go along with the opinion that the censorship is an obstacle to being faithful to a personal voice. For me, that's an obstacle. Although in the past it's been tempting to criticize the people with publications who are responsible for deciding whether my material goes, I blame it on them that they don't use my work. There are a lot of women like me who haven't realized how difficult it is to stick with something, even though people may not give you the support you need. It's important for myself to really have faith in that voice. I believe very strongly in the politics of human relationships. Sometimes that is not always interesting enough, but I like to tell stories about people. I like to put the emphasis on the realness of the characters that I draw, rather than creating boffoyaks gags. I don't mean to dismiss that, because it's a difficult thing to cultivate; I have great admiration for the people who do it. It's important for men and women to create their own way of doing it. In times of economic depression, it's important for people to look at things that entertain them and remind them that they are human, especially in these times when it is so easy to dismiss our rights to think and feel as individuals.

SHARY FLENNIKEN: I published a couple of books myself [*Drought Chic* and *Shary Flenniken's Sketchbook*] and distributed them through underground distributors. I did well in that I didn't lose money on the deal, and I have two nice little things to put in my hand. I did that with a lot of help from my boyfriend. It's amazing how much self-publishing is being done today. I found it really difficult. I don't know whether or not I would try that again. Underground comics, unless they're vastly successful, can't support the artist. This has slumped off and rationalized with a lot of idealism and talk about freedom. I think real freedom is being able to support yourself.

AVIS ROSENBERG: I'm in a different position from everyone else here, but I certainly see this freedom in the alternative press and self-publishing. However, one cannot be idealistic about self-publishing unless one is prepared also to do the follow-up—distribution.

M.G. LORD: As the editorial voice of the tenth largest newspaper in North America, I am not exactly intimately familiar with alternative publishing. The observation that part of freedom is the rent, the car, the house in the country, the valuable beachfront property is really valid. I've never drawn anything that I felt compromised me. I don't necessarily think you have to be a collaborationist to make a good living. Fortunately, I was successful in convincing *Newsday*, Universal Press Syndicate, and, most recently, Little, Brown of that state of affairs. I do have to put up with a certain amount of compromise; I hesitate to say censorship. The trade-off is cash and exposure, and I think that inevitably pays off in the end. [*applause*]

You sign your name M.G. Lord. Is that because you're trying to hide the fact that you're a woman?

M.G. LORD: No. It's just that my name is Mary Grace Lord. [*laughter*] It's not that I don't want to be mistaken for a woman. I don't want to be mistaken for an agent of the Vatican. [*laughter*]

WENDY PINI: Another advantage to alternative publishing is that women who are in it can bring other women into it. Trina Robbins is, of course, famous for her *Wimmen's Comix*.

TRINA ROBBINS: It's not my *Wimmen's Comix*. There is a group of us who work on it.

WENDY PINI: That's true, but certainly you were like the founding—

TRINA ROBBINS: I was one of the founders.

WENDY PINI: Oh, one of the founders? I have a new assistant myself who has been working for me for a few months—Jane Fancher, right over there. Say "hi," Jane. Women have to learn to work together, as well as work with men. It's difficult to work with men. It's difficult to work with other women, also. There really isn't that much difference between men and women, in terms of prejudices, fears, insecurities, in terms of everything that makes us human. This is my perception. I have found as much trouble communicating with my "sisters" as well as my brothers and as much reception from my sisters as well as my brothers. Women now coming into the alternative press are presenting role models to other younger ones who would like to express themselves and perhaps feel intimidated by mainstream companies and corporations.

What do you mean by syndicating yourself? What do you have to do to get syndicated?

M.G. LORD: I was approached by a syndicate. Syndication isn't all that viable. We're in the middle of a depression right now. Papers are folding right and left. Editorial cartoons which go out to a huge number of newspapers may be a thing of the past soon. As more cities have one newspaper, as opposed to two competing features that will draw readers. Syndication seems headed for obsolescence—on a fast train.

NICOLE HOLLANDER: If you are not well known, the syndicate can set its own terms, and they are often quite unbelievable. They sign you to a long-term contract. They don't guarantee you any money. You have to pay part of the expenses. They own your character. You can do *nothing* with that character without their permission. They take fifty percent of everything that you make in every way with that character. My strip was very different from any other strips in the paper. When it didn't sell immediately, there certainly was a lack of enthusiasm after that, and so it was stopped, and the attempt was no longer made. I feel I can do better, and even if I can't do better, even being on my own and only being in the same amount of papers, I will still be making more money, because I won't be sharing it. The comic pages in general are extremely bland. I don't know what it will take to change those pages.

In searching for a self-image as a cartoonist, is there a lack of role models for women?

M.G. LORD: The first short piece in my book addresses precisely that problem—the lack of role models. When I sent my portfolio to a syndicate, they acted as if it had been mailed in by a unicorn. Even now I feel some kind of solidarity because I'm not selling especially well. Everything else in my life is going wonderfully smooth except for the syndication. It's not really a women's issue, but it is an alternative press issue. When *Newsday* would reject a cartoon, I thought, "I still have an outlet. I will send it to my client papers." Then the client papers started to trickle down because of the *alleged* tasteless cartoons I was sending them. It's a frustrating kind of arrangement. For a political cartoonist, I don't feel my work is especially feminist, and it does deal with larger national and inter-national political issues. The only real difference between, say, me and Jeff MacNelly is that I'm not a fascist, and I have two X chromo-somes. [*laughter*]

SHARY FLENNIKEN: I didn't discover I was a woman until I was thirteen years old. [*laughter*] I lived a large part of my life thinking that men didn't draw, that they didn't have the delicate hands and that they didn't sit inside and draw like the women, girls, I knew. It was a real rude shock, and I haven't gotten over it. [*laughter*]

MARY WHILSHIRE: It's so difficult for me to get my type of work out there. I don't do jokes *per se*. I like to draw real people, their real expressions, the way they hold their bodies, the way they relate to each other. I think that's funny. I think that's worthwhile, but that is not marketable. That's been proven to me over and over again. It's so frustrating that I wound up jumping around a lot, so I had this schizophrenic portfolio. The self-image I have is from these women here, especially Trina and Shary. I'm very grateful for that, and I'm still overwhelmed from that slide show we just saw, be-cause it proves to me there are a lot of other women who feel the same way I do. I'm still working on that self-image; it's a real challenge for me.

WENDY PINI: My story is the classic example of the kid who was the odd person out in school. I never really fit in with any of the cliques or the popular kids, but all through my early years the one thing no one could ever get on my case for was my artwork. I was always a darn good artist. I worshipped cartooning, especially animated cartooning, and always tried to get a lot of flow, move-ment and expression into my drawings, and it came across very well. When I began my professional career, I illustrated for science fiction conventions. It was only in 1977 when I actually became a comics artist. Cartooning has always been in my blood. I love it. It is one of the shortest, swiftest, clearest ways of making a point. People lack communication with each other nowadays; cartooning is absolutely vital as a means of communication. It's an international language that crosses all barriers; a picture is something everyone can understand. My self-image as a cartoonist began when I was a very little girl and never did I *not* identify with cartooning.

NICOLE HOLLANDER: I never thought about being a cartoonist; I thought about being an artist. I went to school and studied to be a fine artist, to be a painter. Somewhere along the line, I became a graphic designer and illustrator. I wanted to illustrate textbooks, and they kept getting rejected. I couldn't understand why and they said it was too satirical and nasty. [*laughter*] I redesigned a magazine called *The Spokesman*, a feminist political newsletter, and I started doing illustrations to go with the articles. In the illustrations the figures began to talk to each other, and one day I did a cartoon strip. I can't remember the day or why I did it, but cartooning for me is the first time that my drawing and what I wanted to say and my observations about life and also being funny have come together.

Is there anything about your work that is distinctly female or different from that of men in your field?

TRINA ROBBINS: In researching my book [*Women and the Comics,* co-authored with Cat Yronwode] I've been developing all sorts of theories. I call it the Draws Like a Boy/Draws Like a Girl Theory. This used to be a putdown about certain artists: "Oh! She draws like a girl!" There are people who draw like women and people who draw like men. Not everyone. As a classic example of Draws Like a Boy, I would use Jack Kirby. [*laughter*] As a classic example of Draws Like a Girl, I would use Dale Messick, [*Dale Messick changed her name from Dalia to Dale because of male art editor prejudices against women cartoonists.*] These are just two people who have taken their particular gender styles to the end. Dale Messick is very romantic, very fussy, lots of little ruffles. Kirby is square, everything is solid and squared out—including his women. [*laughter*] This is not to say that anything is wrong with either Dale Messick or Jack Kirby. They have certain styles. I have finally realized after many years of fighting it, because I thought it was a negative quality that I do draw like a girl. Most women draw like girls, and the problem is that it has been looked down on, that it has been out of style. The super-hero problem is why you don't have women drawing super-heroes. Because the style has been very influenced by Jack Kirby, the style has been to draw like a boy. There hasn't been room in the major comics for people who draw like a girl. Again, we have the alternative: Thank God, it's okay to do elves and draw like a girl. [*laughter*] I've forgotten the question now, but this is my theory, anyway. [*laughter*]

NICOLE HOLLANDER: When I started looking at comics, there were few women. If you count the characters, there are few women. I wanted to make a strip where the woman was the important character, where the woman finally got the last word, and where she was independent, self-possessed, heart-of-gold, and also where the interactions were not on a very physical level. You've hardly seen Sylvia stand up, let alone do cartwheels. [*laughter*] She is often sitting across a table from another woman. I wanted to show women interacting with one another, and the kind of conversations that take place with women, and with women's concerns. I have gotten into trouble with the syndicates over panty-liners. [*laughter*] We had a fight where I had a cartoon that mentioned hemorrhoids, and one that mentioned panty-liners. I compromised on hemorrhoids and left in panty-liners. [*laughter*]

WENDY PINI: In women's cartooning, particularly women's comic cartooning, they tend to be more oriented toward facial expressions and body language than perhaps the male artists are— because women communicate more through facial expressions and body language than men do. It's part of our means of getting by. As to Trina's remark about me drawing like a girl: naturally, doing a comic book about elves would have enabled me to do some very fey artwork with curlicues and the traditional elements. That's one thing we wanted to get away from in *Elfquest*. We have no dragons, no unicorns and no flittery, chirpy women in long gowns. We have equality of the sexes. The artwork is very straightforward, not very fussy at all. My artwork is somewhere in the middle in terms of either drawing like a girl or a boy.

TRINA ROBBINS: Wendy, you are misinterpreting what I meant. I'm not too fussy either. And I draw like, and Mary Wilshire draws like, a girl. [*laughter*]

WENDY PINI: Okay.

MARY WILSHIRE: I like to make the emphasis on facial expressions and the body language rather than the jokes. I was even discussing it with a very fine cartoonist who contributes to *The New Yorker*, Bob Mankoff, who was saying, "Women are more interested in the substance of relationships and little idiosyncrasies." I don't want to make any generalizations about men not doing this, because I don't think that's true. There are fantastic men cartoonists who have been that role model for me in a lot of ways.

SHARY FLENNIKEN: I work out a lot of my kind of current fixations and leftover vexations in my work, and it's by nature female— because I am. Sometimes my work is grossly misunderstood. I tried to talk about rape in one strip, and I got a fan letter from a Nazi in Detroit. [*laughter*]

AVIS ROSENBERG: I spend a lot of time working with women. I feel totally comfortable doing so, and I did not working with men.

Many women object to men showing women in sexual situations and consider it exploitative. Why is that different from women drawing themselves in sexual situations?

TRINA ROBBINS: We're not talking about "rape and rescue" here. We are not exploiting ourselves. We're talking about what's in our heads, our hearts and in our bodies—what other women understand. Maybe it will show men that we are into something besides "rape and rescue." We are trying to show that we are people, that this is me, all parts of me, from work, from creativity, from sexuality, everything. This is me—a complete person.

DAVID BOSWELL

DAVID BOSWELL IS STILL ONE OF THE WELL-KEPT SECRETS OF THE COMICS; OUT-side of Canada his comics can only be found in comic shops. His most popular character, *Reid Fleming—World's Toughest Milkman,* is the embodiment of male aggression, and his war on anything that irritates him has the look and feel of classic silent comedy.

This interview was conducted by Joe Sacco.

"I sometimes feel a bit of embarrassment when I'm thinking about what I'm doing for a living," admits David Boswell, creator of *Reid Fleming—World's Toughest Milkman*, "because as one who doesn't read comics, my sympathies are with other people who don't read comics."

You get the impression that Boswell, whose main influences have come from outside the comics medium, would rather talk about cinema, his "first love," or classical music, which he says he might have pursued if he had to do it all over again. In fact, he told me, "I probably know less about comics and cartoonists than anybody you know, including your grandmother."

While this might not be entirely true, Boswell illustrates his professed ignorance by relating a story about a party several years

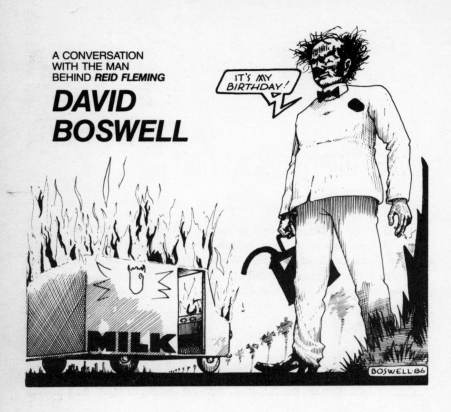

A CONVERSATION
WITH THE MAN
BEHIND *REID FLEMING*

DAVID
BOSWELL

IT'S MY BIRTHDAY!

ago at which he was accused of "basically ripping off" Robert
Crumb's hatching style. At the time, Boswell didn't know who Robert Crumb was, and almost got into a fight trying to make one fellow
believe him.

Boswell, who makes his home in Vancouver, B.C., with his wife,
Kathi, and three children, simply doesn't have the time or inclina-
tion to keep up on the comics world (though he does enjoy Bob
Burden's *Flaming Carrot* and the work of Harvey Pekar, Drew Friedman, and M. K. Brown). "I find when the day's over and I've finished

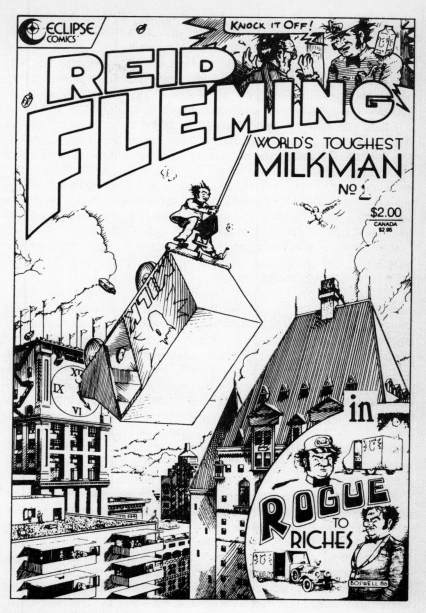

my drawing, I'm not really interested in looking at more drawings no matter how good they are. I just want to have a real change."

Not that cartooning is somehow incidental to Boswell, whose hot-tempered, all but out-of-control Reid Fleming character has the biggest chip on his shoulder of any comics character around. In fact, Boswell would be among the first to point out—and demonstrate—that "you can do absolutely anything in a comic."

But it did take time for Boswell to settle on cartooning as his artistic niche. As a young boy he was "never much into cartooning, per se. I always drew and sketched around in the way ten- and twelve-year-old boys do when they become aware they can make a commentary on cafeteria food by showing people throwing up—that level of wit." Boswell also recalls one summer he spent when he was thirteen copying *Sad Sack* comics. "I really liked that," he says. "Then I forgot about cartooning for years."

And he didn't shed tears when his collection of *Superman* comics simply disappeared, circa 1965. "I didn't really regret it," he says. "It suddenly became very boring to me."

What had begun to interest Boswell in the uninspiring surroundings of his hometown, London, Ontario—the "archetypal Canadian city . . . It's always 1959 there"—was movies, particularly the old silents. "It was the way they looked," Boswell says. "I'll never forget that moment when I became aware of tonality as an ingredient in artistic creations." In comparing a movie still from the 1931 *Dracula* starring Bela Lugosi with one from the Christopher Lee remake in 1958, Boswell noted "the more recent one just looked like a photograph of actors with make-up on—too much lighting and too crisp. And I immediately had a preference for the older one. I began to seek out movies and photos of that vintage, and, as I explored further and further, I found they tended to do things a little more thoroughly and a little more artistically back then."

After devouring the early horror movies, Boswell drenched himself in the comedies of the same period. "I became a Marx Brothers and W. C. Fields fan with a capital F," he says. "I'd go through library books and search the index to find Marx, Marx, Marx, Fields, Fields, Fields."

Inevitably, Boswell began experimenting with his own home-made films, even producing a version of *Robin Hood* at age sixteen. In his adaptation, the arrow Robin shoots to cut the ropes that bind Friar Tuck ends up in the good Friar's belly instead.

After high school—and following a brief flirtation with the idea of becoming a detective because it was "outside the norm"—Boswell ended up at an art school, and eventually in a film program. "I guess all I wanted to do there was use the facilities to make a film," Boswell says, and this he managed in fine style, nabbing sixth place in the student category for a silent, farcical film at the Long Island International Film Festival in 1974.

But a career in films wasn't in the cards for Boswell. After leaving college, he rejected the typical procedure of applying to the Canadian Broadcasting Company for a job as an assistant film editor, "which in reality meant you would drive a truck for a couple of years." Besides, "who wants to work for the CBC and spend twenty, thirty years, maybe, working your way to the top? And then what do you do at the CBC anyway? I mean, ninety-five percent of the stuff they crank out is just crap."

He did try—though unsuccessfully—to have his film aired on a CBC show called *Sprockets*, which featured experimental movies of people "wrapping themselves in forty yards of cloth and rolling around on the floor while Stockhausen plays in the background." He also went to Toronto to apply at film studios for a directing job. "It was an incredibly stupid thing to do," he admits with a laugh, "but I figured I'd start at the top. I couldn't get past the front door and the secretary nine times out of ten. So I said, 'Ah, to hell with it!'

"If I'd been ambitious, I would have been discouraged," he adds. "I was never ambitious. I just wanted to support myself without doing anything too demeaning."

And so Boswell continued the string of odd jobs that had helped him through school and would provide some of the inspiration for *Reid Fleming*.

The first of these was a job installing cable television. "You'd go into a person's home or their hospital room, and you'd talk to them and see how they lived for five, ten, or fifteen minutes. Sometimes they'd give you drinks. Sometimes they'd be real jerks. Sometimes the women would let their tops fall open. You got a real nice cross section of society. So I think that's a lot of Reid Fleming. In fact, Reid's going to lose his milkman job in [an upcoming] book—just for a while. He's going to come back as a cable installer."

Delivering pizzas gave Boswell more opportunities to meet customers in their homes. "One time I went to a delivery at about two in the morning. The house was pitch dark, and I thought nobody was home. A woman answered with a negligee on. She was blond and really attractive. She asked, 'What time are you finished?' I said, 'About an hour or so.' I didn't know what to do. Then I looked down, and I just about died. She had *really* thick ankles. I cannot abide thick ankles. So I went home instead of to her place."

Boswell found further inspiration at the twenty-nine-dollars-a-week dive he rented in downtown Toronto, which would be condemned a month after he left. "It was a really good place to get material," he says. "I met a lot of interesting people. They all went crazy or committed suicide . . . It was really scummy. Nobody [there] you'd call normal.

"The guy who lived in the basement furnished a lot of the stuff for *Reid Fleming* . . . His name was Darryl, and he was doing time on the weekends for armed robbery. When I first met Darryl I thought he was going to kill me. People in the house tended to meet in the basement apartment, which was Darryl's, but we never saw Darryl. He was always in jail or someplace else. I felt after a while it was just like a common room you'd drop into." But one day, when Boswell dropped in looking for a fellow tenant, he found Darryl. "He turned around and said, 'I don't know who the fuck you are, but you get out of this room this second or I'm going to blow your head off.' "

It was an inauspicious first meeting, but Darryl, amused by the patchy comic strips and panel cartoons Boswell was beginning to experiment with, became Boswell's hard and fast friend. They spent time together firing blanks at people on the street for laughs and, in one case, keeping a would-be rock star rehearsing all night while they pretended to be big-time record executives with a spare contract.

With a host of tragic family and relationship problems, Darryl finally cracked in the spring of 1977, trashed his room, and took off with a stolen U-Haul trailer to eastern Canada. "It's been ten years now since I heard anything [about him]," Boswell laments. "He could have gone straight, but he had so many strikes against him that summer. I used to stay up all night and try to talk him into another way of thinking."

Meanwhile, Boswell had begun sending his cartoons around with the encouragement of a friend. "I was always informed by people in the business that no magazine ever bought cartoons the first time out from an unknown person," he says. So Boswell "played the game," hitting slick, top-of-the-line publications with more submissions after each rejection. And he began enclosing a full page of something he called *Heart Break Comics* to go with his single-panel submissions. The *Georgia Straight*, an underground paper based in Vancouver, B.C., bought the page and asked for more. "So I thought, forget single-panel drawings. I'll just do *Heart Break*," he says. "I began to do that on a weekly basis, for twenty dollars a week."

The character Boswell featured in *Heart Break* was Laszlo, a "Slavic lover" in the tradition of the Eric Rhode character in Fred Astaire and Ginger Rogers' movies, who was always "spouting some malapropism. [He was] the stereotype of the foreign lover." Boswell admits that *Heart Break Comics* is "in a lot of ways the fruit of my experience with a certain woman that went on for years and years and years. And the keynote of that relationship was frustration. The same with Laszlo. Things always fall just a bit short of making sense to him."

Reid Fleming was unleashed upon the world in the pages of the *Georgia Straight* for the first time in June 1978. Boswell had only intended for Reid to be a one-shot character, as a break from the continuing *Heart Break* strips. "I had Reid in my sketchbook when I came out to Vancouver, but nobody had seen it, and it was only meant to be a one-off anyway."

That first page (redrawn for *Reid Fleming* #1) has the Man of Milk beating up someone for making fun of his milk truck, pounding down a bottle of rye as he zooms off, pouring milk into a customer's goldfish tank, and then threatening, "Seventy-eight cents or I piss on your flowers!" Says Boswell of that page: "It's the cornerstone of the entire Reid Fleming personality. It's been tough to continue in some respects because everything is summed up in that one page."

Boswell went back to doing *Heart Break* for the rest of the summer, but he received numerous letters demanding Reid's return. "*Heart Break* was the kind of comic you would savor while smiling to yourself. But people tended to laugh out loud at Reid Fleming. It was a whole different response.

"I think one reason many people like Reid is that most of us at one time have had a service job, whether waiting on tables or delivering pizza, and one can relate to that . . . That kind of a job gets tiresome after a while, and inevitably one wonders how it would be to shove that pizza in the guy's face. So Reid's just like you or me, only braver. Or stupider. Or both.''

Boswell is the first to admit that *Reid Fleming* doesn't have the sort of depth Laszlo has. ''Reid is more of a surface character,'' he says. ''I think his entire personality should be evident in his actions. I don't want to explain him too much. I just want him to be . . . I think it weakens the character if you have to say, 'Well, he's like this because his mother beat up on him when he was a small boy, and his father was cold.' That kind of stuff I find superfluous and a bit tedious as well.''

Boswell has managed to add flavor to *Reid Fleming*, which replaced *Heart Break Comics* in the pages of the *Georgia Straight* from the late summer of '78 to February of '79, with a host of foils for Reid. These include Mr. Crabbe, Reid's supervisor and constant nemesis; Mr. O'Clock, president of Milk, Inc., who's getting ''more and more senile all the time, helped along by Mr. Crabbe, who is putting something in his private supply of milk''; Cooper, a.k.a. Captain Coffee, Reid's co-worker, who ''fits in as well as a narcoleptic personality can fit into any situation''; and Lena, Reid's wife, who punches just as well as he does. And just when Reid's angry antics threaten to get out of hand, he takes a break by watching the dead-serene adventures of Ivan, his comatose television hero. ''It's a quiet place in Reid's day,'' Boswell explains. And quiet it is indeed, for Reid stops whatever he is doing to see if Ivan will come out of his six-year coma. ''If Reid didn't have cause to hope . . . he wouldn't bother,'' says Boswell. ''But he's so dedicated and so full of faith. And it's true! One day Ivan does regain consciousness, albeit for only thirty seconds or so. Then he dies.''

After enjoying Reid Fleming's popularity, Boswell decided to tie up the loose ends with Laszlo by producing a *Heart Break Comics* book. He secured a leave of absence from the *Georgia Straight* and moved to his parents' home in Dundas for four months of artistic solitude. ''I realized quickly that I'd bitten off much more than I could chew . . . I got maybe a quarter of the book done in that time, and I came back to the paper to find out, 'Hey! Surprise! There's no job for you anymore!' ''

While Boswell was away, the *Georgia Straight* had metamorphosed into a family-oriented paper running syndicated Mickey Mouse strips, and there was no longer room for the manic humor of *Reid Fleming*. "There I was, high and dry in the summer of '79, with no job. I thought the only way to bounce back was to do a *Reid Fleming* comic book." Boswell moved into cheap student housing with his future wife and spent the next ten months reworking and expanding upon his *Georgia Straight* Reid strips.

In 1980, he self-published 10,000 copies of *Reid Fleming—World's Toughest Milkman*, using $3,000 in inheritance money. "And *then* I began to look for distribution. I didn't know a thing. I didn't know the names of any distributors. And I managed, by talking to people who had some contacts, to find out to whom I should send books. It was a very slow and painful process . . . Last Gasp picked up a couple of thousand copies right away. Within six months I'd broken even on the book and the rest was all gravy. It did sell out eventually."

Boswell next decided to complete his *Heart Break Comics* project. He wanted a more sophisticated look than his *Reid Fleming* work, and he honed his skills with numerous test drawings. The artwork, on which Boswell pulled out all the stops and spent three and a half years, is superbly atmospheric, with painstaking shading. "If you look at my technique, you can see that it's in many ways a modification of the wood-cutting technique used by engravers of the 19th century, with the fine parallel lines," Boswell explains. "It's not as quick as using Zipatone or something like that. That stuff looks so mechanical and dead that . . . I don't see the tone. I just see the time saved. You get a kind of control and a subtlety of variation in tone with a few strokes of the pen that you can't get with Zipatone."

Heart Break Comics' storyline, about a love triangle involving Laszlo, his partner Ken, and their secretary Constance (with Reid Fleming thrown into the plot for good measure), has a texture as developed as its accompanying artwork. "I think if you just want to read the book very quickly, it's got a fast-moving story that has a good line through it. But you can go back, I think, and find other ways of looking at the same material," he said. "And I really appreciate that quality in other work, if I can find it."

Boswell also utilizes dream imagery to emphasize certain points and provide a "weird sort of synchronicity" in which "a certain characteristic can manifest itself at the same time, in different places." When Laszlo dreams he is searching underwater for the object of his infatuation, Constance, Ken cuts off Laszlo's air supply and hooks Constance, in mermaid form, from the water for himself. In the following panels, the same elements repeat themselves in a jumbled way: Ken cuts off Constance's air supply with his flatulence, and Constance, who escapes into the street, is enticed back to water—albeit drinking water—by Mr. Don, the wooden barber. "I'm not trying to do a comic in [psychological] terms," Boswell points out, "but I always like to have that psychological underpinning."

Although Boswell himself feels *Heart Break Comics* is the "better book . . . a real labor of love," he recognizes that *Reid Fleming* is the "real fave, obviously the more commercial of the two."

Though Boswell might resurrect Laszlo in a future *Reid Fleming* comic, he thinks a continuing *Heart Break Comics* series would be "really pointless . . . I think the story is so wrapped up, so resolved, that to carry it on any further would be ridiculous. It would be like bringing Frankenstein's monster back from his watery grave. You can do it, but it might just diminish one's pleasant memories of that first issue."

Besides Reid Fleming's continued comics appearance, Boswell has more than toyed with the possibility of bringing the milkman to the big screen. Negotiations and plans with Dave Thomas, one of SCTV's McKenzie Brothers, went into advanced stages before finally breaking down at the top M-G-M management level. Boswell felt "more relieved than anything else" because the script being considered, which included limited Boswell input, departed from the essence of Reid Fleming. "The first time I spoke to anyone at the studio, he said that Reid would have to be made more sympathetic, which is to totally miss the point of the character. There were scenes of overt pathos, which really bugged me, because Reid Fleming would never feel sorry for himself."

Boswell has had other TV and movie offers and is currently talking to interested parties, but he is taking a wait-and-see attitude. "I'm not in any big rush to make a film or to get involved with one. If something really good comes up, I'll go with it. But until that happens, I'm really not hot to get a film made. It's much easier to get it wrong than do it right."

Even though Boswell would enjoy working in film—his first creative passion—he realizes, "It's so hard to get the kind of control that I already have as a cartoonist."

And, as a cartoonist, Boswell says he has the same sort of problem Reid Fleming does. "For him it's keeping a routine, repetitive job interesting. And he'll do anything he can to prevent the job from being boring. His job is my job. I've got to think up what he's got to do.

"The nice thing is I've got Reid working for me now. He's increasing my standard of living. I suppose I should share things around, get him a new house, let him find a wallet with 5,000 bucks in it, or something like that."

And as for himself, Boswell says, "I'm not ambitious. I don't have high expectations from life. I just want to insure a steady flow of food and good cheer for my family whilst being careful not to become too much like the *bourgeoisie*." And, somehow, one feels Boswell will never quite run out of milk.

JEAN "MOEBIUS" GIRAUD

COMICS IN EUROPE ARE A DIFFERENT STORY ENTIRELY. IT COULD BE SAID THAT European comics are what American comics might have been if they had followed the path of EC rather than falling into the Comics Code. Where American comic books remained a form of children's entertainment, European comics grew up with their audience. A European reader will pick up a western or detective comic in the same way he would pick up a western or detective novel. For the most part, the comic book as Americans know it doesn't exist in Europe; comics stories are serialized in slick magazines and then collected in albums. The costumed character is practically unknown, and standards of draftsmanship are far higher than in the American industry.

Still, European comics underwent developments not unlike their American counterparts during the '60s. The Franco-Belgian comics industry is a prime example. While it was more mature than the American industry, French language comics were still dominated by harmless gag humor and formulaic genre fiction. In the late '60s a group of cartoonists, inspired by American underground comics and the cultural ferment of the times, began expanding the boundaries of comics. While genre comics are still the mainstay of the Franco-Belgian industry, art comics have achieved a strong, vital presence in it. It may well be that Franco-Belgian and European comics in general are now what American newspaper comics were up until the '50s: the creative center of the art form. The best known French cartoonist in the U.S. is Jean Giraud, though he's not known by that name.

Giraud leads a double life. In France he's best known for drawing the

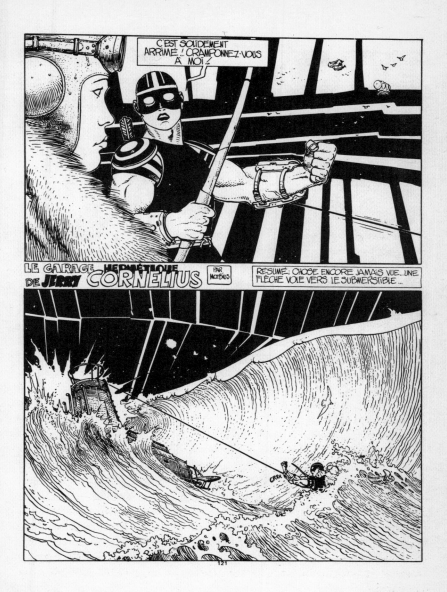

From *The Airtight Garage*

© 1983 JEAN GIRAUD

From *Approaching Centaurus*

popular western series *Lieutenant Blueberry* (written by Jean-Michel Charlier), which he signs "Gir." In the U.S. he's known almost exclusively by his pseudonym Moebius, which he adopted for his science fiction and fantasy comics. In 1975, dissatisfied with the conservatism of the established magazines, Giraud, Phillipe Druillett, Jean-Pierre Dionnet, and Bernard Farkas founded *Métal Hurlant*, a science fiction magazine which shattered the conventions of comics storytelling. It was an instant success, spawning several spin-offs in France and foreign editions in Germany, Italy, and the U.S. The U.S. version was called *Heavy Metal*. Though haphazardly edited and poorly translated, it introduced Americans to European cartoonists and was the first (almost) slick, mass-market comics magazine in this country. As Moebius, Giraud quickly became the star attraction. (Ironically, the U.S. version has survived its parent; *Métal Hurlant* folded in 1987, while *Heavy Metal* continues as a quarterly.) His popularity led to work in the American film industry, and he has done work for the films *Alien, Tron, Willow,* and several others. He now lives in California.

This interview was conducted by Kim Thompson. Jean-Marc Lofficier, Moebius's translator and agent, was also present.

JOURNAL: *How did* Lieutenant Blueberry *come about? Did you request a western, or was that what they offered you?*
GIRAUD: When I went to *Pilote* I was greeted by the editor-in-chief, Jean-Michel Charlier. He'd taken that position so he could check out all the artists who presented themselves in order to grab any he'd like [*laughter*] to work on his scripts. And that's exactly what happened. He saw me come, and asked me if I was interested in working with him—knowing full well I'd say "yes," because he was already a major professional, as well as the editor of the magazine. He'd been working for twenty years and was very famous, having already done some very fine strips in *Spirou*. He was also writing one of the star strips in *Pilote*, namely *Tanguy et Laverdure* [illustrated by Albert Uderzo of *Astérix* fame].

Working with Charlier was extremely beneficial for me. First of all, he was a professional who wrote very good scripts. But the other extraordinary advantage I had in working with Jean-Michel Charlier was that I didn't have to present my pages to an editorial department, and he didn't have to submit his scripts to the approval of an editor-in-chief [*laughter*], since that was his job. Moreover, my stories were reprinted in album format very quickly. Certain artists were waiting five or six years for their albums, while my first one appeared less than a year and a half after the story's serialization in *Pilote*. And collaborating with Jean-Michel was very pleasant. He's a very talented man who also does not work exclusively in comics; he's done screen-writing, reporting . . .

JOURNAL: *Before* Blueberry, *a lot of Charlier's scripts were rather classical—even rightist, militarist at times.*
GIRAUD: True . . .

JOURNAL: *Was there any tension between the two of you as to the direction in which the strip was going?*
GIRAUD: It was a natural tension, a positive tension. But there *was* tension: I was pulling in one direction and he was pulling in the other. It never reached the level of open conflict, however, or even hidden conflict. It was always more of a give-and-take.

JOURNAL: *When you were working with Charlier, would you sit down and discuss the scripts, or . . .*
GIRAUD: After four or five years of collaborating, we started talking more and more. Often we'd discuss themes. I can't say that I brought the themes; that's not true. Each of us brings something. I have a much livelier imagination than Jean-Michel. Jean-Michel has a tendency to rely on rather classical narrative structures; his imagination unfolds slowly during the development of the story. I have a tendency to sketch out a whole concept in my head, very rapidly, but then run into problems when I try to execute it. He was very skillful at executing the concepts.

JOURNAL: *Where does this European fascination with westerns—which you obviously share—come from?*
GIRAUD: I think it's more or less the same as the one that existed in the U.S.

JOURNAL: *But the one in the U.S. has vanished since then.*
GIRAUD: Yes, but it's the same phenomenon. The western represents a certain dramaturgy within a privileged place and time: it's

about the contact with nature, not completely primeval but not yet under the control of man; it's about technology that is already impressive but retains its human dimension; it's about the forces of government trying to exercise pressure but failing.

JOURNAL: *It may be the last period in human history when men weren't in a controlled environment.*

GIRAUD: Exactly. And this is at a time when men already display modern characteristics. The conquest of the West, at the end of the nineteenth century, features character types that can already—you can take modern character types and transpose them into this environment, which is hard to do for earlier periods in human history. As soon as you go back beyond 1860 you have difficulty in identifying with the people. Whereas from 1860 on, you see the emergence of modern man.

JOURNAL: *Of course, the movies played an important role in defining the universe of the western.*

GIRAUD: Yes, but . . . What interested me in the western, what I enjoyed, was this universe of *signs*, circumscribed as a place and a time. As soon as you move a little bit too far north—or south, or east, or west—it's no longer a western. If you go back just ten years, before the invention of the revolver, or if you go past the moment when there's too much barbed wire in the desert, or too many automobiles, or too many roads, or too much long-distance communication—that's it, it stops being a western. The western takes place from 1860 to 1890.

JOURNAL: *At the end of* The Ballad of Cable Hogue, *Hogue is run over by a car . . .*

GIRAUD: Yes, that's very symbolic, a very sharp observation by Peckinpah. One of the first movies he made, *Ride the High Country*, with Joel McCrea and Randolph Scott, is a very beautiful movie.

JOURNAL: *You first used the Moebius pseudonym, in the early '60s, on* Hara-Kiri. *Now, those strips were mostly satirical.*

GIRAUD: In fact, it was a regurgitation of my enthusiasm for the work that appeared in *Mad*. I was a total fan of Elder's—and Kurtzman's, of course. At the time, *Hara-Kiri* was loosely defined enough to include those sort of stories; after May '68, it specialized itself a little more, became more strained, lapsed into desperate provocation . . .

JOURNAL: *Where did the "Moebius" name come from? It's the cleverest pun for a comic strip illustrator imaginable.*

GIRAUD: Yes, it's amazing. It's a coincidence, because I originally took this pseudonym without thinking about it too much. I had to find something that would distinguish this work from my more mainstream work [which was signed "Gir"], and working for *Hara-Kiri*, I wanted to add a more provocative, mysterious side. At the time I had read short stories where the Moebius strip was used as a theme, exploiting its unique spatiotemporal properties; I liked the concept and took that name without really knowing whether Moebius was someone [*laughter*], without realizing that it would pursue me all my life, and without any idea of all the symbolic applications.

JOURNAL: *Two sides, both of which are the same . . .*

GIRAUD: Yes, I was just astounded, in the following years, by the many applications. Not always pleasant ones, for that matter, because the Moebius strip doesn't have nothing but qualities—it also represents a kind of imprisonment in terms of energy, so that one constantly has to make efforts to escape from that eternal circle to begin anew. Otherwise you end up in a descending spiral. [*laughter*]

JOURNAL: *Let's talk about the birth of* Métal Hurlant *and the rebirth of Moebius, which actually began with some strips you did for* Pilote *that were still signed "Gir," like "The Detour." How did you decide that what you wanted to do as Moebius would not be feasible in a magazine like* Pilote? Pilote *was developing at the time, but not rapidly enough, it seems, since there was a great exodus in the late '60s.*

GIRAUD: Over several years *Pilote* had developed what they called the "current events pages." I had too much to do on *Blueberry* to do any work on them, but I went to their meetings and took part in them, tried to contribute ideas. There was a whole gang of young artists starting there, with whom I was friendly. Those Wednesday meetings, with twenty of us sitting at a big round table around Goscinny, and each would throw in ideas he'd been preparing all week . . .

JOURNAL: *I remember Gotlib produced a fumetti on those meetings, which appeared in one of his books.*

GIRAUD: That's just how they went, too. Since I often attended, Goscinny would sometimes say, "So, Giraud, don't you feel like doing something this week?," and I'd say, "No, I have too much work"; but once in a while I'd say, "Okay, I'll take that." I did a couple of pages like that, three or four times, collaborating with various people. But the "current events" pages began to suffer from a certain sameness . . . My idea was that we should break the sameness. I suggested that in addition to the current events, we could also do experimental works. The first reaction, of course, was fear: "Experimental? What does that mean?" Something obscene, or incomprehensible? The only way I could explain it was to do some, so I did "The Detour," the theme of which, to an extent, was what I was proposing, namely to take unexplored roads.

Our proposal was that every week, someone would be given complete liberty to do something, following his dreams, independent of the house style or even comics in general. If he wanted to do a painting, or a sculpture, talk about something that had happened to him, write a short story, do an article on someone—I wanted to throw it wide open. So I did this story, which was also a manifesto of sorts on the subject of freedom and dreams. It was as if I had stuck my finger in a machine: suddenly I wanted to do more. A few others did things in that vein, but it rapidly fell back into routine. People become the victims of success. In fact, success is the biggest danger an artist faces. When you succeed, you want to maintain this success because it's so pleasant.

Anyway, they kept on trying to fix up the current events pages, and when I started working on "The Detour," I felt it moving, vibrating, and I realized something was going on. Later, speaking with the other artists at *Pilote*, we figured out that we had three options.

One was to continue as we were, working in a magazine that combined a traditional, even conventional section with a section that was more alive, with the resultant inconvenience—namely that the strips that were more alive didn't really reflect favorably on the traditional ones, and vice versa—there was a lack of harmony. In fact, the problem wasn't even with the traditional strips, it was with the mediocre strips, by people who had been at the magazine for a long time, artists who were not bad enough to get sacked—because it would have been terrible to fire them, they did their work conscientiously and well. So we ended up in a factory situation rather than a magazine situation. It was no longer quality that enabled an artist to be there, it was the fact that he was there. We were employees rather than artists, with all that that implies in terms of risk and cruelty. And we were suffocating.

The second option was rebellion: forcing the magazine to change. But that wasn't possible in that Goscinny was the publisher, as well as the author of two traditional strips, which were also the most successful: *Asterix* and *Lucky Luke*. And these were still quality strips, mind you.

So we saw the possibility of launching, not new series, but a whole new *press*. That was the third solution, and the one we chose. Our model was the American underground press. But we didn't realize that it would take a radically different direction there, because of the differences between the audiences. In the United States it remained marginal, and bogged down into a sterile situation, while in France, it rejoined an old literary tradition, which is simply that the avant-garde explores a new territory and once that territory is open, everyone heads in that direction.

JOURNAL: *Let's talk about "Arzach." That was really the beginning of the new comics.*

GIRAUD: No, I disagree. I don't think you can say it was the beginning of the new comics. The new comics, when they began appearing in Europe, were something quite different. What they were, oddly enough, was the return of the clear line, the return of traditional dramatics—not the traditional dramatics themselves, but the use of the traditional dramatics on a different level, taken to the second degree. The return to the image . . .

LOFFICIER: Ted Benoit . . .

JOURNAL: *Yves Chaland . . .*

GIRAUD: Yes, all of those. The old images were recycled as vehicles for contemporary thought.

JOURNAL: *Okay, so those were the* new, *new comics. But "Arzach," at the very least, represented a rupture with the classic strips . . .*

GIRAUD: No, what "Arzach" represented was the artist seizing his own freedom. People who came later, like Chaland or Benoit, or anyone else, the people from *Frigidaire*, Liberatore, etc., didn't follow me: they encountered the same phenomenon, namely the open field. And they did what they wanted to do, which was to combine their love for the images of classic children's comics with contemporary concerns, in the same way that I'd dreamed up a world. Other artists did things that were similar or parallel, but "Arzach" was an act of liberation—freeing the artist from an inbred system of production with an excessively standardized style imposed from above. And the result was the evolution of styles of unknown origin, that could not be linked to a school or a person or anything—something almost biological. When analyzing the system, you aren't aware of individual people, except maybe in retrospect.

Now, here in the United States, there have been artists who made an impact in the comic book field, like Adams, Kirby, and so on. They marked a generation, but it was done in a peculiar way. These people would draw and other people would notice the drawings and pick up from them, but there was no contact between the artists. While in Europe, maybe because it's a smaller place, people can belong to the same school without having the same style. It's the *thought* that's the common denominator, not the look. "Arzach" is a fairly interesting example of that, because on the level of the thought, it's the beginning of an explosion. But not on the level of the style.

JOURNAL: *That's true. I didn't mean to suggest that it was simply the style of rendering that . . .*

GIRAUD: But you see, it's not uninteresting to nail this down. A whole "Moebius style" later evolved, but it wasn't based so much on "Arzach" as on "The Garage," short stories like "Rock City" and "The Long Tomorrow." It was a style that was noticed and picked up by several artists—who in some cases went beyond what I'd been doing.

JOURNAL: *"Arzach" was perceived as antinarrative, although upon closer examination, it turned out not to be as antinarrative as one first suspected.*

GIRAUD: It's not antinarrative. Let's call it paranarrative. One avoids a traditional form in order . . . not to fall back into it, but to make the leap into less traditional forms—forms which already exist [in other media]. See, my influences are not all in comics—they're in music, they're in film, they're in interpersonal relationships. Sometimes a ballet will influence a comic strip of mine, more so than any other comic strip. Of course, a critic will have no idea of that. And when I say a strip of mine, it could be anyone's. If I had a piece of advice to give to young cartoonists, it's to extend their field of pleasure as far as possible.

JOURNAL: *When* Métal Hurlant *was running "Arzach," "Jerry Cornelius," etc., there was a reaction against them, no?*

GIRAUD: No. Well, there was a reaction against the idea of stories without plots—or rather, what was perceived at the time as stories without plots. Whereas in fact it was just a different way of finding the plot. The only thing one could react against was my versatility, my ability to go from one style to another. Anyway, when I did "Arzach" it precipitated the hatching of several other artists who tried to do similar things. One couldn't call it an epidemic, but there were artists who were intrigued by the open door attitude and did things of their own—albeit sometimes with mixed results, especially in magazines like *Métal Hurlant*, semimass-market magazines.

LOFFICIER: I think the negative reaction you're alluding to in the United States is mostly a puritan backlash.

JOURNAL: *That's possible, but it's really quite difficult to find even fellow artists or critics who have a good word to say about* Heavy Metal *in the United States. Certain artists, like Moebius, Druillet, and others, are popular, but the vast majority . . .*

GIRAUD: Listen, as an artist and a critic, I find *Heavy Metal* idiotic. It's a hodgepodge. There are no lines in the magazine. It's really an absurd catalog, with no coherence whatsoever, of all sorts of tendencies. One can criticize them for that.

JOURNAL: *Did your graphic experimentation as Moebius reflect back on your* Blueberry *work?*

GIRAUD: A little, yes. There was a spontaneity in the execution of certain Moebius stories that freed my hands and head and showed me that it was wrong for me to be scared, that I shouldn't hesitate to do certain things, to leap without looking from time to time. The only thing you risk is blowing a drawing [*laughter*], and then you just start over twenty minutes later. You're constantly surprised by new elements. I was leafing through a Milton Caniff album, and his blacks are mesmerizing—the way he does his blacks with a brush, it's marvelous, it's so free. That's something I've lost to a certain extent in the last few years, and in the latest *Blueberry* something I tried to regain—blacks and shadows. But it's hard.

JOURNAL: *You've been heavily involved in a couple of full-length animated cartoon projects in the last few years, most prominently*

"Les Maitres du Temps," which unfortunately hasn't turned up over here yet. Do you think your work on the animated cartoons has influenced your graphic simplification?

GIRAUD: The work on the cartoons put me in the kind of situation I was talking about earlier—extremely uncomfortable, almost unpleasant. In fact, I had the same experience when I was working with Jodorowsky on *Dune*. Because when you work for people in movies or in advertising, they'll say, "No, that won't do. Move it to the left, to the right, up, down, make it bigger, smaller . . ." whereas when you do comics as I do, it's utterly comfortable in that I'm totally free. If I want to put a turd in the middle of the page, no one's going to tell me, "No, you can't put a turd in the middle of the page." [*laughter*] I'm the only one who imposes limitations, and as an artist, you always tend toward a certain complacency, even on an unconscious level. You're always giving yourself presents, as Charlier says. Charlier says that artists who do their own writing have a tendency to draw things they enjoy drawing. As a result, the stories don't always go where they should in terms of dramatic logic: they go where the graphic whim of the artist takes them. I admit this is quite true. In my Moebius stories, there were a lot of ideas I had, directions I would have liked to explore, for instance in the "The Airtight Garage," that I didn't because it would have been too complicated to draw it. I wasn't able to do it. [*laughter*] So I really, basically drew what I enjoyed drawing. Sometimes the logic within which I'm working forces me to draw things I'm not as keen on, but I always try to find an escape so that the following drawing will be just as pleasant to do as the previous one [*laughter*] Maybe that's one of the secrets of Moebius, I'm sorry to say! [*laughter*]

HOWARD CRUSE

WHEN HOWARD CRUSE ENTERED THE FIELD IN THE MID-'70S, HE HAD THE greatest handicap an underground cartoonist could have: a gentle sense of humor and a "cute" style of drawing. As time went on he developed an ingenious solution to the problem: he began to present the most horrendous events in the most charming way imaginable, thus satirizing and deflating underground pretensions. More importantly, he began to explore gay themes in his work. Indeed, "coming out of the closet" could be a metaphor for his whole career; abandoning a safe but sterile life for a less secure but more vibrant and fulfilling one. Cruse edited the first five issues of *Gay Comix*, perhaps the last truly pertinent underground comic, and continues to do his strip *Wendel* for *The Advocate*. His work has also appeared in *Heavy Metal* and *The Village Voice*.

This interview was conducted by Steve Ringgenberg.

JOURNAL: *How old were you when you realized: "Hey, I'm gay"?*
CRUSE: Well, you don't just wake up one day and know you're gay. But I first began to have fears about it when I was eleven, I guess.

JOURNAL: *Right around the onset of puberty?*
CRUSE: Yes. That's when the sex drive starts manifesting itself, and you notice that the feelings you're supposed to be having

about girls, you're having about boys instead. Not just sex feelings, but romantic feelings, crushes. Except for budding lesbians, of course, where it's the other way around. Anyway, some people accept the fact easily, but others are like I was: terribly scared.

I would try to find any books I could about homosexuality, but most of them that were available in the '50s were homophobic crap. But they were usually written by doctors, and I thought doctors were supposed to know what they were talking about. The thing I learned from surviving that period of my life was: Don't automatically trust authority figures. Examine the facts and think for yourself.

Anyway, the kindest thing these books had to say was that homosexual feelings were just something that "normal" youngsters pass through, but they outgrow it. "It's just a phase," is a sentence you'd run into over and over. So I spent several years waiting for the phase to end. Every time I'd have the slightest sexual stirring about a girl, I'd get all excited and say to myself, "Oh boy! I'm coming out of the phase! Now I'll get to be normal!" From my adult perspective, knowing how phony most of the issues about gayness are, I can't help but be pissed off at all the unnecessary pain I went through.

JOURNAL: *Coming from the background you did—having a minister father, growing up in the South during the '50s—that must have been pretty heavy.*
CRUSE: It was. When you're a kid, you believe what the world tells you, so all the prejudices people have about gays become part of the way you view yourself. It was years before it hit me that there's nothing wrong or unnatural about being gay, and that all those bad feelings had been pointless.

JOURNAL: *Why don't we talk about your strip* Wendel? *You drew it for* The Advocate, *and now it's been collected into a big paperback book.*
CRUSE: I proposed *Wendel* to *The Advocate* around the tail end of '82, I think. It started running kind of irregularly early in 1983. As readers indicated they liked it, it ran more often, until it finally started appearing in every issue.

Actually, I originally proposed a series using Luke and Clark, the characters from "Dirty Old Lovers." But the editors suggested they'd rather have a strip featuring a younger central figure. I think they were concerned that older gays would think they were being satirized. I don't think that concern was well founded; all of the older gays who've contacted me have responded very positively to Luke and Clark.

But I was happy that *The Advocate* wanted a strip at all, so I started from scratch and came up with Wendel Trupstock. When the strip first started, I thought it was going to be in the mold of *Little Annie Fanny*—except with gays. I figured I'd satirize the craziness of the gay subculture and do lots of stories about gay bars and the singles scene. Three of the first four strips centered on bar pickups or sex ads. The fact that the strip ran in the classified sex ad section of the magazine tended to influence the overall tone, if you know what I mean!

However, that was about the time it started hitting me what a tremendous crisis the AIDS epidemic was becoming. Jokes about pickups in bars and sex with strangers started seeming a lot less funny.

JOURNAL: *I guess it could have been perceived in some quarters as bad taste.*

CRUSE: Well, it certainly would have been hard to keep up a jolly tone and ignore all the anxiety and danger that was suddenly surrounding the whole idea of recreational sex. I didn't want to be in the position of getting laughs out of behavior that was killing people.

So the focus of the strip changed. I introduced the character Ollie Chalmers, and the strip started being about the developing relationship between Wendel and Ollie. I more-or-less backed into the change, but it turned out to be much more interesting than just continuing to do sex gags. I was burned out on doing sex gags anyway, from all those years in underground comics. I mean, I'll do a sex gag or a serious sex scene if it reveals human nature, but I don't want to be stuck in that rut of trying to be shocking or outrageous all the time. I want to do strips about the way people feel and behave in their everyday lives, and sex is only a small part of most people's everyday life.

Wendel developed the way Barefootz did: first I had the image, and then I slowly discovered who the person was behind the image. Wendel has some things in common with Barefootz. In many ways he's an innocent, or at least he's naive. But he's much more connected to the real world than Barefootz ever was. When Ollie came into the strip, he was hard for me to get a handle on at first. But then I found the part of men that he's based on. Wendel and Ollie are like two sides of Howard Cruse's personality. Wendel's an idealist who thinks anything is possible. I think idealism is important for a person to hold onto. But I've also been kicked round the block enough to have some scars and some pessimism about the human condition. That part of me is like Ollie. Ollie is older than Wendel, and he knows a lot about disappointment and frustration.

There's a panel where Ollie is musing about the differences between himself and Wendel, and he says something like, ''Wendel thinks we can have a gay president in 1988. I just wanna keep us out of concentration camps.'' If you're a gay in America in the '80s, you get bounced back and forth between these extremes a lot!

So I can identify easily with both of these guys, and it's been interesting seeing how their romance spins itself out. And exploring a gay male relationship in detail is something that, if it's been done before in comics, I never ran into it.

JOURNAL: *One thing you're pretty forthright about in your work is your drug experiences in the past, as in ''My First Acid Trip'' [in* Dope Comix—3]. *Are you ever concerned that being an admitted drug user is going to undermine the credibility of your insights in the minds of some of your audience?*

CRUSE: Well, I can't change history. I was part of the '60s and the '60s was a time of experimenting with psychedelics. Furthermore, I'm a believer in telling the truth, and the fact is that—even with all the dangers that may exist with psychedelics—they did *me* a world of good. They helped clarify my thinking about a lot of things and gave me a much more spiritually rooted attitude toward life.

Now I don't *recommend* drugs to anybody. And I'm personally bothered when drug-taking becomes a way of life, particularly when it's drug-taking that doesn't teach you anything, such as drugs that are all about physical sensations . . .

JOURNAL: *Something like heroin, for instance, which just feels good?*

CRUSE: Well, never having had it, I don't know, but . . .

JOURNAL: *I'm not speaking from personal experience either.*

CRUSE: The point is that you never hear somebody coming back from using heroin or cocaine or a whole array of downers or stimulants people take for fun—you never hear people coming back and saying, "I really feel like I learned profound things about myself or got real insights into the nature of the universe!" Usually they talk about, "Gee! I felt good! I really got a buzz! It was exciting and fun!"

I don't want to be a puritan about it and say I'm going to scorn somebody for some experimentation. But you need to be aware that there are dangers in drug use. There are risks. Also, they wear down the body. The body isn't intended to metabolize all these substances.

I was almost exclusively a psychedelics person. I didn't even care that much for grass.

JOURNAL: *Did you try psilocybin mushrooms as well as acid?*
CRUSE: Yeah. And mescaline. All the stuff under the psychedelic umbrella that was popular in the '60s and early '70s. I continued to draw on the experiences long after I quit taking them.

But they began to wear me down. My nerves got fragile; I was tireder and tireder after the trips. And of course, drugs don't do great things for your immune system, so it's not a great thing to be doing when there's an immunity-related epidemic going around!

To be responsible, I would say to somebody the same thing I'd say if they came up to me and said, "I've decided to take up skydiving as a hobby." I'd say, "That's very dangerous. Are you really sure you want to do this? I'm not sure I'd recommend it." But I'd also know that people who skydive feel that it gives them a very important lift that means a lot to them. It can be a spiritual experience to be free from gravity for a period of time. They're willing to risk being killed to have the experience. And of course, they try to educate themselves, if they're smart, they can do it safely.

JOURNAL: *In "My First Acid Trip," you showed the LSD experience as essentially a joyous, transcendent one. Except for the ending [laughter]. I wanted to ask you about that ending. You built the story up to a certain point, and then the ending was kind of a shaggy-dog payoff. Had you intended to do that all along, or did you come to the last page and you were stuck for an ending?*
CRUSE: No, I knew how it was going to end. The story was based on an actual acid trip where we had a guy along who wasn't tripping. He was sort of an observer who was going to protect us from doing foolish things and harming ourselves. And he was really trying to be part of the scene, to provoke us with funny, trippy

thoughts, and to show us interesting things that we could hallucinate on. He really wanted to be involved with the trip, but unfortunately he didn't understand the psychedelic experience, and it was just awkward and embarrassing! Everybody loved him, but we just wanted him to go away so that we could relax and have our trip!

So anyway, much of the story was taking off on that experience. And then the ending was a take-off on all the drastic horror stories spread by the media about the terrible things that would happen when people did psychedelic drugs. There are probably some people who came out of psychedelic experimentation the worse for wear, and of course there are truly tragic stories to be told—although in those cases you'd have to look at the individual biographies of the victims to see whether the psychedelics were really the *reasons* those tragedies happened. But for the most part, those of us in my crowd who spent some time experimenting got what there was to get from it and went on to relatively drug-free lives. That's certainly been the case with me.

JOURNAL: *I guess you haven't done psychedelics for years.*
CRUSE: I think I've done LSD twice in the last ten years.

JOURNAL: *In your biography you mentioned tripping on acid and being down in the West Village when the Stonewall riot occurred.* [In June, 1969, a routine police raid at the Stonewall Inn, a gay bar in Greenwich Village, met with unexpected and violent resistance. The riot that followed became a landmark event of the gay rights movement.] *That would seem to be a pretty intense experience. Why didn't you ever do a story on that?*
CRUSE: I did a comic strip about that.

JOURNAL: *Oh, did you?*
CRUSE: Yeah. It was just a little six-panel item that I did for a Gay Pride Week issue of the *Village Voice* a few years ago. I didn't do a whole story about it because there wasn't that much to it. It wasn't as though we were actually involved in the riot.

It was just a funny coincidence to stumble upon an historic event in the middle of something as unhistoric as taking an acid trip. Some friends and I were just bumming around the Village after having been up in Central Park listening to a Tiny Tim concert . . .

JOURNAL: *Oh, that's terribly " '60s"!*
CRUSE: Right. So we were winding down at the end of our trip by strolling around the Village, and there was all this excitement!

JOURNAL: *So you were coming down as you ran into this?*
CRUSE: Yeah, it wasn't at the peak. I'm not sure I'd want to be in a riot with bricks and bottles flying when I was peaking!

JOURNAL: *Was it pretty violent when you wandered into it?*
CRUSE: It was violent, but contained within a space, sort of. Actually, things could have flown out of that crowd and hit us, but they didn't. Y'know, we used to have this glib little phrase: "God protects happy trippers!" Somehow or other, most of us came out okay even when we were in situations where we could have been very vulnerable. In this case, we just stood on the fringes of this riot and watched it as though it were a movie or a play. We didn't know what the significance was. I thought the government was being overthrown!

JOURNAL: *That was your stoned perception of it?*
CRUSE: Yeah. I mean, I didn't know! We wandered away after a while. Then the next morning we got a *New York Times* and there was a little story about this riot at the Stonewall. Of course, nobody perceived instantly that this would come to be considered a turning point for the gay civil rights movement.

But looking back at it, you can see why it was important. Gays had resisted harassment and oppression before, but it had all been very civilized. It had taken the form of debates and arguments, very business-suit civil-liberties protests. But by the time of the Stonewall riot, people were fed up, and the protests took on an angrier "Hell-no!-We-won't-go!" kind of attitude. People who were used to being treated as second-class citizens gained a sense that they could have some control over their lives instead of simply being carted off whichever way the police chose to cart them off.

JOURNAL: *Well, I know that you've been living with your steady lover Eddie Sedarbaum for a number of years, and I was just wondering . . . did you get into the bar scene much? That sort of casual sex?*
CRUSE: I've had plenty of casual sex, and I think casual sex is a great thing. However, we happen to be at a point in history when, for practical reasons, we have to think about the ramifications of casual sex. In particular, we have to think about what things we *do* when we have casual sex, because of the AIDS epidemic. But philosophically I feel it's ridiculous to have all these walls around people, all these rules and regulations about who touches who. I

think the world would be a better place if more people had sex with each other. I also believe in the importance of long-term relationships. But the kinds of things you get from being in love with someone and having a deep, long-term relationship are very different from the things you get from having a quick fling. And there's something to be said for quick flings.

Y'know, there's *this* kind of food and *that* kind of food, *this* kind of nutrient and *that* kind of nutrient. And different kinds of sexual experience offer different kinds of nutrients.

The epidemic has put a horrifying demand on gays that they quickly learn how to avoid spreading AIDS while still having meaningful emotional lives. Sex remains an important part of a healthy person's emotional life. As a result, a lot of thinking has been done about how to have safe sex. This is something that straight people are going to have to learn, too; the AIDS virus doesn't care who's gay and who isn't.

JOURNAL: *You yourself did an AIDS story called "Safe Sex." Which I liked a lot, by the way.*
CRUSE: Yes, I did. Of course, it wasn't a narrative. It was an explosion of feelings. It was working through the jumble of feelings that hit me and many other gay people when we were first confronted with the AIDS epidemic.

JOURNAL: *When did you do the story?*
CRUSE: As I recall, the story was drawn in 1983. I was preparing *Gay Comix* #4 and I realized that if something called *Gay Comix* came out in the year 1983 and did not mention AIDS—which was the single most traumatic event the gay community had been going through—then any claim the comic might have to relevancy would be a farce. Nobody had submitted an AIDS story, so I knew it was going to fall on me to do something about it.

I made several tries at doing a narrative, but felt that everything I came up with was trivializing the disease. This was something that people were dying horrible deaths from. I couldn't just make it a casual comic book plot device. Also, the disease itself hadn't been part of my personal life. No close friend of mine had gotten it; I'd be faking, not drawing on direct experience. I felt this was too serious a matter to fake about.

But one thing I *had* experienced along with so many people was the alarm, panic, anger, fear, outrage—the feelings that add up to what we call "AIDS Anxiety." So I was sort of working through all that when I drew "Safe Sex."

JOURNAL: *The cumulative effect was pretty shattering. That last page was a real zinger.*

CRUSE: Yeah. That panel where the guy says, "Billy's dead"— that's the Billy in "Billy Goes Out." That's the behavior—the Billy that we all came to like in that story was doing exactly the kinds of things that we all later learned were dangerous. Not dangerous in themselves, but dangerous because a virus had entered the picture.

Early in "Safe Sex," there's a panel with the caption: "Going downtown isn't what it used to be." That panel is lifted directly from "Billy Goes Out." The connection between the two stories is subtle and you could easily miss it, but I put it there because I wanted to make a point.

"Billy Goes Out" is about what you do when you're lonely. I have no apologies for Billy's behavior in that strip. He hadn't always been lonely; he'd had a lover before. But the lover was gone now, and he was in transition. His pain was too great for him to relate to opportunities for significant relationships, but he still needed to be touched and held, and that's what the strip was about.

JOURNAL: *It was kind of a sad strip.*

CRUSE: It was sad, but not because Billy was a tragic figure, because he's not. He'll recover from his losses. He'll have new relationships. Or he would have, if things had taken their course normally.

JOURNAL: *It just seemed like he was going through a low period, and you communicated that.*

CRUSE: I'm very sympathetic to Billy in that strip. I've had those feelings and done those things. I didn't get AIDS from it, thank God. But I could have. And Billy did.

I had very deep feelings myself when I drew that "Billy's dead" panel because, if I hadn't drawn it, I might have entertained the idea sometime of doing more strips about Billy. Now I have a sense of mourning, because I can't do another story about Billy. My friend has been taken away by death.

Unless they're burdened by homophobia, I think most people would have to come away from "Billy Goes Out" feeling that Billy was kind of a friend. I felt that way, from drawing it. So when we learn that Billy has died in "Safe Sex," there's a bit of real grief. I wanted to bring home a suggestion of that awful pain of the AIDS epidemic: losing friends.

THE HERNANDEZ BROTHERS

MARIO, GILBERT, AND JAIME HERNANDEZ WERE BORN IN OXNARD, CALIFORnia, just north of Los Angeles. They grew up in a standard '60s media bath of rock and roll, monster movies, TV wrestling, and most of all, comic books. As the oldest, Mario was the leader, passing down his comics and helping his brothers teach themselves cartooning. In 1981 Mario recruited his brothers in a self-published comic called *Love & Rockets*. They sent a copy to the *Comics Journal*, hoping for a review. They got not only a glowing review but a publisher as well. Mario dropped out after the first few issues, though he did collaborate with his brothers on the first four issues of *Mr. X,* which have since been reprinted in paperback.

Gilbert and Jaime both credit punk rock with widening their horizons and giving them the nerve to do their own kind of comics. Indeed, one could almost say that *Love & Rockets* is about what you do after you've been a punk. In Gilbert's case it took the form of an exploration of his Latin American roots. His "Heartbreak Soup" stories about the citizens of the Central American town of Palomar have been compared with the work of Luis Buñuel and Gabriel Garcia Marquez. Jaime, on the other hand, explores the community-in-spite-of-itself that surrounded punk rock. He began with a tongue-in-cheek science fiction series called "Mechanics," which had a more realistic subplot about one of the mechanics and her friend who played in a punk rock band, under the title "Locas Tambien." As time went on, the science fiction became less interesting to Jaime and the "Locas" storyline took over. *Love & Rockets* was acclaimed from the start, and its audience has grown slowly but steadily. It is perhaps the best marriage so far of the polish of commercial comics and the concerns of alternative comics.

This interview was conducted by Robert Fiore.

LOVE & ROCKETS

No. 20 ■ **$2.25** (*$3.40 in Canada*) Recommended for mature readers

JOURNAL: *I'd like to start out with your family background. You got into comics through your mother, right?*

GILBERT: Yeah, our mom collected comic books in the '40s, and it's the old story, her mother—our grandmother—threw them out, so she didn't have any left and she'd always tell us about the old comics. [*To Mario*] Actually, you were the one who started collecting comics.

MARIO: Yeah, when I was five.

GILBERT: Did she encourage that or—

MARIO: I just started picking up comics. I'm not really sure, I just know I started collecting comics when I was five years old.

JOURNAL: *So the rest of the family followed your lead.*

MARIO: Yeah, because comic books got passed around, and we started drawing our own pictures.

GILBERT: Jaime and I were born into the world with comic books in the house. That was normal to us.

MARIO: Comics were everywhere. You'd go to the bathroom with comics, you'd eat dinner with comics, it was pretty lax. You could get away with something like that, just be reading all the time.

GILBERT: It's because our mother did read comics was, I imagine, why she let us. Nostalgic for her, I guess. So, comics were always normal to us, it was an everyday thing. It wasn't until school started that we realized that we were abnormal.

JOURNAL: *What were the comics you liked most when you first started reading them?*

MARIO: Just the super-hero stuff, *Superman, Adventure Comics,* all the DC stuff. And things like *Hot Stuff, Richie Rich.*

GILBERT: Almost anything that was out there, with a few exceptions, like westerns. We didn't read too many of those. The DCs, Harvey comics, like *Richie Rich* and *Hot Stuff, Dennis the Menace* comics, and *Archie* comics. I guess the strongest influences were those. Still influence us now.

JOURNAL: *Jaime, your work is constantly compared to* Archie *comics. How much of an influence is there, really?*

JAIME: Not influenced so much by the stories, but the characters themselves. Believe it or not, they worked. They had a lot of sides to them. And the body language, and things like that, because Dan

DeCarlo and Harry Lucey, the two big artists, had a great way of showing body language.

JOURNAL: *How did you get started reading underground comics?*
GILBERT: *That* was a turning point.
MARIO: I'd always seen Bob Crumb drawings in articles—I used to get *Rolling Stone* secretly, because anything with "fuck" in it or anything I couldn't get into the house, I had to hide these things from our mom. [*laughter*] I'd always wanted to read them, they looked really intriguing. As I got older, I just didn't care anymore, I started smuggling these things into the house. They were a really great inspiration.

JOURNAL: *Did you start trying to draw like Crumb?*
GILBERT: No, I think that was subliminal, because when I tried to copy Crumb, it was flat, I knew I didn't have what he had, even though it was easy to draw like that. I was more impressed with the stories, because he could get away with anything, I mean it was anything goes. And at that time, I was at the age of starting to hang around with the teenage and a little bit older kind of crowd, and they had them laying around all the time.

JOURNAL: *Did you draw strips from the start?*
GILBERT: We were pretty young. Mario did a comic book of Superman, and I did one of my own called Spaceman. It was really crude, of course. We did it for a while, we did it for maybe a couple of years, and then we just stopped doing it, for a long time. And then one day Jaime and I picked up and started doing it. What we'd do is fold a piece of typing paper in half, did a cover, and it had art on the inside and a back cover with scribbling on it.
MARIO: The thing was, that Superman thing was just a lark. It was just a fun thing to do for the day, and then I just dropped it, and everybody picked up on it. And then later on, I remember seeing they were still doing it. I go, "Wow, you guys are still drawing this stuff?"

JOURNAL: *When did you start doing your own kind of characters?*
JAIME: When I was seven or eight years old, we really got hooked on the *Peanuts* cartoons.
GILBERT: Yeah, we started swiping those.
JAIME: We started swiping them, and slowly they evolved into our own thing, where we wouldn't go by the rules of storytelling, we would just go crazy, go wild.

JOURNAL: *So Mario brought in the first* Zap *comic. Who brought in the first Sex Pistols record?*

GILBERT: Actually, this goes back to when we were little kids. I think my mother was expecting Jaime [*laughter*]—this is a true story—and next to her was a teenage girl expecting a kid, and she would listen to the radio all day long. It drove my mom crazy at first, but after a while she started getting into the songs. This was like '59. After she came home, every day she would put the radio on a major pop station, which was KRLA at the time, and we heard pop music, rock music, all day long. That was another thing. Just like comics being normal, we just heard that music in the background.

JOURNAL: *So all through your youth all that was going on.*

GILBERT: It was always there.

JAIME: And it was all normal to me.

JOURNAL: *So you were also music geeks?*

GILBERT: No, music was different.

JAIME: Actually, I gave up on music in the late '60s. I started getting back into it in the early '70s, when Mario and Gilbert started getting into the glitter groups. Iggy, Roxy Music, T. Rex, Mott the Hoople, New York Dolls. I would listen through Mario's door, because these guys were big guys, I was just a little guy, I couldn't hang out with them. [*laughter*] Their hair was longer than mine was.

GILBERT: That was really strange, though, why we got into that glitter-type punky stuff, because before we were listening to Jethro Tull records, I bought the first Paul Simon record.

MARIO: It was pretty diverse.

GILBERT: But then, the one that really changed us was *Slider*, T. Rex. We listened to it and we thought it was the world's silliest record, and we kept listening to it and listening to it, and our tastes were ruined forever. [*laughter*]

JAIME: Naturally, when punk came out in the late '70s, it just fit.

GILBERT: It was the same kind of music, except it was real fast.

MARIO: A breath of fresh air.

GILBERT: For some reason, I always thought rock and roll, comics, wrestling, and horror movies all sort of mixed, in a way, and when punk came out, that was all those things I suspected were alike.

JOURNAL: *Before punk came in, were you involved in any kind of music thing? Did you go to shows?*

MARIO: Yeah, we went to shows, we saw Blue Oyster Cult, we'd go once a week to the [Hollywood] Palladium.

JAIME: And when disco started coming over, I started backing off. And I almost gave into it before punk came along. [*laughs*]

GILBERT: We actually got into punk a year late. The Sex Pistols had already broken up before I bought the album.

JOURNAL: *It wasn't that long between the time the album came out here and they broke up . . .* [laughter]

GILBERT: That's true, but my wife Carol was into it the day the first single came out. But then again, she was around fourteen, and that makes a lot more sense. Because we had already gone through glitter and all that shit, through Kiss, and all that superficial stuff made us think, "Oh, here comes another one." So when punk came we thought it was another circus thing, I kind of backed off on it, I didn't want to get burned again. I thought I was getting too old—I was *twenty* and I thought I was getting too old.

JOURNAL: *So punk rock had an effect on your world view?*

GILBERT: Yeah, I took it a little too seriously, I was really gung ho with the Clash, it was like, "Yeah, yeah, yeah, we're going to take over the world!" And after a while I realized it was just music. It was just the Johnny Rotten snotty attitude. I was never really snotty—well, I guess I was—but I didn't really have anything to back it up. These guys were snotty and they sort of had something to say, and I kind of liked that. Wow, you could be snotty and smart.

JOURNAL: *So where did you fit in?*

GILBERT: Just audience, really. We never really had hair—well, Jaime had a mohawk and stuff—but I never went out and hated my mother. I liked my mom. That's the part I never understood about rebel rock and roll, you had to hate your parents . . .

JOURNAL: *That was more of a '60s thing, wasn't it?*

GILBERT: Yeah, but a lot of kids adopted that. A lot of kids said "Ah, I hate hippies," but they were exactly like hippies, just different costumes.

JOURNAL: *But punk rock affected your outlook on things other than music.*

GILBERT: Yeah, hard to explain. I had a bad attitude about everything.

MARIO: Just had an opinion about everything.

JAIME: Also, it made you realize that you could do what you want.

GILBERT: Yeah, it made me cocky enough to believe that I could do a comic book, and it was good and it was all right, as opposed to being intimidated by the Marvel guys. As lousy as they were, at least they could draw buildings. I couldn't draw buildings unless I made it up, and that intimidated me. And so with punk, I took that musical anarchy to comics.

JOURNAL: *You did the first issue of* Love & Rockets *what year?*

GILBERT: Was it '82 or '83?

JAIME: We drew it in '80, '81.

JOURNAL: *So, in 1980, what were you doing?*

GILBERT: [*laughs*] I wasn't doing anything.

JAIME: You were working at the . . .

GILBERT: Was I working in 1980?

JAIME: During "BEM" you were.

GILBERT: I got a job after stalling for five years.

JOURNAL: *What were you doing?*

GILBERT: As soon as I got out of high school, I did do comics for myself, vaguely similar to *Love & Rockets,* but they were just for myself. I used some of the characters from *Love & Rockets,* that would be Inez and Bang, but I just got bored with that, because it didn't seem to be going anywhere. I didn't know what to do with it.

MARIO: Even people we asked didn't know what to do with it. There was no place to put it.

JOURNAL: *Now, Mario, you were married, and I suppose you were working in construction?*

MARIO: Yeah.

JAIME: And me, I wasn't doing anything. I was being a full-on punk rocker.

GILBERT: You were going to college.

JAIME: I was going to college, and they were paying me, so I didn't have to work. [*laughs*]

JOURNAL: *You had a scholarship?*

JAIME: It was some kind of Social Security deal from when my dad died.

JOURNAL: *When you left school, were you considering any kind of career in art?*

JAIME: I didn't. I didn't think what I had to show was any good. I didn't think it was professional.

JOURNAL: *But by the time that the first* Love & Rockets *came out in '81, it was obviously professional work.*
JAIME: But I didn't know that.
GILBERT: Because it still didn't look like a Marvel comic.
JAIME: And because we were doing it our own way, and we thought, well, we're doing it wrong. So maybe this will be good for a fanzine . . .
MARIO: That's why the first *Love & Rockets* was like a fanzine.

JOURNAL: *Also, there weren't any undergrounds then that were going to publish new people.*
GILBERT: And we weren't interested in doing the "Dealer McDope" stuff that underground comics were doing at that time. What undergrounds wanted seemed pretty narrow.

JOURNAL: *Did you ever look into that?*
GILBERT: Well, no, because we're the world's laziest human beings and we knew you'd starve if you were an underground cartoonist. I knew that right away.

JOURNAL: *It kind of makes you wonder just how much talent gets pissed away like that.*
GILBERT: Oh, yeah. We lucked out, it's that simple. We were doing our stuff, but we were sort of not into it that much anymore, and Mario says, "I have a friend that works at a college, and she works in the print shop."

JOURNAL: *Why don't you let Mario tell the story. How did* Love & Rockets *get started?*
MARIO: Like I said, we used to do our own stuff, and once in a while Jaime would let me ink some of his early stuff, his early *Mechanics,* and then Gilbert would let me ink his Inez and Bang stories, and we did some things we took to conventions that nobody knew what to do with. We had a dry period for a long time, but they seemed to be keeping at it. I kind of lost touch with it. But I was starting to see that Gilbert was getting pretty good, more professional. And Jaime—you were doing "How to Kill a—", was that the first thing you did?
JAIME: That was one of them.

MARIO: I remember you handed me something that had your current style.

GILBERT: You were just preparing your little universe.

JAIME: Yeah, I had my little universe, but I didn't think it was going to go anywhere, so it was going to be my own.

GILBERT: We'd created all these little universes before [*laughs*], and we didn't think they'd go anywhere.

MARIO: But the thing is that Jaime's talent went from sort of fannish-looking art to this chairoscuro style. I picked it up and I was doing flips in my head. I thought, "This is professional art."

GILBERT: Jaime's talent blossomed within a year. It just went BOOM, like that.

JOURNAL: *Within a year of what?*

GILBERT: From his previous style.

JOURNAL: *From little fanzine drawings?*

GILBERT: Yeah, it was his characters like Rand Race and Maggie, but they were drawn in the style we came up with when we were kids, without any influence from anybody else, and his style just changed completely.

MARIO: It became so professional.

GILBERT: This was a surprise to me, too. I didn't know Jaime could draw like that. That's what's really funny. He was already living outside of our mom's house, he was living with our cousin. And one day I went and saw his artwork, and I go, "Oh, I didn't know . . ."

JOURNAL: *So it was Jaime's work that made you think it was possible?*

MARIO: It kind of put it over the top. If this is this good, he'll hold up the book at least. He'll hold it up for everybody else. So I told Gilbert, "We're definitely going to do this." And Gilbert started working on his "BEM," and his stuff was getting really polished, and I thought, "Oh, Jeez, this is going beyond." So I badgered this girl to get us into the print shop at the local college, and made up negatives of the first issue. Then we went and got a printer to print the pages for us, and he did a lousy job of it. [*laughter*]

JAIME: And when Mario asked us, or asked me, I had no idea of what I was going to do. I just did it as I went along.

MARIO: We used to see ads for these little fifty cent comic books that guys self-produced, and it had been years since I'd last seen one, but I assumed it was still going on.

JOURNAL: *Like mini-comics?*
MARIO: Yeah, but before they were just rip-offs of super-hero comics. So I just took it from there, I figured we could always sell it through fanzines.

JOURNAL: *You also sent a copy to the* Comics Journal.
GILBERT: That was me. We'd been reading the *Comics Journal*; Jaime had a subscription. I thought, "God, these are the meanest son of a bitches in the world [*laughter*], if we can take their abuse, we could take anything." See, that was my punk attitude working. I said, "Fuck these guys, I can send this to those guys; they can't do nothing to me." I got up the courage to send a couple copies straight to Gary [Groth], I was thinking, "Well, maybe they'll review it." Being really naive about it. I figured that would be advertising, because we couldn't even afford ad space or anything. I sent them and I forgot about it. Two weeks later, Gary writes a letter saying, "Wow, this is great, we want to publish our own comics, how would you guys like us to publish you?" For a minute I say to myself, "No, we could still do it ourselves," and then I say, "Am I crazy?" [*laughter*] Because, from the beginning Gary was supportive. "I like this, do it your way." Everybody else had told us we had to change. He was the first person from the beginning who said, "Do it your way, this is the way I like it." That appealed to us, of course. We could do anything we wanted. Then we slogged out a year of adding thirty-two more pages to it, because he wanted to put a sixty-four-page book out. Well, actually, it just fell into place. As soon as we got it to Gary it fell into place.

JOURNAL: *What do you mean, fell into place?*
GILBERT: Doing *Love & Rockets* as we do now. It's been the same since the first issue he published.

JOURNAL: *There was some development from the first issue, wasn't there? Even then, I think I've heard you say, you thought you had to put what you were doing in some sort of fantasy context.*
GILBERT: Yeah, because I was already doing "BEM" . . .

JOURNAL: *Explain what "BEM" is.*
GILBERT: "BEM" was the first story I did for *Love & Rockets*. It was a quasi-*Heavy Metal*-type story . . .

MARIO: Yeah, because we were still influenced a lot by *Heavy Metal.*

GILBERT: The magazine *Heavy Metal.*

JOURNAL: *How did "BEM" turn into "Heartbreak Soup"?*

GILBERT: I always had "Heartbreak Soup" in the back of my mind. There was my movie geek period, when I started watching every movie [made] before 1950 that was on TV. I'd watch anything from before 1950, because there was a romantic feel to those films, good or bad. I had no taste, I liked them all. Then I progressed to '50s movies, and I got into foreign movies, and when I would watch Sophia Loren movies like *Yesterday, Today, and Tomorrow,* or when I saw *Black Orpheus,* I always thought, "This would make a great series." Sort of like *Gasoline Alley,* but use an exotic locale, so I could draw girls in tight skirts with baskets of food on their heads. It was a boyish fantasy.

JOURNAL: *You've also said you'd become interested in your roots . . .*

GILBERT: That was falling into place, too. There were always great stories that we heard from our uncles and aunts and our grandmother. They told these great stories about when they were living in Mexico or when they were living in Texas, where my mother's folks were from.

MARIO: And even Mom.

GILBERT: And we thought, "If we could just tell those stories somehow . . ." But we figured that nobody white could understand this. We were naive. But, then, at the same time, there were movies about white kids with elements like that, and I thought that if [white people] could get that, maybe they could get this. So, all this was in the back of my head, even though I was still churning out fantasy stories, because I figured fantasy was what people read in comics. Then I put that little element of "Heartbreak Soup" in "BEM", when they have this big party for the solar eclipse. The reason I jumped from that to "Heartbreak Soup" was because Jaime's stories were getting really good response, and mine were getting sort of mediocre response. It wasn't because they were jealous, it was because they were *right.* They were pointing out things in Jaime's stories, and I was saying, "Wait a minute, I could do that."

JOURNAL: *What were they pointing out?*
GILBERT: They were talking about Maggie and Hopey's relationship, and how Maggie seemed like a real person even if she was in a strange background, and I had been doing stuff like that before with Bang and Inez. I thought, "I understand this, I know this is better, and if they're willing to accept it, I'm willing to do it." But he'd already done Maggie and Hopey, and if I'd used Bang and Inez it would have been the same thing. I had to stand on my own, I had to have something on my own that I hoped was just as good but was completely different. So all that stuff, all those Sophia Loren movies and all that stuff came back to me. I dared myself to do "Heartbreak Soup."

JOURNAL: *So "Heartbreak Soup" is a combination of stories you've heard, movies you've admired, and elements from your own life?*
GILBERT: Yeah, elements from my own life. Like, when I have the teenage guys talking, that's usually just me and my friends when we were young, talking about girls about whatever. But I understood I had to change it a bit, to make it like a Central American village.

JOURNAL: *Did you do any studying on that?*
GILBERT: No, no, if there's one thing I can't stand, it's research. [*laughter*] That's another reason that it's an imaginary town, because I'd hate to do the research.

JOURNAL: *The main holdover from "BEM" to "Heartbreak Soup" is the character Luba, who is the center of the stories in many ways.*
GILBERT: Yes, because I was originally doing "Heartbreak Soup" as a sort of a roundabout way of doing a "BEM" sequel.

JOURNAL: *So what was Luba at the start?*
GILBERT: In "BEM" she was just a voodoo woman, an island lady who wanted power, wanted to take over the world. You know, it was just bullshit. [*laughter*] She was sort of like Corben's queen bitch in *Den.* I just did it, I didn't think about it at all. At the end of "BEM" Luba becomes a revolutionary leader, and so in "Heartbreak Soup" there's one panel that gives it away, where her cousin Ofelia says, "I told you not to mingle with the locals." She says, "I know what I'm doing." That's because she was hiding out from the government. And there was a point in "Heartbreak Soup" when I thought, either I take this seriously, or I chump out and make it a "BEM" sequel. So

I just threw out the "BEM". I said, okay, forget it, I'm going to go all the way and make this a straight story.

JOURNAL: *Was Luba this Sophia Loren/earth mother character from the start, or is that something that changed once she got into Palomar?*
GILBERT: Yes, I think at first she was just, you know, a lady I liked to draw. I didn't really think about that—what was the question?

JOURNAL: *How did Luba evolve from the character in "BEM" to the character in "Heartbreak Soup"?*
JAIME: She was this generic character in "BEM", but the longer we did these characters the more they evolved personalities of their own.
GILBERT: She almost wrote herself. I put her in this different situation, and I have to deal with it, because at the time I was very sensitive to what feminists were saying about movies, comic books, how women were portrayed in popular culture. At the time I was thinking, how could I draw a character like this and think I'm doing something progressive? So I had to try real hard to make her a good character. And there are still people who won't read it because Luba's tits are too big.

JOURNAL: *The "Locas Tambien" stories replaced the "Mechanics" stories over a longer period of time than "BEM" was replaced by "Heartbreak Soup".*
JAIME: Oh, yeah. "Mechanics" started out a little like "BEM", where Maggie and Hopey were these generic punk teenagers. But as I got more involved in the storytelling the Race and the rockets became less important than the girls' lives, because they started writing themselves and started getting more complex. So I got more into the "Locas" aspect.

JOURNAL: *But this took place over two or three years, didn't it?*
JAIME: Yeah, because I had a lot to tell before I moved on.

JOURNAL: *You had these "Mechanics" stories saved up in your mind?*
JAIME: I don't know, to tell you the truth. For me, it just turned out the way it did. There was no timing in it or anything. It's still going day by day as I think of it. Maybe that's why it takes longer; Gilbert has more of a plan for his characters. That's why he can jump years ahead.

GILBERT: Because I know my characters are going to get old and croak, whereas Jaime's not sure where they're going to go.

JOURNAL: *What made you pick this particular subject, the lives of these girls?*
JAIME: Going to L.A. punk shows and seeing these little punk girls who I just fell in love with.

JOURNAL: *What struck you about them?*
JAIME: They were so full of life. They weren't like any I knew. They were so full of life, they were cocky, they didn't give a shit about anything, they were nice.
GILBERT: Then again, Southern California, they happened to be really beautiful, too, a lot of them. [*laughter*]
JAIME: That helped.

JOURNAL: *How did you get to putting these girls, or Maggie at least, into this "Mechanics" storyline?*
JAIME: That was an idea I had since high school. I thought, I'm going to draw a woman wearing a tool belt. I thought that would be really sexy—drawing a woman in a man's uniform. And I drew her on a telephone pole. And then I thought it would be good to do it in space, because at the time that's what I was interested in. Maggie was at first a middle-aged woman, but by the time the comic came out, she was seventeen or eighteen years old. These were ideas I had stored up. When Mario asked me to do a comic I asked myself, what do I have to show? And so I took all these old ideas and threw them all together.

JOURNAL: *Was there any one point where the "Locas" part became more interesting to you?*
JAIME: The first issue. [*laughter*]

JOURNAL: *Oh, really?*
JAIME: The second "Mechanics", the forty-page one that was so successful, was all the "Mechanics" ideas I had before. I wanted them all to be in one story, and by the time I was done I was burned out on "Mechanics."
GILBERT: The reason we did the science fiction things first, and I think this goes for Jaime, too, was that it's so easy to do. You can please the audience so easily with that stuff. Like, there's a monster in this scene, and we'd do it our way. Most people would have a monster tearing people apart; we'll have a monster asking for

change or something. It's so simple for us to do. All I have to do is draw a monster. If you draw a bum doing that it won't have the same impact with comic readers.

JOURNAL: *I understand that from that day to this, there's been a lot of pressure on you to return to science fiction and fantasy.*
JAIME: I'm stubborn. The more they want me to do it, the more I say, "No, no, I'll show 'em, I'll show 'em. I'll do it *my* way, they're going to see things my way."

JOURNAL: *I remember a story where these kids are hanging around their parents' house when the parents aren't present, and it's almost like a world where adults have disappeared. Is that just the way it is?*
JAIME: With those kids, I imagine. It's just that that's where I am right now with the book. Maybe later I'll show more of the adult point of view. Like, I do want to show that Hopey's mother isn't just a bitch, that there's her side of the story, because all you hear are horror stories. Maggie says her mom's crazy. I don't want to make this like some John Hughes film, where the teenagers know everything and the grown-ups are evil.

JOURNAL: *So Maggie does have parents. I'd gotten the idea that Maggie had more or less grown up on her own.*
JAIME: She was raised apart from the rest of her family. I got that idea from my mom's oldest sister. She might as well be a cousin, because she was raised by her grandmother rather than her mother, and she's so apart it's like she's not part of the family.

JOURNAL: *There seems to be an economic difference between Maggie and Hopey. Maggie apparently comes from a somewhat poorer background, Hopey comes from more of a middle-class background, and Hopey is more of a free spirit.*
JAIME: Yeah, it's like Maggie grew up more traditional. Traditional ways, old ways of the Mexican culture, and Hopey never had a family, really. She's reckless. There's nothing to keep her down, like family or love.

JOURNAL: *I was never particularly close to it myself, but I'd gotten the impression when I was living in Hollywood that there were ugly aspects to the lives of punks that I don't see in the "Locas" stories, and I was wondering whether that was just the difference between Hollywood and Oxnard or . . .*

JAIME: Yeah, basically. There's a lot of stuff that I don't know about Hollywood punks who live in abandoned hotels. That's how they live all the time. Well, I went home every night. Or, if I stayed overnight somewhere, I was home the next day. It's just something I don't know that much about, so I don't get too deep into it. I've just started a story where Hopey's living on the streets, and she's having a miserable time, because where she was she had all these people to support her, if not her parents, her friends. She thinks she's pretty hot, but now she's seeing what it's really like.

JOURNAL: *With all the continuing characters and long-standing situations, many of them still developing, do you ever worry that new readers will have trouble getting the hang of* Love & Rockets?

GILBERT: That's why I'm planning to end the segment of "Heartbreak Soup" I'm doing now, to get away from it for a little while and start again later on. I want to be able to write stories that use the characters, but in such a way that you won't have to know them beforehand.

JAIME: Yeah, I'd like to get away from it, too—not from comics but from the "Locas Tambien" characters. Like maybe take a minor character and spin off a whole new series. But I still have too much left to do with these people. You think, "Okay, I'm finally done, this is the last story I will ever write about her and then I can break away." But as I'm doing it, I'm thinking of new stuff. It just never stops.

GILBERT: It got to the point in "Heartbreak Soup" where I had to end this particular segment, get away from Palomar for a while, and come back in five or ten years, like I did once before.

JOURNAL: *A few stories, like Jaime's series last year on gang violence, don't just explore character. They have "something to say."*

JAIME: I don't like to get too preachy, though. What I basically do is lay out the facts. I say, "This is what this character thinks, this is what this character thinks, and it's up to you now. You take it from here."

SELECTED BIBLIOGRAPHY

The following is not intended to be a comprehensive list but a selective introduction to the best currently available comics. It includes several notable cartoonists not interviewed in this book. One thing that the newcomer and returnee will notice is that comic books (or at least collections of comic book comics) have gone from being the cheapest publications on the market to the most expensive. For instance, Russ Cochran and Another Rainbow publish beautifully produced three- to five-volume (200-250 pages per volume) slipcased sets of EC, Walt Disney, and *Little Lulu* comics at prices ranging from $75 to $125 per set. This phenomenon is conditioned by two factors: small print runs and the collectors' market. The sets Russ Cochran and Another Rainbow publish will often have print runs as low as 2,000. Collectors who are willing to pay $40 to $100 for a single issue of an old comic book will not balk at paying $125 for a high-quality reprint of the whole run. Single volume hardcover comic book collections can run from $20 to $30. Trade paperback collections will run from $10 to $16. Current comic books will run from $1 to $3.25 an issue, "graphic novels" will run from $5.95 to as high as $15.95. It can become an expensive habit.

ORIGINATORS

The best single introduction to the first twenty years of comic books is *A Smithsonian Collection of Comic Book Comics*, edited by Mike Barrier and Martin Williams (Abrams/Smithsonian), a marvelous collection with generous samplings of Will Eisner, Harvey Kurtzman, Carl Barks, John Stanley, Jack Cole, Otto Binder and C.C. Beck, Basil Wolverton, Sheldon Mayer, George Carlson, Walt Kelly, and others. That book aside, cartoonists from this era will generally be reprinted either exhaustively or not at all. The best book about the early days of comic books is still Jules Feiffer's *The Great Comic Book Heroes* (Bonanza).

Carl Barks

In the days when comics version of Walt Disney properties bore no signature but Disney's, Carl Barks was known to his young readers only as "the good artist." It was clear even to the youngest that a special talent was at work. Since the '40s, the world-spanning adventures of Barks's impossibly wealthy Uncle Scrooge McDuck, his hapless nephew Donald, and various other waterfowl have amassed a world-wide cult not unlike that of Sherlock Holmes. Unlikely as it may seem, they are probably the best adventure comics ever done. The best place to start is Gladstone's series of color albums. Titles to look for include *Back to the Klondike, King Solomon's Mines*, and *Terror on the River*. Gladstone also publishes Barks in

comic book format, but the reproduction is rather poor, as comic book reproduction tends to be. For the true addict, *The Carl Barks Library* (Another Rainbow) collects all of his Disney material in a series of beautifully produced three-volume sets. Of particular interest are Set III, collecting the Barks stories from the first twenty issues of *Uncle Scrooge,* and Set I, collecting his earliest extended stories starring Donald Duck. Abbeville Press has published two large volumes of Barks stories, *Donald Duck* and *Uncle Scrooge,* but they were heavily edited and recut, and are not recommended.

John Stanley

The Little Lulu Library (Another Rainbow)—Another anonymous toiler, John Stanley prefigured *Peanuts* in his captivating *Little Lulu* stories. While older readers will find a surprising sophistication and irony here, above all Stanley was a brilliant comedy writer, and a well-nigh inexhaustible one. Stanley was remarkably consistent over a long period; Set IV covers what was probably his peak.

Will Eisner

The Art of Will Eisner (Kitchen Sink) edited by Cat Yronwode—An excellent overview of Eisner's career.
Hawks of the Seas (Kitchen Sink)—A reasonably rousing pirate story from 1937, done in the mock-Sunday newspaper style.
The Spirit Color Album, Volume 2 and 3 (Kitchen Sink)—Still available from the publisher at remainder prices, these beautifully colored hardcover albums reprint the best of the Spirit stories. Kitchen Sink also publishes a monthly *Spirit* comic book, which reprints the postwar stories in sequence.
A Contract With God (Kitchen Sink)—A series of linked semi-autobiographical stories, still the best of his later work.

EC

The Complete EC Library and *EC Color Classics* (Russ Cochran)—Russ Cochran set the standard for comic book reprints with this series, which reproduced every single EC comic book from the original art (which William Gaines fortuitously kept). The newcomer would want to start with *EC Color Classics*, a series of sixty-four page color albums. Be warned: Dr. Wertham wasn't fooling; they are awfully gory. Though somewhat biased towards its subject, Frank Jacobs's *The Mad World of William M. Gaines* (Bantam) includes an excellent and entertaining history of EC comics and the early days of *Mad.*

Harvey Kurtzman

Hey Look! (Kitchen Sink)—Kurtzman's pre-EC gag pages for various comics gave a preview of the anarchic humor of *Mad.*
The Complete Two-Fisted Tales and *The Complete Frontline Combat* (Russ Cochran)—As *Two-Fisted Tales* includes pre- and post-Kurtzman issues, the *Frontline Combat* set is probably the better buy. Kurtzman's artwork has always been underrated in relation to his writing (not least of all by Kurtzman himself), but the

war stories he drew show him to be a visual storyteller on the level of Milton Caniff and Roy Crane. *EC Color Classics* #3 reprints his Civil War stories. There were also a few excellent Kurtzman stories in EC's science fiction comics.

The Complete Mad (Russ Cochran)—All 24 issues of what was arguably the best comic book ever. As a bonus, high advance orders and anticipated sales allowed the publisher to reprint the entire set in color (other Complete EC sets had been in black and white with only the covers in color). If you've got $125 to spend on a comic book, this is the one to spend it on.

Jungle Book (Kitchen Sink)—Between *Humbug* and *Help!*, Kurtzman wrote and drew the first all-original cartoon paperback. *Jungle Book* continued the pop culture parodies of *Mad*, but with a savagery that the comic book never allowed. The choice for Kurtzman's best single work would either go to this or . . .

Goodman Beaver (Kitchen Sink)—Will Elder was Kurtzman's favorite collaborator, and this was the peak of their collaboration. Goodman Beaver is a modern Candide walking blithely through the moral chaos of postwar America. Elder clinched his reputation as the cartoon Brueghel with his intricate portraits of a world cheerfully going mad. After *Help!* folded, Kurtzman and Elder created *Little Annie Fanny* for *Playboy*, where it continues to this day. Annie is essentially Goodman Beaver with huge breasts and no brain. *Playboy's Little Annie Fanny* (in and out of print from Playboy Press, mostly out these days) has its moments, particularly in the early episodes.

Betsy's Buddies (Kitchen Sink)—Another strip for *Playboy*, this time in collaboration with Sarah Downs, it shows more of the original Kurtzman spirit than *Annie*.

Robert Crumb

Like most of the underground cartoonists, very little of Crumb's work is collected in book form. This will be changing over the next several years with *The Complete Crumb Comics* (Fantagraphics Books), a collection of all his comic art, illustration, and hundreds of pages from his private sketchbooks. The series is expected to take up more than twenty-five volumes. At present many of his underground comics are still in print and are available in larger comic shops or through the mail from Last Gasp and Kitchen Sink, among others. Titles to look for include *Despair, Mr. Natural #1* and *2, Home Grown, The People's Comics*, and *XYZ*. His best recent work can be found in *Weirdo*, published three to four times a year, and *Hup*, published twice a year, both from Last Gasp.

MEN IN TIGHTS

Frank Miller

The Dark Knight (Warner Books/DC) inked by Klaus Janson an colored by Lynn Varkey—Effective but shrill crime melodrama, marred by the cliches of the *Dirty Harry* school of reactionary cinema. *Batman: Year One*, (Warner Books/DC) art by Dave Mazzucchelli, a modern retelling of the hero's origin, is a better treatment of the material.

Daredevil—Born Again (Marvel) art by Mazzucchelli—One-man-against-the-mob story, closer in spirit to Jimmy Cagney than Clint Eastwood, and better for it.

Elektra: Assassin (Marvel/Epic) art by Bill Sienkiewicz—Ian Fleming Meets Paul Krassner in the Twilight Zone. Miller's best comic.

Howard Chaykin

Hard Times and *Southern Comfort* (First Comics)—These albums collect the first six issues of *American Flagg!*, a satirical science fiction version of *Gunsmoke*. Reuben Flagg, a former video porn star on Mars, is drafted to keep law and order to protect the status quo in corporate-owned Chicago. He has other ideas.
The Shadow (DC Comics)—Clever though bloody updating of the pulp and radio hero.
Time²: The Epiphany and *The Satisfaction of Black Mariah* (First Comics)—Those hoping for more substance behind the flash will be disappointed. Plenty of flash, though.
Blackhawk, (DC Comics)—A somewhat cluttered romp through World War II mythology, featuring Chaykin's best artwork.

Alan Moore

Shocking Futures and *Time-Twisted Tales* (Titan Books)—Short stories from the British weekly *2000 A.D.*, featuring Moore's funniest (and smartest) writing.
The Saga of the Swamp Thing, (Warner Books/DC) in collaboration with John Totleben and Steve Bissette—About as intelligent and entertaining as a comic book about a swamp monster can get.
Watchmen, (Warner Books) in collaboration with Dave Gibbons—Referred to in the text.
The Killing Joke, (DC Comics) art by Brian Bolland—Moore's twisted valedictory to the costumed character genre, featuring the most twisted costumed character of them all, The Joker.

UP FROM UNDERGROUND

As we said earlier, at the moment the best place to find underground comics is still in underground comic books. Underground comics were never considered throw-away periodicals, and their publishers kept them in print as long as there were buyers for them. Because of this and their relative unpopularity with collectors, prices of old underground comics are not inflated as much as their commercial counterparts, and some are still in print to this day. The first place to look is in the anthology comics, the best of which are: *Zap* (Last Gasp, thirteen issues), *Bijou Funnies* (Bijou Publishing Empire and Krupp Comic Works, eight issues), *Arcade* (Print Mint, seven issues), *Rip Off Comix* (Rip Off, continuing), *Anarchy* (Last Gasp, four issues) and *Young Lust* (Last Gasp, six issues). *Weirdo, RAW*, and *Prime Cuts* frequently publish the current work of these cartoonists. Mark Estren's *A History of Underground Comics* (Ronin Publishing) is a disorganized, profusely illustrated overview of the peak years of the form.

Jay Lynch

Appears in: *Bijou, Arcade*. There have been two issues of *Nard 'N Pat*, the second still in print from Kitchen Sink. Kitchen Sink also published three issues of *Phoebe and the Pigeon People* by Lynch and Gary Whitney.

Gilbert Shelton

Appears in: *Zap, Bijou, Arcade, Rip Off,* and *Anarchy*. Shelton is one underground cartoonist whose work does get collected regularly, if only because he collects it himself. As we said in his introduction, *Wonder Wart-Hog and the Nurds of November* (Rip Off) was his satirical statement on the '70s. His satirical statement on the '80s is *The Idiots Abroad*, (Rip Off) in collaboration with Paul Mavrides, in which the Freak Brothers take a trip through terrorism, imperialism, anarchism, Thatcherism, fundamentalism, and nuclear brinksmanship. Any issue of Freak Brothers is a sure bet, and *Give Me Liberty*, (Rip Off) in collaboration with Ted Richards, was about the only thing worth remembering about the bicentennial except for the tall ships.

Manuel "Spain" Rodriguez

Appears in: *Zap, Arcade, Anarchy, Young Lust, Weirdo,* and *Prime Cuts*. Fantagraphics books plans two Spain collections in 1988: *Trashman Lives!*, collecting the Trashman stories; and *Spain—An Anthology*, collecting his fantasy, autobiographical, and historical stories.

Kim Deitch

Appears in: *Bijou, Arcade, Young Lust, Weirdo, RAW,* and *Prime Cuts*. *Hollywoodland* (Fantagraphics Books) reprints his strip from the *L.A. Reader* probably his finest extended work to date. *Beyond the Pale* (Fantagraphics), a collection of his earlier stories, is planned for 1989.

Justin Green

Appears in: *Bijou, Arcade, Young Lust, Weirdo, RAW,* and *Prime Cuts*. Last Gasp plans a trade paperback collection of all the Binky Brown stories, along with new material. Until then, the original *Binky Brown Meets the Holy Virgin Mary* can still be found without much trouble.

Bill Griffith

Appears in: *Arcade, Rip Off, Young Lust,* and *RAW*. The longer Zippy stories are generally the best, and some of them can be found in *Zippy Stories* (Last Gasp). Collections of his weekly and daily strips include *Are We Having Fun Yet?* (Dutton), *A Nation of Pinheads* (Last Gasp), *Pointed Behavior* (Last Gasp), *Pindemonium* (Last Gasp), and *Kingpin* (Dutton). *Griffith Observatory* (Rip Off) is not difficult to find as an underground comic. Fantagraphics plans a collection of Griffith's non-Zippy material, including all the *Griffith Observatory* strips.

THE NEW COMICS

art spiegelman

Breakdowns (Belier Press)—Reprints spiegelman's shorter pieces, which are some of the wittiest explorations of the comics form ever. Out of print and probably expensive if you can find it.

Maus: A Survivor's Tale (Pantheon)—The first six chapters of *Maus*, plus additional material. As of this writing, it's sold more than 60,000 copies. Subsequent chapters appear in *RAW* #8 and Vol. 2 #1.

RAW

Read Yourself RAW (Pantheon) edited by art spiegelman and Francoise Mouly—The best of the first three groundbreaking issues of "The Graphix Magazine for Damned Intellectuals," featuring the cream of modern cartoonists from around the world.

Any Similarity to Persons Living or Dead is Purely Coincidental (Fantagraphics Books) by Drew and Josh Alan Friedman—Hilarious and totally untrue revelations about the stars of 3 A.M. television, taken from the pages of *RAW, Weirdo, Heavy Metal, National Lampoon*, and others. The Friedman brothers generate such an air of conviction that their wildest inventions can have the reader wondering if they're true.

Hard-Boiled Defective Stories (RAW/Pantheon) and *Big Baby* (RAW) by Charles Burns— Unnerving stories about the outer reaches of human behavior, so outer that it's hardly human any more.

How to Commit Suicide in South Africa and *X* (RAW Books and Graphics) by Sue Coe—Political pamphlets as art and art as political pamphlets. Powerful, impassioned agitprop.

Agony (RAW/Pantheon) by Mark Beyer—The Edvard Munch of comics, going on perhaps a bit longer than is good for him.

Weirdo

As edited by Aline Kominsky-Crumb, *Weirdo* (Last Gasp) is the nearest thing to *Arcade* since *Arcade*. All issues are still in print and available from the publisher. Crumb is featured in every issue. With *RAW* coming out sporadically if at all, *Weirdo* is the best continuing alternative comics magazine. Also of interest is *Prime Cuts* (Fantagraphics), a bi-monthly that falls somewhere between *RAW*'s highbrow and *Weirdo*'s lowbrow.

Peter Bagge

Neat Stuff (Fantagraphics)—A continuing razor job on mall culture. *The Best of Neat Stuff* (Fantagraphics) also includes Bagge stories from *Weirdo* and elsewhere.

Harvey Pekar

American Splendor and *More American Splendor* (Doubleday/Dolphin)—Collecting Pekar's stories in book form only heightens their effectiveness. The magazine version continues, more or less annually.

Gary Panter

Jimbo: Adventures in Paradise (RAW/Pantheon)—A punk manchild in a land that's more of a threat than a promise.
Invasion of the Elvis Zombies (RAW Books and Graphics)—Elvis returns to wreak an inconclusive revenge and ask where time goes when it passes.

Matt Groening

Love is Hell, Work is Hell, and *School is Hell* (Pantheon)—The thematic series Groening created for these books bring out the best in him, but sticking to these themes tends to leave some good strips out.

Lynda Barry

Girls + Boys (Blue Comet), *Big Ideas* (Blue Comet), and *Everything in the World* (Perennial Library)—In these collections of her weekly *Ernie Pook's Comeek* strips, Lynda Barry prosecutes her end of the sexual wars with a sly, earthy wit reminiscent of middle-period Rolling Stones, but with an empathy they would never have dreamed of. Her best *Ernie Pook* strips, however, might be her long series on childhood, reprinted in *The Fun House* (Perennial Library). *Modern Romance* (Harper & Row) collects her full-page strips from *Esquire*.

Bill Watterson

Calvin and Hobbes and *Something Under the Bed is Drooling* (AMP)—Outsell the Bible in some states.

David Boswell

His best book, the self-published *Heart Break Comics*, can still be found at larger comics shops. Eclipse has reprinted the first issue of *Reid Fleming*, and also publishes the new Fleming series *Rogue to Riches*.

Moebius

Upon a Star, Arzach and Other Fantasies, The Airtight Garage, The Long Tomorrow, The Gardens of Aedena, and *Pharagonesia* (Marvel/Epic)—These six albums collect the bulk of Giraud's fantasy and science fiction work, with new translations approved by the cartoonist. Of particular interest are *Arzach and Other Fantasies* and *The Airtight Garage*. Epic is also translating Giraud's (pardon the expression) epic *Incal* series, written by film director Alexandro Jodorowsky (*El Topo, the Holy Mountain*).

European Comics

Tintin (Atlantic-Little, Brown, twenty-three volumes) by Herge and *Asterix* (Dargaud, twenty-two volumes) by Rene Goscinny and Albert Uderzo—Though they've never made much of a dent in the U.S., Tintin and Asterix might well be the most popular comic characters in the world (the latest *Asterix* album sold two and a half million copies in France alone). Tintin is a boy reporter whose world-spanning adventures are similar in spirit to those of Barks's ducks (though Hergé was there first). Hergé (pen name of the Belgian cartoonist Georges Rémi) is probably the one person most responsible for giving Franco-Belgian comics their unique character. Asterix and his large sidekick Obelix—members of a village of "indomitable" Gauls, last holdouts against Roman rule—travel the Roman Empire, giving Caesar trouble. *Asterix the Legionary* and *The Seven Crystal Balls* are the best places to start.

Sinner (Fantagraphics) and *Joe's Bar* (Catalan Communications) by Jose Munoz and Carlos Sampayo—New York as a Third World city, with imperialism coming home to roost.

Evaristo: Deep City (Catalan Communications) by Carlos Sampayo and F. Solano Lopez—Stories of political and police corruption in Argentina during the '50s, setting the stage for the repression that Sampayo escaped and Solano Lopez survived.

Indian Summer (Catalan Communications) by Hugo Pratt and Milo Manara— Gorgeously drawn story of tragic misunderstandings between settlers and Indians in Puritan New England.

Hungarian Rhapsody and *Orient Gateway* (Catalan Communications) by Vittorio Giardino—Spy stories in the Eric Ambler vein, tracing the roots of World War II.

The Magician's Wife (Catalan Communications) by Jerome Charyn and Francois Boucq—This collaboration between an American novelist and a French cartoonist won France's highest comics prize in 1986.

Gods in Chaos and *The Woman Trap* (Catalan Communications) by Enki Bilal—A grim, engrossing two-part story about a decadent future Paris by Europe's foremost science fiction cartoonist.

The Cabbie (Catalan Communications) by Marti—Spanish cartoonist Marti appropriates Chester Gould's style, which turns out to be thoroughly appropriate for this wicked satire of corrupt mores during the Franco era.

Lady Chatterley's Lover (Knockabout Comics) by Hunt Emerson—The wild man of English comics simultaneously savages Victorian morality and D.H. Lawrence.

Outrageous Tales From the Old Testament (Knockabout Comics)—The cream of British comics (including Emerson, Alan Moore, Dave Gibbons, Brian Bolland, and token Yank Kim Deitch) join to show why the church fathers kept the Bible in Latin for so long.

Howard Cruse
Dancing Nekkid With the Angels (St. Martin's)—The best of Cruse from *Heavy Metal*, *Gay Comix*, and elsewhere.

Wendel (Gay Press of New York)—Collects the *Advocate* strip about gay night life and home life.

The Hernandez Brothers

Love & Rockets (Fantagraphics) has been collected in two formats. *The Complete Love & Rockets* (five volumes so far) collects strips by all three brothers and is sold mostly through the mail and comic shops. The solo volumes *Love & Rockets* and *The Lost Women* by Jaime Hernandez and *Heartbreak Soup* and *The Reticent Heart* by Gilbert Hernandez collect the same stories in a smaller format aimed at bookstores.
The Return of Mr. X (Warner Books/Vortex) by Mario, Gilbert, and Jaime Hernandez, based on concepts created by Dean Motter—An architect returns to the "perfect city" he designed, only to find that his plans were dangerously compromised. Their best story in the fantasy vein.

Chester Brown

Yummy Fur (Vortex)—The best comic exploration of Christian mythology since Justin Green's *Binky Brown*. It combines a disturbing, phantasmagorical comedy of Christian guilt with a quiet, moving, almost childlike retelling of the Book of Mark. Together they form a bemused commentary of how ideas get distorted over time; it's as if to say that "the Good News of Jesus Christ" was quickly followed by the bad news of human beings.

ADDRESSES

Books published by Doubleday, Pantheon, Dutton, Warner, Abrams, and some published by First Comics and Fantagraphics should be available at regular bookstores. Others can be found at comics shops (look under Book Dealers or Hobby and Collectibles in the yellow pages) or through the mail from their publishers.

ANOTHER RAINBOW/GLADSTONE, P.O. Box 2206, Scottsdale, Arizona 85252
CATALAN COMMUNICATIONS, 43 East 19th Street Suite 200, New York, New York 10003
RUSS COCHRAN, P.O. Box 469, West Plains, Missouri 65775
DON DONAHUE, (Co-publisher of *Zap* #1 and one of the foremost dealers in out-of-print underground comics), P.O. Box 3199, Berkeley, California 94703
ECLIPSE COMICS, P.O. Box 1099, Forestville, California 95436
FANTAGRAPHICS BOOKS, 1800 Bridgegate Street Suite 101, Westlake Village, California 91361
FIRST COMICS, 435 N. LaSalle, Chicago, Illinois 60610
KITCHEN SINK ENTERPRISES, No. 2 Swamp Road, Princeton, Wisconsin 54968
LAST GASP ECO-FUNNIES, 2180 Bryant Street, San Francisco, California 94110
RAW BOOKS AND GRAPHICS, 27 Greene Street, New York, New York 10013
RIP OFF PRESS, P.O. Box 4686, Auburn, California 95604